THE COLLECTED POEMS

OF A. M. KLEIN

To the memory of the poet's daughter,
Sharon Klein
December 8, 1945 — May 30, 1973

A. M. KLEIN

I lift my visor. Know me who I am.

from SONNET XIII *(unpublished)*

THE
COLLECTED POEMS
OF
A. M. KLEIN

Compiled and with an Introduction
by
MIRIAM WADDINGTON

McGRAW-HILL RYERSON LIMITED
Toronto Montreal New York London
Sydney Johannesburg Mexico Panama Düsseldorf
Kuala Lumpur New Delhi São Paulo

Casebound ISBN 0-07-077625-3
Paperbound ISBN 0-07-077626-1

1 2 3 4 5 6 7 8 9   (D74)   3 2 1 0 9 8 7 6 5 4

Printed and bound in Canada

ACKNOWLEDGEMENTS
Hath Not a Jew . . ., Behrman House Inc., New York: 1940.
Poems, The Jewish Publication Society of America, Philadelphia: 1944.
    Dedication: *To the Memory of My Father.*
The Hitleriad, New Directions, New York: 1944. In the series The Poets of the Year—New Directions.
The Rocking Chair and Other Poems, The Ryerson Press, Toronto: 1948.
    Dedication: *For my wife.*
The Second Scroll, copyright 1951 by A. M. Klein. A Borzoi Book published by Alfred A. Knopf, Inc., New York, and simultaneously in Canada by McClelland and Stewart Limited.
The previously uncollected poems were published in the following periodicals:
    Accent; The Canadian Forum; The Canadian Jewish Chronicle; The Canadian Mercury; The Canadian Zionist; Contemporary Poetry (Baltimore); Contemporary Verse; Dalhousie Review; Haboneh; The Harp; The Jewish Standard; The Jewish Tribune; The Judaean; The Menorah Journal; The McGill Daily; The McGilliad; New Directions Annual; Northern Review; Opinion; Poetry Chicago; Poetry Year-Book; Preview; Saturday Night; The YMHA Beacon

Frontispiece and cover photo: Associated Screen News Ltd., Montreal, courtesy Public Archives of Canada.
Foreword to *Hath Not a Jew . . .*, by Ludwig Lewisohn, by permission of Behrman House Inc., New York.

TABLE OF CONTENTS

INTRODUCTION

Abraham Moses Klein was born in Montreal on February 14, 1909. He was the surviving one of twin sons born to Kalman and Yetta Klein, who, together with their older children, had fled Russia four years earlier. Klein grew up in the east end of Montreal where he first attended both a Protestant primary school and a Hebrew Talmud Torah, and later, Baron Byng high school. A scholarship in classics enabled him to go on to McGill University. After obtaining a Bachelor of Arts degree in 1930, Klein enrolled in law at the Université de Montréal and was admitted to the Bar in 1933. Two years later he married Bessie Kozlov, the friend and sweetheart of his adolescence, and for a short time afterwards practised law in Noranda, Quebec. He returned to Montreal in 1939 where he established himself in the law firm of Chait and Klein. Here he remained to the end of his days, pursuing his interests and activities as a writer and public figure at the same time as he earned his livelihood as a practising lawyer. It was during these same years that much of his energy and rhetorical virtuosity were devoted to writing and editing a weekly newspaper, the *Canadian Jewish Chronicle*. Klein also acted as an occasional public relations consultant, lectured frequently on Jewish subjects, and affirmed his unswerving socialist views by running for Parliament on a CCF ticket in 1949.

His law practice was briefly interrupted in 1946 when he was appointed Visiting Lecturer in English at McGill university, and at about the same time he found a broader base for his literary activities as a contributor to several new Canadian magazines—*Preview, First Statement, Northern Review* and *Contemporary Verse*. It was during these busy years of writing, teaching, and community activity that three children, Colman, Sandor and Sharon, were born to him and his wife.

Like many brilliant and gifted artists, Klein was subject to emotional depressions, and in 1954, his illness became severe enough for

vi

him to retire from his law practice. At the same time he gradually withdrew from literary activity and publication. He died quietly in his sleep on August 20, 1972, a year and a half after the death of his wife.

Such are the factual events which define the outer life of the poet A. M. Klein. His inner imaginative life, however, is more profoundly defined by his writings. These consist, not only of the four books of poetry which he published during his lifetime—*Hath Not a Jew, The Hitleriad, Poems,* and *The Rocking Chair*—and his poetic novel *The Second Scroll,* but also of all the scattered uncollected poems, book reviews, essays, editorials, speeches, plays and short stories that he published in journals and newspapers.

It was only after Klein's death in 1972, when the copyright of his work reverted to his children, that the publication of this book became possible. I am indebted to Colman, Sandor and Sharon Klein, and to the wives of Sandor and Colman, for allowing me to study the A. M. Klein manuscripts in the spring and summer of 1973 before they were acquired by the Public Archives of Canada. I would also like to express my thanks to Usher Caplan, a postgraduate student at State University of New York at Stonybrook, for his help in finding and reproducing many of the early uncollected poems.

In putting together this edition of Klein's collected poems I had three goals in mind. My primary concern was to bring together the large number of poems which Klein had published in the years between 1927 and 1952 in periodicals and newspapers all over Canada and the United States, and to bring all these published, but hitherto uncollected, poems into conjunction with the four published books, so that the whole work would present an overall chronological picture. I decided not to include in this volume either Klein's translations from Yiddish and Hebrew or any of his unpublished poems. There are a large number of the latter which were written prior to 1934, but few, as far as I know, that were written after 1940. Klein collected most of his early poems and had them bound into three volumes which he then inscribed to Bessie with his typical aphoristic wit: "This edition, like the author, is limited to one."

My second aim has been to present the work in such a way as would facilitate the reader's access to the poems. The chronological arrangement, by its very nature, fulfills part of this aim, but in order to carry it further, I eliminated italics wherever possible; that is, in cases where a whole poem was originally set in italics, in the pages which follow, it has been set in ordinary type. When a poem was set partly in italics and partly in ordinary type, I have arranged it so that the main body of the poem is set in ordinary type. I have also eliminated the numbering of stanzas from several long poems where such numbering seemed to interfere with the sequential flow of the poem or the rhythm of the reader's eye.

With regard to Klein's frequent use of French, Hebrew, Latin and Yiddish words and expressions: only those which cannot be found in an ordinary English dictionary have been italicized. Otherwise, I have made no changes in the text, either in the books, or in the published versions of the poems which appeared elsewhere, except to correct typographical errors.

In cases where a poem was first published in a periodical and later incorporated into one of the books, I have not attempted to place it in its original chronological position but have left it in the later position which Klein gave it in the book. With regard to the uncollected poems, I have, in each case but one, reproduced the first published version, even though it often happened that Klein published the same poem a second and even a third time in different magazines, often making changes in the text and the title of the poem. The exception is the two versions of "Not All the Perfumes of Arabia" where I have disregarded the chronology in order to place both versions side by side for the convenience of the reader.

I have isolated, but not displaced from their general chronological order, the group of radical poems, because of their importance in Klein's development. Since I have fully discussed the reasons to which I ascribe their importance in my earlier study of Klein's work,* I need not repeat them here.

Finally I have based my arrangement of the poems not on chronology alone, but also on the desire to make a book where the poems can live, find room, and speak for themselves. This is the most important and least tangible part of an editor's task and perhaps his most serious responsibility. A book should be more than a mechanically assembled aggregation of poems and then, if the writing is any good at all—and Klein's writing is—the book becomes a living thing and the poems can move out of it into the reader's mind where they may continue to live and grow long after he has read them.

My work would have been greatly lightened if I had been satis-

---

*A. M. Klein, by Miriam Waddington, Toronto. The Copp Clark Publishing Company, 1970.

viii

fied to simply reprint all the books in one section and all the uncollected poems in another. But that is not how Klein conceived or wrote the poems. Even so, the chronology of publication can only approximate the chronology of actual composition. This is because whether or not a poem got to be published in one of the books depended on such extraneous factors as the number of pages available, or the poem's topical and thematic appeal. This is more readily understandable when we recall that two of Klein's four volumes of poetry, *Hath Not a Jew* and *Poems* were published by Jewish publishing houses in the United States who addressed themselves chiefly to a Jewish audience. They were therefore not likely to be interested in either Klein's radical poems of the nineteen-thirties or his Joycean experiments with language in the poems of the nineteen-forties. The latter had to find a home in publications like *New Directions Annual, Poetry Chicago, The Canadian Forum, Northern Review* and *Contemporary Verse*.

Indeed, anyone reading Klein's work in its entirety cannot fail to notice what he called the twinship of his thought. There seemed to be, throughout his writing life, two main sources from which he drew for his language and his themes—the Jewish and the Canadian. This is as true of the very early poems which were published in the *McGill Daily* and the *Menorah Journal* in 1927 as it is of the later ones which were published in the appendix to *The Second Scroll* in 1951.

More than the work of any other Canadian writer, Klein's poetry shows how a poet's use of cultural tradition—and in Klein's case it was two cultural traditions—moves from the general and literary to the specific and individual, and how the cultural experience of the group finds expression in what is ultimately the local life and voice of the poet. This voice, at its most personal, nevertheless includes the most essential and representative aspects of the artist's culture: its history, beliefs, legends, customs and religious ethics.

With Klein the problem, though he never perceived it as such, was to bring together the culture of his familial Jewish heritage with the culture of his English school and university, and to bring them together, moreover, in the Montreal locale where the language of his profession and of most of the people was French. There is no question but that such a richness of language background—Yiddish, Hebrew, English and French—was one of the chief sources of Klein's linguistic virtuosity; it also made him, who loved order and exacti-

ix

tude, aware of some of the dangerous and chaotic forces that might be hidden in language.

Klein started out as a Jewish poet incorporating into traditional English verse forms the stories, legends, folklore and sufferings of his own people. He did this sometimes with love, sometimes with anger, and often with a mixture of both. And simultaneously, even in the earliest poems, he was dealing with the broader, secular and even conventional subjects of romantic love, death, landscape and social satire. Klein's landscapes were, right from the start, human and psychological. This is as true of the early and faltering "Haunted House" as it is of the later and fully realized "Portrait of the Poet as Landscape."

It was in his last volume of poems, *The Rocking Chair*, that Klein finally found his true tongue and voice; here he put into poetry his double and sometimes triple tradition, extending ancient biblical metaphors to include modern grain elevators in a northern landscape, and finding a new metaphysic in such folk objects as rocking chairs and spinning wheels. In "The Sugar Bush" he moved freely and unselfconsciously into the use of Roman Catholic imagery, while the early Jewish scapegoat motifs were transformed to reappear in his compassionate portrayal of old maids and displaced antiquarians. In "The Break-Up" he concedes the presence of death and decay, but at the same time reaffirms his messianically rooted faith in life and in the seasonal renewal of it.

Klein finally emerges from these pages as a poet whose sense of community reached beyond the shabby realities of pawnshops and political meetings to envision the national "unity of the family feature, the not unsimilar face," a poet who celebrated language as the miracle through which the writer became "the nth Adam, naming praising" and eternally seeking to bring "new forms to life, anonymously. . . ." It was this awareness of the possibility of new forms as they symbolize the future that made Klein, in the fullest sense, modern and a poet of his time; but it was his understanding of the paradox that the poet's self must always remain submerged and anonymous in his community, his country, and his world, before he can speak for it, that made him the remarkable, intellectually passionate, and moral artist who lived and wrote among us as A. M. Klein.

MIRIAM WADDINGTON
Toronto 1974

x

POEMS

1927-1937

EPITAPH FORENSIC

Here lies a lawyer turbulent
Who fought in every case anent
Prolonged unjust imprisonment
Of men accused, yet innocent
With sole and only argument
Habeas Corpus—You may have
    the body.

And so debating life he spent
With this one only sentiment
And even in last testament
That laid him in this monument
He wrote with a resigned lament
Habeas Corpus—You may have
    my body.

BOREDOM

Blasé nihilities encompass me. . .
    And dullness is adventure of today. . .
    (The gilt edge of the moon is worn away. . .)
And I inhale and exhale ennui. . .
I will disguise the drab in mystery,
    Kill tediousness with euphemism-play
    (The full moon is a gold ambrosial tray. . .)
And weariness will no more weary me.
    I will contrive to fill days with strange words:
I will contrive to strangely masquerade
    My fantasies in gay fantastic hordes. . .
But only then, when I, in coffin laid,
    Will listen to the clods clap on the boards,
Then, only then, will I call spade a spade.

2

THE MONKEY

(With apologies to Chesterton)

When fishes soaped, and forests danced,
    Though at their feet grew corn;
When moon was frozen lemon-juice
    Then surely was I born.

With half-bald pate and hairy hide,
    And tail-lassoo that swings;
The devil's walking parody
    On all two-footed things.

The slandered scapegrace of mankind,
    Unwilling sire of men,
Write books, deride me, I am dumb—
    A better time I ken.

Fools! for I also had my hour.
    When I, a celibate,
Had not produced a progeny
    That me do degradate.

THE LAY OF THE LADY

He stuttered when he spoke, and then
He toppled o'er his tongue;
He gurgled hordes of broken words
That to his gullet clung. . .

He loved a lass; the brainless ass,
He loved her pretty looks;
At last she said, "I will thee wed."
She loved his fat bank-books. . .

3

But he smelt that there was a rat,
So asked in begging tone—
"Tell, is it me that's loved by thee
Or is it what I own?"...

On bended knee I ask of thee,
Of thee, my fiancee;
Wilt thou still be betrothed to me
Without my finance, say..."

So she complies and him replies
With voice that hotly mocks—
"Despite your stutter, sputter, mutter,
It is your money talks...."

OBITUARY NOTICES

RHEUMATIC

His pillow knew all that he sigh'd;
    Had heard his last soul-struggling groans;
Had felt his last clutch.... He had died.
    The wind had broken his bones....

STRABISMUS

His squinted eyes at strife,
    As everyone still saith,
He looked thus at his Life,
    And bumped right into Death....

4

NARCOSIS

Whenever he wanted some sleep
    To go to the Land of Suppose,
He took some narcotics . . . Quite cheap
    And the best was Death's free-offered Dose.

APHASIA

All he muttered was the same,
    He babbled in a trance;
Remembered but a single name—
    And that was not a man's.

LUNATIC

The moon in his head was a strain.
    The moon attracts the tide;
    And as a consequence, he died
With water on the brain.

LOCKJAW

A microbe sewed her lips, this monger
    Of gossip's slander spleen—
Even before she could die of hunger,
    She died of vex'd chagrin.

HEART FAILURE

He gaily jaunted down the street,
    With not a thought of Death—
His heart did sudden stop to beat—
    Surprise knocked out his breath!

LA BELLE DAME SANS MERCI

"O, what can ail thee, flashy sheik,
With head thus drooping downward bent? . . ."
"I spent a blissful night with her,
And my last cent."

"O, what can ail thee, flashy sheik,
With eyes insomniously red? . . ."
"The jazzing symphony has ceased—
I seek my bed."

"I see white powder on your suit.
Your lips bedaubed with scarlet press . . ."
"A blushing witness there you have
Of her caress."

"I met a flapper in the hall.
Full beautiful—a druggist's child . . .
Her fingers long . . . her head was light . . .
And I was wild.

Hers was a very floral name,
Her suitors called her Marigold. . . .
The reason she was merry was
That I was gold.

She had insatiable wants,
I had to keep up wealthy tone. . . .
She revelled in the silvered sound,
And I made moan.

She had a ready store of hints,
She shrewdly could insinuate . . .
I took the hints, she took the rest . . .
We osculate.

I danced with her the whole night long,
Apostrophised her, 'Peaches. . . . Honey. . . .'
And in my heart the echo came—
My money.

The saxophone wailed loud and long . . .
The pianist shook his shoulder-blades. . . .
We danced . . we stamped . . we suffered our
Own bastinades.

I tripped with her at quarters close,
My blood within me hotly tingling . . .
We hugged each other to the tune,
Of money jingling.

I took her home in taxi-car. . . .
In thought and otherwise was lost. . . .
I wondered why she lived so far . .
How much the cost?

Suspense was past . . . at last we reached
Her very distant residence.
I turned the corner . . . chauffeur paid—
Left with two pence.

I have not money left to me
To buy a fare on the tramway,
And that is why I homeward plod
My weary way.

And this is why I am so sad . . .
My head thus drooping downward bent . . .
I spent a blissful night with her
And my last cent."

THRENODY

O weep your tears, you crocodiles! the great
     McGilliad is dead . . . is gone . . . is not . . .
     (Please punctuate this with the triple dot.)
The great McGilliad is now the late . . .
No more will it rave, rant, or wildly prate;
     No more will it turn many a naught to aught;

ore will it throw the deeper thought
nt's simpletonic pate.
ides have lately been increased;
iccumbs unto the fatal fad . . .
So weep, O crocodiles, let be appeased
The melancholy which may drive you mad . . .
And you, ye little worms, prepare to feast
Upon the corpse of the McGilliad.

FIVE CHARACTERS

AHASUERUS

Set in the jewelled fore-part of his crown
A naked innuendo cameo
Of his loved empress shone in purple glow. . . .
And when a ray of light was on it thrown,
It smiled as if it knew what was not known. . . .
The king arose, and swaying to and fro
Raised up his goblet, quaffed it. . . . Let wine flow!
And then he sank upon his cushioned throne.
Drink! drink, my satraps! drink my nobles! drink!
And let me fill again this cup of wine. . . .
He rose again but once again to sink,
And drooped his head, his whole crown making shine,
And stared into the bottom of his drink,
And saw his Vashti smiling from the wine.

VASHTI

The chamberlain burst on the royal feast
Of Vashti, and he caught the women flushed
With wine and maiden-pleasure. They all blushed.
But Vashti did not blush, not in the least.

8

The chamberlain, as solemn as a priest,
  Delivered the king's oracle, and hushed
  The hall. Then Vashti's blood boiled, rushed
Into her face, but she was pale as East
  Before the worshippers may praise the dawn,
As pale as Shushan-lilies in moonlight
  "The king shall not see me, a naked swan . . . ."
She faltered, weeping almost, but not quite.
  The chamberlain looked closer; deathly wan
She was, not pale. No. She was leprous, white.

ESTHER

Queen Esther is out walking in the garden,
  Yet all the wise men, knowers of the seasons,
  Are watching for some new star's sudden naissance,
While Esther is out walking in the garden. . . .
Hadassah is out walking in the garden,
  And every rose is wafting forth its reasons
  For love of life, and the entire pleasance
Is whispering the secrets of her pardon. . . .
  The king has seen his queen, alone, and facing
His palace and the moonlight. He does not lust her,
  —So beautiful and mine— His wild love racing
Into his lips, how Persian-hot he kissed her,
  Giving her his sceptre, and embracing:
"What wilt thou? What is thy request, my Esther?"

MORDECAI

He reverenced no idol, nor of gold,
  Nor silver, certainly not one of flesh.
  He was not snared within the common mesh
Of hero-worshipping, by being told.
Had he not justly loyally revealed
  The plot of Bigthana and loud Teresh?
  Were they not hung upon a single leash

9

From either end? Had he not thus unsealed
    The king's death? Was he not a king's grandson?
So Mordecai was bold and cringeless proud.
    And now when Haman passed, though everyone
Fell prostrate in a belly-walking crowd,
    Haman and Mordecai erect alone,
No one could tell for whom the people bowed.

HAMAN

How lividly he looks, obliviously!
    How eagerly he stares at endlessness,
    Enchanted by the accolade-caress
Of hempen rope swung from a gallows-tree . . .
Whenever breezes shake him carelessly,
    Dangling, he remonstrates a brief distress
    By clicking teeth, and gurgling to express
A last thought . . . Starkness stiffens cap-a-pie.
    And that is Haman whom the king delights
To honour . . . He has raised him and assigned
    Him place amongst the high . . . the raven-flights.
There's his coveted horse. — Where? — Are you blind?
    Do you not see him sway in startling plights,
Curvetting on the Charger of the Wind?

CONJECTURES

The snow-flaked crystal stars fall fast—
Age of miracles not past !

These whitish flighty airy things—
Are feathers clipt from angel's wings ?

These are silk remnants God casts down,
Snipt from the new-made saintly gown ?

10

A widow dies—in heaven weds
Her husband—these confetti shreds ?

Linnaeus is dissecting now,
White butterflies—The proof? White snow.

Some Patriarch clips, trims his beard—
And these the furry hair just shear'd ?

Aaron now in abstract mood
Is whittling off his Blossom-rood ?

The Shepherd Lord flings down earth's alms—
The fleece shorn off the Holy Lambs. . .

They whirl and swirl, through heavens stray—
White curd dropped from the Milky Way ?

The snow-flaked crystal stars fall fast—
Age of miracles not past !

JOSEPH

"Behold the dreamer cometh!" . . . They beheld
The lad, well-favoured, good to look upon
Hurry towards them eagerly, as one
Who feared his news might be too long withheld.

"Let him no longer work his little schemes
Upon us. Let him in this pit think now
A star is lord, a sheaf stands upright . . . Now
Let scorpions interpret him his dreams."

They stript him off his coat; and in this wise
They left him in the wilderness. They slew
A kid and took the coat of many dyes
And steeped it in its blood to make a clue . . .
And held before old Jacob's dimming eyes
A coat of one red retribution hue.

MATTATHIAS

Of scabrous heart and of deportment sleek,
And reeking like an incense superfine,
The Hebrew renegade laid hold the swine
And raised it as a flattery to the Greek . . .
His dagger flashed, truly a lightning streak;
The blood gushed from the swine-heart which, in fine,
Did the Lord's altar all incarnadine . . .
In truth, there is sore vengeance now to wreak!
And Mattathias, Man of Modin, cool
With old age grew all warm with wrath; he threw
Discretion to the winds like a false jewel,
And on the instant, zeal-possessed, he slew
The knave. Behold within a single pool
A swine's blood and the blood of traitor Jew!

TO THE JEWISH POET

You cherished them as ancient gems, those tears
    Of Jeremiah; through that night for you
    These only shone; these jewels of the Jew,
With which he graced his sorrow all the years.
But now forget them! Spurn them! The dawn nears!
    The Dawn arises, tinted white and blue,
    Upon a land, lean to the parvenu,—
Make fat that land with sweat, and not with tears . . .
    Do purge your voice; suppress the groan; abate
The weepings; cleanse the whimper; choke the whine . . .
    You make grimaces, cast complaints on fate,
And speak about a cup of bitter wine?
    That cup now has a crack, a crack as great
As the whole length and breadth of Palestine.

12

CANDLE LIGHTS

Dead heroes ride the chariots of the wind;
Jew phantoms light the candles of the sky.
Old war-cries echo in my memory;
The ghosts of five brave brothers stalk my mind.
And this because my father and his kind
Are lighting heirloom'd candelabra, aye,
Are singing praises to the One on High,
This night in which past battles are enshrined!
As sweet as were the sweet songs of degrees
That David sang rejoicing, is this rite
My sire rejoicing sings; and as the sight
Of almond blooms that burst on spring-time trees
Is sight of this *menorah,* and of these
Eight blossoms breaking on a winter night!

AUTUMN

Black crows are pecking at the carrion
of Summer. Worms enter themselves in dead
leaves. White birch branches sing the song a swan
sings before its silence sings. Dull lead
and heaviness are heaven's *sine qua non.*
Sad leaves all day commit their suicides;
such puny tragedies even till dawn
Throw little echoes in the wood . . . Death hides
its cross-bones in the branches . . . Halcyon
breeds maggots in the brain . . . The huddled owl
doth sometimes hoot his profane requiems . . . Gone
is pleasure and the year has donned a cowl.
And lo, with twiggen fingers, one on one,
Autumn, a pious ghost, wrapt mistily
in winding-sheets, stalks onwards, onwards, on.

BALLAD OF SIGNS AND WONDERS

Every burgher is a feaster;
Prague is welcoming the Easter
And the *Judengasse's* over—
Joyed with *Abib* and Passover . . .
April arm in arm with *Nissan*
Doubles beauty of the season . . .
    And upon the market-curbs
    Lilies are sold, and bitter herbs.

Prague did vaunt a lone apostate;
Had a Jewish soul and lost it;
Saw and coveted the Christian
Gold, and so he razored his chin . . .
Hated all his former brethren;
Longed to see the fleeting Death run
    In amongst them, with his dance
    Bringing his inheritance.

He, the money-hired liar,
Taught the monk and priest and friar
Twisted lore; they did imbibe all
Proving thus the text of Bible:
"From thy womb will come Jew-baiters!
From thy loins thy people's haters!"
    Maledictions on his fame.
    May the earth forget his name!

She was tall and she was fair;
She had long and golden hair;
Lovely as the lilies are
She was loveliest, by far,
Of all virgins then or since;
She was daughter of the prince
    And in April she did seem
    Verily an April-dream.

14

The accursed traitor lusted
After her; his iron heart rusted
With his passion; and he sought her,
Sought to steal the prince's daughter—
When, in struggling, flashed a dagger!
Pale and blood-stained he did drag her
  Under cover of the dark
  Night, into the Holy Ark.

Dawn arose like blood; "And where is
One who was preserved by furies?
Foul deed done! We will avenge! Hence!
Seek the culprit! Wreak the vengeance!
Find him! We will screw his thumbs off!
Pluck his gizzard! Tear his limbs off!
  Be his carcass-remnants fried!"
  So the wrathful burghers cried.

Spoke the nameless: " 'Tis the Hebrews
Who have need of strange bloody brews!
Wring confession out with torture!
Roll them in spiked barrels! Nurture
Them upon their own horse-radish!
Make each son of theirs a *Kaddish*!
  With each *Kaddish* feed a hog!
  With me to the synagogue!"

As the cantor strove to rival
Spring-time birds, in wild arrival
Rushed the angry horde and "Slaughter!"
Cried they, "or the prince's daughter!"
The apostate then did pick on
One of all the terror-stricken,
  Clenched the Rabbi's bearded hair:
  "Open us the coffin there!"

Down he pulled the hangings, and
Lo! he raised a blood-stained hand!
Lo! upon the Holy Scroll
Lies a body but no soul . . .

15

Lies the princess, golden-haired . . .
(Adonai, thy flock be spared! . . .)
        Slowly under every breath
        Creeps the whisperer called Death.

"Death!" they shouted and their words
Glistened on the fast-drawn swords.
(Hear, O Israel, God is One! . . .)
When behold there stood upon
The stained threshold of the Ark
She, the princess who did mark
        With her finger him the snake.
        Jew-apostate . . . Thus she spake:

"In the sweetness of my dream
It was thy blade that did gleam;
Thy blade it was that did rest
In the sheathing of my breast.
It was Spring! and life was mine . . .
I am dead! The deed was thine."
        Spoken; and she closed her eyes.
        May she rest in Paradise.

Israel, blow the *shofar*; Oyez!
Praise the Lord with hallelujahs!
Foes will ever seek to sunder
Life from Judah! God is wonder!
Miracles our way of living!
Raise your voices in thanksgiving!
        Let the sky and let the sod
        And all between now praise our God!

16

FIVE WEAPONS AGAINST DEATH

FOREWORD

If you are joyous now, omit
These whining sonnets; pass this black
Page over; overlook this writ.
It will recall the song you lack.

Turn you this leaf, and you ensconce
Yourself in graveyards, hear the dull
Stroke of the spade against sheer bones,
Against a once-familiar skull.

ARROW OF ALOOFNESS

This last week I have shunned mortality;
    Advisedly eschewed the mentioned dead;
    Shut both my eyes to graven tombstones; fled
From the small horrors of a cemetery ...
Worn epitaphs this last week were to me
    Menacing omens ominously read;
    This week there was no sound I did not dread,
No sound was there that was not threnody ...
    Strive as I could, I could not flee it, I
Could not from Death keep utterly aloof;
    The least worm's turn—a threat; the slightest sigh
Upon the wind—a soul's last good reproof ...
    O, this last week, this last week—even the sky
To me was like a fretted charnel roof!

IRONY OF FOURTEEN BLADES

Striking the melancholy attitudes
They laved his body in feigned tear-drops—O
These staid mechanic mourners, and their throe!
They nailed his coffin with sad platitudes.

17

Lo, the post-mortem praiser—he exudes
　　Stock phrases such practitioners all know;
　　Commiseration made to order—woe
Delivered of manufactured moods!
　　The merchants weep—they have one less to cheat;
The gossips whine—they have one less to doom;
　　Old women, for the sake of bleating, bleat;
And sorrow bubbles from the eyes like spume.
　　All have performed the sad incumbent feat—
The undertaker gloats behind his gloom.

SWORD OF THE RIGHTEOUS

And they have torn their garments; and have turned
　　The portraits to the wall, and hid the bright
　　Reflections of a mirror in a white
Cloth; they have stared on Sorrow and discerned
Fatality; and they have truly mourned . . .
　　And ceased to mourn. On stools in stolid plight
　　Shoeless they sit; suddenly stand upright
And chant the *Kaddish* they have lately learned.
　　For why be desolate, and why complain
Seeing that Death has always his last say?
　　Let rather piety accept his reign.
Rather let worthy unconcern allay
　　The anguish, iterating the refrain:
He who has given, He has snatched away.

SLING FOR GOLIATH

Never let me behold her so again . . .
　　Where happiness should be, no happiness.
　　Woe on her lips all rouged with bitterness,
Tears on her face like acid etching pain,
And fingers knitted in lamented strain
　　Inversely broken out of great distress;
　　And weeping, weeping and sad bitterness—

18

Never let me behold her so again.
   Let me not think upon her father's death,
And certainly not think of her strong sorrow;
   Let me not brood upon that knavish Sleuth
   Contriving clever frightfulness to harrow
      Body and soul, and take away the breath
   My hand cannot stay steady, chiseling Sorrow.

CLUB OF FINAL PAIN

There lies a corpse upon your memory, plus
   A headstone heavy on the corpse—O shun
   Consortments with your memory of one
Whose pain no longer shrills as querulous.
O my beloved, do not sorrow thus.
   The moon has lost no lustre, and the sun
   No sunlight; nor like you is it undone.
And dawn arises still to call to us.
   Surely there is no difference, no change
   In this our love since he passed by the door
   And kissed no worn *mezuzah* . . . Why estrange
Yourself from happiness, and why implore
   And coax the heartache? Surely there is no change,
Only that in your grief I love you more.

AFTERWORD

The crow upon the hawthorn bush
Pecks at the haws until they bleed;
Or watches some red earthworm push
Himself along a slimy weed;
Or meditates the autumn leaf
Turning to powder and to dust . . .
He caws in arrant unbelief.

KOHELETH

Koheleth, on his damasked throne, lets weary exhalation follow
The weary inhalation. He finds breath a toil of no reward.
As hollow as the rotted gourd is the heart of the monarch hollow . . .
His weakened voice drops weariness, that slowly falls, word after
     word:

"Take your black quill, O Scribe, and write in wormwood and with
     gall—
That I am but erected dust that flutters to a roofless tomb;
That even on the loveliest the unparticular worm will crawl;
And that this sun, this splendid sun, is nothing more than whitened
     gloom."

Death is a tall, a stripped and oil-anointed Negro chamberlain
Standing behind the lion-guarded throne and rustling leaves of palm
Over the royal crown to cause cool ripples in the royal brain . . .
Death is an oil-anointed slave, exuding an inebriant balm.

"Take your black quill, O Scribe, and write in wormwood and with
     gall,
That I who have known the speech of birds, the love of the fair
     Shunamite,
The import of the thorn-pierced rose, that I do spurn them all . . .
My days are cawing crows, O Scribe, yea, cawing crows in darkened
     flight.

"Speak of the pleasures of the wise, verily I have known these once;
The glories of the goblet, yea, these, too, have been a part of me,
The ecstasies of damosels, these also have been Solomon's,
Who waking and who sleeping cries: These things are wind and
     vanity.

"Many the provinces I rule, but weariness rules over me;
Strong are my gem-crammed coffers, yet compared to coffins weak,
     infirm . . .
A thousand concubines are mine—a thousand reasons for ennui . . .
There is naught new beneath the sun; beneath the earth the ancient
     worm!

"In wormwood and with gall, O Scribe, write these embittered
　　words, to wit:
King Solomon on boredom sups, and on satiety he dines;
His nights are poisoned cups; his days are blossoms bruised; his life
　　is but
A throne built out of coffin boards, and tapestried with death-
　　designs."

Death is a tall, a stripped and oil-anointed Negro chamberlain
Standing behind the throne; he makes grimaces underneath his
　　palm;
Behind the royal back he scoffs; his gestures they are more than
　　plain . . .
Koheleth turns his head, and lo, Death stands most dignified and
　　calm.

BUSINESS

And for the sake of you I am become
A trafficker in stars, and barter my
Knapsack of constellations for some high
Rare compliment for you; I am become
A hawker of the moon, who, never dumb,
Runs through the streets and shouts his wonders; I
Am certainly a magnate of the sky—
I lay before you all my glittering sum.
Yes, I would sell the flora of each clime
For price of metaphor; and I would dole
Out riches for the sake of one sweet rhyme
To sing its solo in a sweeter whole.
And I would buy a poem any time
And gladly pay it with my only soul.

FIXITY

Amber opaque are autumn skies—
And autumn trees and autumn men
Are as so many captured weeds
And as so many fossiled flies.

HAUNTED HOUSE

Let the storm rage;
No better way is there
To ecstasize an autumn midnight
Than lavishly to stage
Fury climbing up a broken lightning stair . . .
Or to arrange
Elemental pyrotechnics as a preconceived affair . . .
The window-seat in this deserted house
Will frame us in still contrast to the wind's carouse;
The window-seat
Accords us cosy circumvision of the universe
Replete
With noisy mourners following a creaking hearse . . .
Are you not comfortable? Do you fear
The thunder storm as night is borne upon a bier?
Draw you then closer to me—how it storms
That tempest in your heart, and how your bosom warms!
See you the sky—an oriflamme tattered,
  A bowl of amethyst shattered,
  An inky hieroglyph spattered
  Against a parabolic wall. . .
This is too strong to last; this heavy fall
Will weary as a madman pounding on a cell.
  For since the wind goes clutching
  At the shutters, wrenching
  The hinges, whistling
  In the attic, climbing

The chimney, and pirouetting
On its top, and since lightning
Piles its sudden stitching
Of the sky, the rain drenching
The weedy garden, the leaves rustling
In the feeble groan of trees
At each wetting,
It must cease.
It ceases.
And lo! the clouds have passed; the moon
Stares at the world, an actor who
Fumbling his cue, has come too soon.
Do not you fear then; the wind grows calmer,
And thunder has laid down his hammer
Ceasing to nail the stars in grooves invisible.
Only the poplar drips, sweating from his great struggles;
Only the vine-leaves rustle, catching their quiet breath;
Only—but what is that sound that silence seeks to smuggle
Into this room, like stealthy footsteps of a death?
There must be someone in the upper attic,
A bird-brained ghost moving with step erratic,
Trying the door-knobs, pressing the wall's buttons. . .
His slightest footstep threatens
Tranquility, until he too is static.
His movement ceases.
Silence collects its broken pieces.

It is quiet in this house;
There is nothing else to do
But to listen to the mouse
That is listening to you.
There is nothing else to stage
But the spider in his hunger
Growing fat, and growing younger
In his age.

There is nothing here for thought.
Silence nullifies the sane.
And dust settles on the brain.
Here is naught.

Nothing is here save you, my love and your
Flaming companionship consoling me
In this lone dust-infested house which we
Have entered, pushing on a latchless door.
Nothing is here, my love, except a poor,
A niggard modicum of empery
And four walls crumpling into meagre three,
The fourth being exit. Here is nothing more.
Nothing and no one save we two, my dear,
Watching a rain-drop, think of a tear,
And foiling sorrow with elaborate dictions,
Therefore so evident, it is, so clear
Life is a haunted house, haunted by fictions.

But let me not change breath to breathing words,
Seeing that zeros transfer into nils.
Let me not be Polonius to love,
Fixing a definition in a phrase,
Adorning small nihilities with frills
Of fancy circumlocutory praise.
Let me not fashion thought in tiny pills,
But let me say, in one of many ways:
Life is a haunted house through which two lovers
Holding warm hands are bravely sallying,
Ransacking cluttered bookshelves, lifting coffers,
Opening dusty cupboards, wandering,
Through rooms uncarpeted, up stairs unsteady,
Reaching at last the attic, and unclasping
The attic window, showing the full sky
With stars expectant of the frenzied grasping,
And splendour calling forth the heady
    Exclamation, and the single cry.
There goes the wind again, again the rain-drops
Riddle the wet leaves, falling from the branches;
Again is the moon torn into indistinguished
Leaves like the fall's; again the storm wind wrenches
Trees from their sockets, and once more the wind
    Rides like a witch upon a broomstick,
    Rides like a witch upon the poplar trees. . .
    Yet as I speak it is all over.

24

Quiet again skulks in this room;
The thunder shower, a rowdy spirit,
Returns unto his unknown tomb.
Only thick gouts fall from the eaves
Upon the loud-resounding leaves. . .
And once again within the upper attic
The bird-brained ghost moves with his step erratic;
His slightest footstep steps upon the mind,
Until he too is static.
His movement ceases.
Silence collects its broken pieces.

A SEQUENCE OF SONGS

EXULTATION

My blood shouts very joyous news
Into my heart; and then
Hurries upon a lively cruise
To come and shout again.
Whose is the gladness that can vie
With mine? Once more, for spite,
Who is so happy as am I?
I see my love tonight!

EXIT

The street is great festivity;
Snow is a royal canopy
Made for a lover, made for me.

This is the way that love should go:
Winter an orchard-walk where blow
Blossom-petals of white snow.

25

Kisses of mine which lent a grace
To summer, run a frozen race:
Snowflake-kissing all my face.

LOVE CALL

Now she awaits me at this time we made—
I'll ring the door-bell as my serenade.

TREMBLEMENT DU COEUR

Footsteps are bringing beauty hither. She
Opens the door. Why do you start,
Why do you leap the stairs
Ahead of me, my heart?

FIRST SIGHT

The beauty that my love wore all the seven
Days I did not see her is now told
Upon her face, her face which is a heaven
Of beauty sevenfold.

SONG OF LOVE

I will make a song for you,
    And will sing it new.
I will not name any rose
    In my passion-throes;
Nor repeat a single word
    Of a singing bird;
Nor remember any tune
    Which will rhyme with June.
Silence will be the words of this
Song set to music of a kiss.

26

QUARREL

If so,
Then I will go. . .
(Downstairs a waiting wind is whistling for me.
Behind me there is sorrow; and before me?)

NEW VERSION

The moon is a golden hoop
    Whence bursts, whence bounds,
Straining for the fatal swoop,
    A pack of hounds.

DOUBT

And yet the doubt is hither-thither cast—
Will the last kiss I gave her be the last?

HOME

Love is become a memory,
A bitter, bitter memory,
Love is become a memory—
Where did I put that key?

FINALE

Love is an ache
    Keen and long. . .
Let my heart break
    Into song.

DIALOGUE

The two shawl-covered grannies, buying fish,
Discuss the spices of the Sabbath dish.

They laud old-country dainties; each one bans
The heathen foods the moderns eat from cans.

They get to talking of the golden land,
Each phrase of theirs couches a reprimand.

Says one: I hate these lofty buildings, I
Long for a piece of unencircled sky.

I do not know the tramway system, so
I walk and curse the traffic as I go.

I chaffer English, and I nearly choke,
O for the talk of simple Russian folk!

The other says: A lonesomeness impels
Me hence; I miss the gossip at the wells.

I yearn for even Ratno's muds; I long
For the delightfully heart-rending song

Of Reb Yecheskel Chazan, song that tore
The heart so clear it did not ask for more.

They sigh; they shake their heads; they both conspire
To doom Columbus to eternal fire.

THE WORDS OF PLAUNI-BEN-PLAUNI TO JOB

Thou dost not know thy deeds, O Job, when thou
Dost call on Death as one who calls upon
A maiden in the Spring at early dawn . . .
Thou dost not know thine heart, O Man of Uz
When thou dost waste thy days with perjured use
Of darling names for Death and for his crew
Of slimy mariners that eat and spue . . .

Has bitterness plucked out thy brain, that thou
Dost knock upon the doors of sepulchres
Crying, that thou canst not regard a hearse
But thou must mind thyself of royal steeds?
Has pain so scabbed thy heart that thou must need
Be gladdened at the sight of the black hue?
Is this Job jubilant that once I knew?

O Job, bethink thyself; it is not good
To look upon the flowers of the field
As sown and grown and nourished but to yield
Sweet strewings on the grave, it is not right
To hold the moon as but a lamp to light
Half-shadowed pits in which a ghost doth brood,
And it is false to think the sod a shroud . . .

Surely thou dost not believe that spices were
Ordained for the embalmer, and for him
Alone; surely it is no futile whim
That eyes are bright and skies are brighter still?
We are not born, we are not born to fill
A banquet-board for glutton maggots, nor
Are navels cut to make death easier . . .

Forsake the stars; forget the moon; forego
The beauty of a sky;—consort with worms!
Behold two boards are thy horizons; germs
Thy concubines; and nails in coffin-head

Serve as thy constellations—thou art dead!
Is this the end of thy desire: O
Is this thy longing? Wilt thou have it so?

There is no spring there, but the roots do clutch,
The fingers of the new roots clutch the hair
With twist and turn; there is no summer there;
Only strange stirrings in the earth; there is
No autumn save in heavy raininess
That trickles through the rot with clammy touch;
There is no winter, there is naught of such.

Bethink thyself again, O Job, again
Consider and give over all these sighs.
These beckonings to catch the Angels' eyes.
Put thine imaginings within the grave,
Emptied of all its charmed enticements, save
Its emptiness, and then, Job, think again—
That in the tomb there is not even pain.

CHRISTIAN POET AND HEBREW MAID

The nightingale proclaims no creed;
    The urgent thrush reiterates
No catechism: and the freed
    Canary holds no dark debates.
These sing; their exhalations cede
    The homage that the sky awaits.

The rose is pollened by no themes
    Spiritual; the lily pales
Before the import of her dreams.
    The lilac blossoms, and then fails.
They spread their fragrance: the Lord deems
    Such cups so many hallowed grails.

And roars no litany the pard;
  The elephant trips lustily;
The antics of the ape are marred
  By no meek genuflexions; the
Beasts of the field inflame no nard;
  And still the good Lord lets them be.

The ant reviles the dantine threat;
  The snail supports no gothic roof;
The larva and the cherub met
  In no cocoon's fine warp and woof;
The moth adores no altar; yet
  From these the Lord is not aloof.

Even as does the turtle-dove,
  And even as the skylark's tongue
Praises the permanence above,
  So can you pour from your full lung
Your vassalage to him of love,
  Your worship to the throne in song.

Blow ram's horns; make a joyful noise;
  Acquaint the seven-throated wind
Two hearts are set in perfect poise,
  In perfect poise the double mind;
And these assail their private Troys.
  On nectar they have both been wined.

The cross and double-triangle
  Are morticed; rosary and thin
Pendule are twined; the shield weds ball;
  The vulgate and the scroll are twin;
The spire and dome advance their call;
  Mary and Miriam are kin.

Blast trumpets, therefore; let doom crack;
  Heralds, announce, and make it known
That one has watched a comet's track
  And seen it brighter than a sun,
And he has spied in the Zodiac
  Virgo and Leo fade in one.

SATURDAY NIGHT

It being no longer Sabbath, angels scrawl
The stars upon the sky; and Main Street thrives.
The butcher-shops are as so many hives,
And full is every delicatessen stall.
Obese Jewesses, wheeling triplets, crawl
Along the gibbering thoroughfare.
Fat wives
Lead little husbands, while their progeny dives
Among this corpulence in shouting frisky sprawl.
The whole street quivers with a million hums.
Hebraic arms tell jokes that are not funny.
Upon the corner stand the pool-room bums.
Most valiantly girl-taggers smile for money.
From out a radio loud-speaker comes:
    O, Eli, Eli, lama zabachthani!

FALSTAFF

In these prosaic days when lovers ask
    Permission for their suit from ministers,
    It is to Falstaff, loosest of bachelors,
That I lift up this ischiadic flask,

Regretting only that I have no cask
    Wherefrom replenishment might further course:
    "Here was warm flesh, and much of it, my Sirs,
Here was a wight in whom a wench might bask!"

    Who left his fire and sack and went to woo
Gay wives innumerable? Who, one dark
    Night for the sake of Venus did endue
Himself with buck's horns in old Windsor Park?
    Falstaff it was, none other; Falstaff, who
For love's sake, raised a ditch's watermark!

FUNERAL IN APRIL

His voice may tear the sky to shreds,
His requiem cause worms to creep,
His wail may shake a hundred heads,
And make a hundred mourners weep.
But we, my love, will heed no knell,
No crow-frocked cantor and his caw,
For all we care, he may, as well,
Sing fiddle-dee and tra-la-la.

CALVARY

Upon these trees was Autumn crucified. . .
Do you not see the thorns, the ready bier
Of leaves, the stains of blood? . . . Do you not hear
His *Eli Eli* echo? . . . It has died.

ANGUISH

The moon
Is sudden grief
Across a star-pricked sky . . .
It is an interjection crying
O! . . .

OLD MAID'S WEDDING

Autumn
Is an old bride.
She wears a veil of mist.
Upon her are thrown confetti—
dead leaves...

EXORCISM VAIN

The tongue has faltered. Hence, revoked the demons,
Scattered the essence, th'incantation futile,
The ghouls return to fructify their lemans;
And pandemonium again is motile.

The circle broken; bird-feet traced but slightly
Within the dust upon the book-shelves; magic
On hallowed midnights murmured eruditely
Wholly discomfited; the terror tragic,

The mispronouncement of the syllable
Conclusive renders the good deed undone—
Alas, the hesitancy in the call,
The stutter in the tetragrammaton.

ON THE ROAD TO PALESTINE

Upon the road to Palestine
    I met a little Jew,
A pomegranate in his hand
    He sometimes stopped to chew,
And sometimes stopped to praise the Lord,
    Whereat I said, *Baruch Hu!*

34

Where do you come from, little Jew?
　　I come from Palestine.
The land is full of clover-fields,
　　The fields are full of kine:
And babes drink milk from flowercups,
　　And old men vats of wine.

O, there are blossoms everywhere,
　　Swinging with tongueless bells;
And when the land is not in bloom
　　'Tis that the fruitage swells:
Oranges drop from orange-trees,
　　And almonds from their shells.

O, why do you leave this Palestine?
　　Then quoth the little Jew:
I come this way from Palestine
　　To find and welcome you
To come to old Jerusalem,
　　And Palestine the new.

YOSSEL LETZ

His mother's bribes,
His father's threats
Could breed no manners
In Yossel Letz.

He twiddled his thumbs;
He turned up his toes;
He ate with his fingers;
He drank with his nose.

Seated at table
In spite of guests,
This Yossel made
Uncouth requests.

A fork, a spoon,
A knife—were toys
With which a boy
Might make a noise.

But on Passover
When he ate
Horseradishes
From off a plate,

Or wrapped the *matzo*
Round the *moror,*
No person screamed,
None shouted: Horror!

And when this Yossel
Asked four queries
And got as answers
Twenty theories,

Or when he dipped
His fingers in
The wine at Pharoah's
Every sin,

Or when he sprawled
On cushions and
Stretched each wild leg,
Each frivolous hand,

His mother glowed,
His father shone;
A Hebrew prince!
A royal son!

MESSIAH

Aleph, Bais,
Son of my race,
Gimmel, Dalid,
With lean face pallid,
Hai, Vav,
My scholar-dove,
Zain, Chess,
Your words will bless
Tess, Yud,
The heathen brood,
Caf, Lamed,
The sons of Mohammed,
Mem, Nun,
And your holy rune,
Samech, Eyon,
Will glow from Zion.
Pai, Phai,
Angels will play
Zaddick, Koof,
On your golden roof;
Raish, Shein,
And God will lean,
Toff, Sauf,
From His throne above,
Patach, Tzaira,
While you will wear a
Kometz, Segal,
Crown viceregal.

INVOCATION TO DEATH

O think, my Love, of what we two will be
In two score years from now, and how we will
Offer our prayers together. List to me:
Better it were to be beneath the hill.

Think of thyself in pious grey perruque,
Through rims beholding little with much praise,
Staring upon an heirloom prayer book:
The saddest weeper on high holidays.

And think of me, a graybeard Jew, and cold,
Reading the psalms all day, a shivering ghost;
Kissing with fingers that will soon be mould
The worn *mezuzahs* on each Jew's door-post.

O let us die before we will be old.

ECCLESIASTES 13

The worm doth make the earth a labyrinth
Full of small chambers and cool passages;
The bee doth buzz his nectared business,
Thinking the sky a bell of hyacinth.
Around some cobwebbed long-deserted plinth
The spider dwells in his thin loveliness;
The caterpillar in his furry dress
With hundred feet doth clasp the terebinth.
And with a lordly calculated tread
The snail moves, moves his marble spiral room.
Thus are the meanest vermin often bred
In riches it is not theirs to assume;
Yea, maggots batten even in the head
Of some great monarch in a gilded tomb.

HEROIC

Avaunt the nightingale! Perish the rose!
Superfluous the moon, that gilded fraud!
Vanish the ermined ladies, satin-shod!
Deafen the rhymes and the poetic prose!
Let music have no aphrodisiac throes,
And let no elves beat sandals on the sod!
Who seeks these subtle scene-shiftings of God,
Fashioned for pining belles and perfumed beaux?
For me and for my love, these bearded Jews
Praising the moon, are goblins now grown old;
The cats, being lyrical, brew no abuse;
Music the shrillness of a Jewish scold . . .
O love casts roses beneath broken shoes,
And paves this ghetto street with burnished gold!

SENTIMENTAL

How will you phrase regret when I depart,
When I am laved upon a naked plank,
Made clean for worms, most clean and deathly dank,
And trundled in an ostentatious cart?
What acid word, what sentence wryly tart
Will leave your lips before your world goes blank?
If it does that. In what terms will you thank

The Lord before the sombre horses start?
For when it will occur which must occur,
It matters not what wailing load the wind—
But now I query while I yet do stir:
Will you weep, dear, when sextons grow unkind?
And will your weeping be the bitterer,
Knowing I leave no *kaddish*-voice behind?

39

NEHEMIAH

The incense, rising, curls the nostrils with its scent:
The music leaps in mountains and in valleys:
The monarch on his purple dais sits intent—
The damsels dance and show their wanton bellies.

Standing beside the Royal One, apparelled royally,
He hears no music; and he sees no dance . . .
He only pours the wine into its goblet. Silent, he,
This cup-bearer of the gloomy countenance.

He dreams he sees dead streets and yawning jackals roam
Through the lone city, hears the lonely whine . . .
There is a sepulchre where once there was his home.
The king will drink a tear-drop in his wine.

FESTIVAL

Ho, maskers, fix your noses, strike a posture,
Squeak out your ditties in a thin falsetto,
Flutter your torn hermaphroditic vesture,
And dance the dances of the vinous ghetto.

If you are thirsty, lift your masks with caution,
And drink this red exultant wine; if hungry,
Here are the cakes, and here the *haman-taschen;*
Guzzle and glut, or else your host is angry.

To-night God loves his Jews a trifle tipsy;
He looks upon the sober with displeasure,
Trundle your limbs in joyful epilepsy,
Carol the catches of a lusty measure.

Tell us, Ahasuerus, anent your harem,
What does a maid to make her royal booty?

How many in a bed-room is a quorum?
Wherefore did Vashti Queen refuse her beauty.

Zeresh, mimic your consort's antic bellows
The time you crowned him with the pot mephitic?
Mimic him, too, upon the lofty gallows,
Gallows designed for carrion Semitic.

Rattle, you rattlers, at the name of Haman,
Ordure to be expelled with sonal senna;
The young men curse him, and the old cry Amen.
And he becomes a whisper in Gehenna.

ARABIAN LOVE SONG

Brown are your eyes, as brown as the gazelle's,
And black your eye-lashes, as thin and black
As the curved lines with which the scribe casts spells
Over illumined script; your eyebrows track
The paths of serpents in tall asphodels.

For colour of asphodel is on your brow,
And on your cheeks rose-petals pink and white.
Yea, even as cool plums in moonlight show
Passing of paleness with the least wind's flight,
So does your skin in beauty, even so.

Your lips are rubies rendered flesh; your smile
Is pearl made quick; your laughter has the sound
Of gems dropped slowly in a glittering pile.
The beauties of your small full mouth confound
Me utterly, and for no little while.

Your lovely breasts are cream upon which float
The petals of the jasmine. . . . Small and smooth
Is the round compass of your waist. . . . Your throat
Is marble, and your marble thighs make youth
Return to those who drivel and who dote.

Four are the beauty spots upon your face
Like black seeds in the luscious melon; four
The beauty spots and one the dimpled place,
Oh, loved one, I am curious for more,
I hunger to give others their soft praise.

LITANY

Because the Lord was good to me, and gave
Me happiness that runneth from the brim—
Because the love of you to me he gave,
I worship Him.

Because I am still young, because the moon
Beneath my ribs has not yet known eclipse
Because with this sure youth I know my boon
I worship Him upon your lips.

FOUR SONNETS: MY LITERATI FRIENDS
IN RESTAURANTS

My literati friends in restaurants—
Platos exhaling smoke from cigarettes—
Assail the virtue in their maiden aunts;
Annul the Jew with paragraphs from Graetz;
Between slow smoke-puffs fumigate a seer,
Settle a war in spitting olive-pips;
Snap at nobility, at honour sneer;
Damn the apostles in twelve coffee-sips.
I toy with a blank menu and a pen:
L'amor che move il sole e gli altre stelle—
Where I did come by this, or how, or when

Only our love can say. Here it sounds silly,
Now that my friends call one another asses,
In shouting their love for the working-classes.

FOUR SONNETS: WERE I TO TALK
UNTIL THE CRACK O' DOOM

Were I to talk until the crack o' doom,
Impeccably maintain you in debate
The loveliest guise that beauty can assume;
Were I to split my heart, a pomegranate,
Showing the unambiguous blood; were I
To scour the se'en seas, scale the mountainous moon,
Forage the archipelago of the sky,
Hoping to bring some eloquent gems as boon,
Still would my largess shame the worth of you,
My mighty words still turn to paltriness.
I shall but say: Your eyes, though grey, seem blue;
Your laugh is joy in blossom; your caress
Sweet to the touch; your lips are soft. In fine,
You are my heart's desire. You are mine.

SEASONS

SPRING

The thin and delicate etching of Jack Frost
Is blurred upon the pane; his fingernail
Is broken from the eaves; his argent mail
Is vanished so it is not even dust.
Preserve the heavy tuque in cedar; thrust
The mittens in the chest; forget the tale

43

Heard by the pine-wood fire; all these fail
When April makes the woods a holocaust.
Before the cabin-door the robins gobble
Worms from the wet soil; sparrows go and come
Rifling dead leaves, and twigs, and barren rubble.
The maple buds are red and thick with gum.
And barefoot boys display from last year's stubble
The three-leafed and three-petalled trillium.

SUMMER

The ants repair to cooler galleries;
The crickets ply their plaints against the sun;
From grass to weed, from weed to tree-trunk run
Grasshoppers vaulting into shaded ease.
The wayfarer is lowered to his knees.
Even the heat-mad sparrows, one by one,
Seeking the jaundiced leaf, have flown and gone.
Most lazily thick bovine tails chase fleas . . .
The wind ignores this slow, this solar slaughter,
And takes his siesta in the hammock hung
Nowhere. The thought of heat makes heat grow hotter.
While mind is bent on dreams of crystal water,
While fevered Sirius droops his parched tongue,
Merely to breathe now is to scorch the lung.

AUTUMN

Autumn, you dement; you wrench from my throat
Plaudits of incoherence, lo, I cry:
You are an oriflamme against the sky;
You are the memory of Joseph's coat;
Vermilion lines that Omar Khayyam wrote;
A molten rainbow; Bergeracian lie;
Jester in motley gibbeted on high;
You are a red hand catching at my throat!
One phrase erupts another. Oh, you paint
The dull brain gaudy as a brilliant totem;

44

Havoc you wreak with speech. Logic you taint.
Futile is praise before your splendour, Autumn.
Splendour that renders my voice small and faint,
Until I am left mumbling, Autumn . . . Autumn.

WINTER

What is this seasonal nonentity?
This pale and shivering shadow? What this white,
This bleached continuance of coloured light?
What is this interlude of leprosy?
Winds from the north rush in most hurriedly
Crying some terrible news, some cryptic fright;
Suddenly die. And suddenly a flight
Of new-born winds speed on and cry their cry . . .
Unto this earth will ashes always cling?
Will the sky always seem of sack-cloth now?
Why this demurring of the days that sing?
And why this loneliness upon the bough?
Has earth forgotten how to stir the Spring?
Give me the magic. I remember how.

EARTHQUAKE

"I think I hear a trumpet overhead.
    A thumping on the lid—a white ass ride. . ."
The corpses murmured, stirred, "We are not dead!"
    And turned and slept upon their other side.

PHILOSOPHER'S STONE

"So have I spent a life-time in my search
 To make, as it is said,
Noble from base. Life left me in the lurch,
 And dropt me with the dead;
And now I find it, buried in the church:
 It stands right overhead . . . ."

WOOD NOTES WILD

INDICTMENT

I said: Autumn
 Is an unfortunate hyperbole,
 An exaggeration in chrome;
 A wench too rouged,
 Or a clown too motley.
Autumn, I said, is Summer
Carried to its *reductio ad absurdum.*

STYLE

This last July a crazy caterpillar
Displayed a miniature raccoon-coat; and
This late October I discovered him
Frigidly lying on a bed of state,
Attired in ermine.

AESTHETIC CURIOSITY

Does an owl appreciate
The colour of leaves
As they fall about him
In the staggering nights of Autumn?

MUTE HERALDRY

An ant shouldering a light straw;
A squirrel nibbling a chestnut
And even a house-fly, solitary on a ceiling—
These are the heralds proclaiming
The tread of white midgets
In a distant sky.

PRIDE BEFORE FALL

Summer had raised herself
To the top-most tree-tops
And had scoffed at rainbows—
Now is she fallen
To the roots,
To the stubble,
To the black wet earth.

IMAGE CELESTIAL

Autumn
Is an insane Japanese
In a gorgeous but torn kimono
Threatening to commit
Hari-kari at my door.

HEAVEN AT LAST

I have seen a lark
Swallow a worm, soar, and disappear
In a blue oblivion.
Wherefore I consoled myself, saying:
It is not too terrible to die
To be eaten by worms,
Provided
Considerable skylarks bear the worms aloft
And lay them at the Upper Gates.

DIVINE TITILLATION

O, what human chaff!
Trying to tickle my feet
With spires . . . what conceit!
Indeed you make me laugh!

DESIDERATA

Three things I long to see:
                    A lustrous moth
Torment with envy bulky behemoth . . .
                    An elf and ant
Conspire to affright an elephant . . .
                    A manikin
Murder the superman of his own kin.

KALMAN RHAPSODIZES

i

The old Jews greet the moon
With triple elevation of the heel.
They stand before the synagogue; they croon.
They laud the gold round shield of David.
From their beads their muted praises steal.
Their words are Hebrew characters which fly
To take their places with the other stars,
That are as annotations in the sky,
As annotations to the Cabalistic wheel.

But we, my love, we praise the moon sufficiently;
We gild it with an alchemistic stuff.
In that we let its splendours be
A mirror to our kisses, we
Flatter it enough.

ii

Reb Kalman contemplates the good and evil
And weighs God in the small palm of the hand,
And in the other balances the Devil.
He finds the burden of the Lord as light as sand
And that of Satan heavy as wet sod
For simple reason that in weighing God
He has forgotten the Angelic Band.

WHERE SHALL I FIND CHOICE WORDS

Where shall I find choice words to mention Sorrow
That Sorrow may not be a pain to you?
That Sorrow may not jewel your eyes with tear-drops
Nor twist your once-resigned lips anew?

Where shall I find such delicate, such tender
Phrases as will slide off your heart, and not
Open the wound that I had said had vanished?
Where shall I find that soft word, that mild thought?
Such words there are not, nor such harmless phrases;
Even the word innocuous sometimes sears.
I found the phrase, designed and well-aforethought
Brought a quick memory, and lavish tears.

MURALS FOR A HOUSE OF GOD

SCATTERBRAIN SINGETH A SONG

On bane big-bellied mothers feed;
    Poison is suckled at the paps;
Hatred is roted with creed;
    And swilled at mine host's taps.
The moon is pricked, and it will bleed;
The sky will flame like an evil screed;
    Demons wear feathers in their caps.

The world is daft. Shrewd Satan walks
    Unknown, his tail between his legs.
At the gate a bleeding knuckle knocks,
    A poor man begs.
A poor man, fie! In his golden crocks
    Are gems; and deeds in his wife's socks;
    And coins in his kegs.

AT THE SIGN OF THE SPIGOT

Emmerich, Count, of the stentorious voice
Rattles his bellicose glaive, and makes such din
His breath befuddles even the tapster-boys
And sets a-quivering the red bush of the inn:

50

"Sirrah, quit counting of thine apron-stains!
Bestir thy stumps! A flagon! a keg! a cask!
Bring hither a brimming tun! And here's for thy pains!
Empty thy cellar, if needs be, on ten wains!
Go to, ere I render thy whey-face a red mask!

Dost gape! Dost thou read a rune on my nose? Ho, ho,
'Tis the state of my purse that pops thy rat's eyes so!
This wallet holds ducats and marks enough to buy
Thyself, thy master, and all such varlet fry.

Save the Jews, the Hebrews . . . these maggots in Holstein cheese,
These spiders in Rhenish wine, these frogs who croak
In our lilied ponds, these bats who are at ease
In mansions edified of stone and oak.

For thirty pieces of gold they sold Him. Now
On usury thereof they have become a folk
Of the golden fist and of the brazen brow
The while we wights get gangrened 'neath their yoke.

Here are the deeds: to Aaron of Mayence, such;
To Isaac of Worms a like sum; to Abraham
A similar warrant for a similar touch:—
What maws their coffers have, and how they cram!

Instance thyself; dost pawn thy silver and plate,
The Jew smiles into his beard; thou art his thrall,
Thence to the tavern to forget thy fate—
Anon, thy wealth is water on a wall.

Holla, the wine! My throat is burnt to a cinder!
Let every heart upon a red sea sail!
Quaff it, my hearties, wine is the soul's tinder!
With *groschen* left, we will still guzzle ale.

Our purses lined with merest shreds; our debts
Advancing minatory cap-a-pie,
I know how we can thwart the bailiff's threats:
The Hebrew chests will open to a key!

51

A lustrous key, a golden key, a bright
Opener of locks, a key of burnished fame,
Defying gates, bars, locks of triple might,
Climbing up ramparts, bursting walls—a flame!

So raise your tankards, let us have a toast—
O let us toast the Hebrews a good brown—
Ho, they will crackle, they will fritter, they will roast,
And with them their vile bills—Heigho, a toast!"

FROM THE CHRONICLES

Wherefore, upon the twenty-seventh May, ten hundred ninety-six
years since our Lord, a mob, in venery of heathen prey, and
purposing to put Jews to the sword, burst on Mayence. The town
was all agog. Some Jews were slain. Some knelt at the blessed font.
Books, writ by Talmud, were burnt in the synagogue. In sooth,
Christ's soldiers made all Jewry their loud haunt.

The Archbishop, soft-hearted beyond belief, opened his palace to
the Jews, to which they did repair, midst roaring of their grief.
Moreover at the gate before the ditch some well-accoutred swains as
guards were set. Ask not: *Quis custodes custodiet?*

JOHANNUS, DEI MONACHUS, LOQUITUR

No pulpit talk in ale-houses; no sermons
Over one's cups; no anthems at the board.
This is mere infant's lore, not fit for Germans.
I, faring here to wet the tip o' my tongue
Must now perforce enounce the Holy Word.

Well-spoken, Count, well-spoken of Jew-dung
This scab upon the body politic,
This pestilence, this threat to Christian quick.
These infidels within the Christian state,
Like lice inhabiting a tonsured pate
Must be outrooted and in fire flung.

52

In vain your genuflections in your pews,
In vain your wafers, masses, churches, altars,
In vain; in vain; they are befouled by Jews,
By Hebrews working such unhallowed filth
A thousand purgat'ries can not redeem you; no,
Nor prayers mumbled from a thousand psalters.
Christian, indeed, this state, a state for scoffers
To laugh in their sleeves beholding Jews who keep
The Christian hostages within their coffers.

Sir, you are faring to Jerusalem
To chase unfaithful toes from Christ's footsteps,
And set your candles on the sacred tomb;
So do you pluck the thorn and leave the stem;
Abort the child, and spare the fruitful womb.

Your spires balance the clouds, but Hebrew homes
Support the silver roofing of the sun.
The Holy Ghost is borne through our streets—
Over hooked noses Jew-eyes look thereon.
And while I pace my cloister, telling my beads,
Bargaining jargons interrupt my creeds.

Before you cast the beam from Palestine
Pick out the mote from Mainz; perish the Jews!
Burn them in fat of pork; stop up their whine
With lard; feed them to flame; disperse their ash
Unto the seven winds; let us be rid
Of these bats clutching at a praying throat,
And of these frogs, croaking from a Teuton's moat.

BALLAD OF THE HEBREW BRIDE

"Why do you set the candlesticks,
Six on this side, on this side six?"

"For that it is my wedding-day,
My lover gallops on the highway."

53

"O sister, you are lily-pale,
And yet you don white robe and veil!"

"Not in my mother's bed tonight
Shall I lie down, so slim, so white."

"O where is the ring your lover true,
On your betrothal gave to you?"

"Upon my finger, it did not fit;
In the deep earth, he buried it."

"Who are the guests at your marriage-feast?"
"Three hundred soldiers, and a priest!"

"Where are the fiddlers that will play
A ditty on your wedding day?"

"There will be only a sad song.
Church-bells will sob: Ding-dong! Ding-dong!"

"O who is your lover, that you fear
His bed as if it were a bier?"

"He has a quiet step; he comes
With legions bearing muffled drums."

"His lips are red; blood-red his lips
And there is blood on his finger-tips."

"When he will clasp you to his side
With what name shall you hail him, Bride?"

"O, I shall run, and have no breath,
I shall not even whisper: Death!"

AN ELDER COUNSELS SELF-KILLING

Unsheathe the blade; transgress your nail
Across its thin edge; be it keen.
This day it cries a soft wassail
To many a throat; this day makes clean
Of its red contents many a grail.
This day blood stains the gaberdine.

O grind your necklaces to dust,
Matrons; O ancients, meet the blade
With the beard combed and pointed.

Must,
Must I teach you, pale-throated maid,
You too, how cold steel breeds warm rust,
And sucklings, you, the slaughterer's trade?

Before this gleam there quailed good fowl,
The barnyard feared this flash of woe.
Now that Death comes beneath a cowl,
Let this heft hail him, bid him go.
To-morrow he may justly howl,
And the blithe cock may crow.

A YOUNG MAN MOANS ALARM BEFORE THE
KISS OF DEATH

Spit spittle on the rose? fling gravel at
The splendour of the sun? prevent the moon?
Acclaim the dark dominion of the bat?
Embrace the cypress? Perish at high noon?
Depart while yet the shadow is still tall?
Ah, bitterer than gall upon the tongue,
More bitter than the bitterest of gall,
So to inhale into the jubilant lung
The poison powdered on the rose, and so to fall.

Oh heart, consider not how from her tears
April now smiles, and how on every branch

55

The song-birds bud; consider rather how he leers,
Death on the juvenal cheeks that pale and blanch.
Are these the stalwart words that I must say?
Is this the stoic sentence I must mouth?
My tongue cannot utter it; its phrases stay
Choked in my throat; my lips are dumb with drouth;
And me only tempestuous syllables can allay.

There is a price upon our beards. Sleek fell
Of cub, gaunt wolf's head gets no more. Death hawks
His Hebrew wares. His voice is a church-bell.
Cradles are tombs a Jewish mother rocks.
Beneath disastrous stars we live. And yet
The Lord Omnipotent, Omniscient, He—
Blasphemy! Blasphemy! Let me choke it! Let
No sacrilege foam at my mouth, no plea
Assault the sky, assail the heavens no vain threat!

Forgive me, Lord, for that I am too much
Enamoured of thy world; too much in love
With sight, smell, hearing, taste and touch,
These to forego; forgive me from above.
Yea, though Thou loudly bid me, saying: Draw
The purple line across the pale white throat
For My sake perish, and for the one Law,
Humble I am; before Thee, less than a mote—
Yet find it not in me to kiss the funest claw.

THE CHRONICLER CONTINUES

Now that the guards, in homage to our Lord, unbarred the gates,
the soldiery, full-armed, into the palace of the bishop swarmed,
raising a pious shouting and the sword.
Alas, the Jews had taken their own lives! They lay there, making
moan, calling the devil. Two only, spurning their old heresies and
evil, asked for baptismal grace, they and their wives.
Howbeit, these treacherous knaves, no sooner ducked, but to the
synagogue they hastened, and beating their breasts, scampering like
chicks half-plucked, put fire to the synagogue with a brand. While
the loud flames still scurried up and down Count Emmerich and his
soldiers left the town.

56

SCATTERBRAIN'S LAST SONG

Heigh-nonny-no!
The wind will blow
The flames through the town
And burn it down.
   While post turns taper
   And plinth turns cinder
   The flames will caper
   On good hot tinder.
The flames will dance
On the roof of each manse;
The flames will browse
On the beams of each house.
   So will they run
   From the synagogue
   Until the town
   Will be one log,
   And the town's folk—
   a scrawny dog.

LEGEND OF LEBANON

Nigh Lebanon, nigh lofty Lebanon,
   The perfumes of the apple-blossom yield
Their fragrance to the wind, which comes as one
   In garlands odorous, in beauty veiled,
A bride within the garden of the dawn.
   And unto this white fragrance of the field
Do virgins, treading unbent grasses, list . . .
As though a song were made of petalled mist.

Full is the land of songsters, and of song;
        Branches of trees are budding musick; and
Even the mountain-streams, that, featly, throng
        Down from the rocks, raising the silver band
Of their laced skirts, light-hearted sing their song.
        And in this airy joyance of the land
Golden noises of bells are heard, as though
An unseen priest were moving to and fro.

And in the garden pools the lilies grow
        Pale with the spring, swoon utterly away
And rest their cheeks upon the water-flow,
        As in a dream of neither night nor day . . .
And in the garden plots the roses blow,
        And with remembrance of some sweetheart fay
Blush, and think of hot lips pressing hot,
A year ago upon this very spot.

O comely are the girls of Galilee
        Awaking in the earliness of morn;
And in the heat of noon-time, wearily
        Sighing away lone thoughts as they are born;
And damsels at the wells are verily
        Most fair to look upon when they adorn
A shoulder with the erst-filled water-jar
Wherein there glistens now the evening-star.

What are the yearnings which the young men nurse?
        Why do the smooth-faced youths find spring an ache?
And why do shepherd lads chant wistful verse
        Upon the hill-side? Why, and for whose sake?
Why are the young men such brave warriors?
        For that those maidens who do oft-times make
A welcoming for them with timbrel'd dance,
Are beautiful, and past all excellence!

Yea, they are lovely, but far lovelier,
        Even the loveliest in all the vale
Is tall Shoshannah of the jet-black hair,
        Which falls upon her throat—O jasmine pale—

58

Like shadow of a raven's wing in air;
Shoshannah at whose mention breathings fail,
Shoshannah at whose passing many hearts
Hasten and languish in uncounted starts.

'Tis noon; no person walks abroad, for full
Upon the brow of heaven fever beams.
But in the chamber of the wall, the cool
High-latticed chamber of the wall, she dreams,
Couched upon silk, most calm and beautiful,
Her face caressed by amorous sunbeams:
A maid ensorceled by a witch's wand,
A lily sleeping in a darkened pond.

Flutter of voice, and doves beneath the eaves
Ruffle the air, and brush upon her sleep
And she is wakened from the dream she weaves:
Its queen is left in empty hall to weep,
Its king lies headless, his meek spaniel grieves;
And frogs about his upturned footstool leap . . .
Alas, that she will never rede this dream
Unto its ultimate light, its final gleam.

Now, like a dream of her own dreams she doth
Arise, and scarcely do her white feet tread
The couchant carpet-woof'd behemoth,
Ere nigh unto the algum-casemented
Window she doth hover, seeming loth
To sense the sun heap kisses on her head;
There in the sun-motes she is even as
An incense-pillar of faint fragrances.

Lo! from the east, a caravanserai!
From rich Damascus lazily it moves.
The camels, treasure-humped against the sky,
Nodding their jewelled halters, raise their hooves.
What pleasant freight is this that now comes nigh
The spice whereof flows out, as though fresh groves
Of aloes and of spikenard and of myrrh
Hither were conjured by yon voyager?

59

Reclining in his gilded chariot,
       Upon soft cushions of a gorgeous dye,
Arrayed in gem-clasped purple, he is caught,
       The prince is caught in distant reverie,
Thinking on the bounties he has brought
       From lands where earth is mingled with the sky,
Musing on the givers and the gift,
The while the slave-held palm-leaves fall and lift.

And in the covered chariots there were
       The concubines the royal princesses,
Glad in their hearts and odorous of myrrh,
       Loved in the farthest of the provinces . . . .
And there was many a valiant warrior
       Guarding the prince and all this loveliness;
And there were peacocks vaunting heavens on
Their wings, and birds whose plumage was a dawn.

These marvels pass the ancient orchard wall
       From which the drooping blossom branches smile,
When suddenly the prince is made a thrall
       Of a faint vision seen a fleeting while
Through the high lattice of the vine-clad wall.
       He felt it like a shadow on the dial
Of his own heart, and as he looked above
The maid found favour in his eyes, and love.

Though she did flit away and was no more,
       Still in his heart he bore the memories
Of two full lips as red as is the core
       Of ripe pomegranates, and of two great eyes
That shone like precious stones both fashioned for
       An Ashtaroth, and of the round surprise
Of pearl-white ear-rings winking from dark hair,
And of a shadow that was standing there.

What guest is there within Shoshannah's heart
       That there is in it drunkenness of wine?
And musick playing with a cunning art?
       And dancing of a body serpentine?

60

What are these fancies that so often start
    From out her soul, like echoes from a shrine?
And why, amidst her troubled fantasies,
Doth she hold converse with herself in sighs?

A moon had pined and dwindled, and a moon
    Had waxed anew with plumper loveliness,
And now saw the bright pride of *Iyar* strewn
    Upon that vale, and saw the winds caress
The curtained tents on which was spilt its shoon
    Like honey spilt in generous excess,
The curtained tents wherein the prince sojourned
Whilst he did woo that one for whom he yearned.

Lo! in her sleep a midnight moon doth walk
    Across the sky; now doth the screech-owl sit
Upon some branch and weirdly doth mock
    The silence; from some quiet lake, moon-lit,
The mountain-pard laps water; demons stalk
    And cast a shadow and do follow it . . .
But brave of heart the prince doth mount his horse
And unto sweet Shoshannah speeds his course.

Clasping the moonlight and the climbing vine
    He lithesomely climbs up the trellis'd wall.
There is a goblet-moon of marriage-wine
    That hangs aloft; there is a beautiful
Maiden who sleeps within yon upper shrine . . .
    Can flesh stay upon earth, and earth not pall?
Can hearts still rest within the ribb'd mew?
He rises aloft, his sandals gemmed with dew.

"Shoshannah, sweet Shoshannah, lovely one,
    Twin of my heart, and secret of my soul,
O fairest daughter of fair Lebanon,
    Awake, arise, and let us both console
The weariness that love has cast upon
    Us, let us with soft blandishments cajole
Some beauty out of night, some unknown bliss
Out of the night in one unbroken kiss . . ."

61

And he beheld the hangings on the wall
    To flutter near the cushioned carven head
Of her soft couch, as if good Uriel
    And Gabriel were moving near her bed . . .
And he beheld long fingers, long and pale,
    The fingers of the moon caress her head,
The while she breathed at the frail moonbeams
A breathing laden with a thousand dreams.

The dew falls from the lips of God, and lifts
    The petalled eye-lids of the blooms; the sun
Uncovers preciousness in sudden rifts,—
    So did his honeyed whispers fall upon
Her, even so did her eyes fill with gifts
    Of glad surprise and speechless benison,
When she beheld him and did hear his voice:
"O come with me, my dearest, come, rejoice!

The night is full of incense of the moon;
    The night is laid before us even as
A royal carpet nuptially strewn
    With stars; the night has beauty and it has
Silence and loveliness of lovers. . . . Soon
    The dawn will break upon our words, and pass
Across the shadow of our eyes, and take
Love from our hearts and leave an empty ache.

For soon the cock will crow against the night,
    And will begin his worship of the sun . . .
Sweetheart, the stars slide down the sky, and light
    The heavens; soon a waking but a drowsy one
Will from a corner watch the sunlit sight,
    But now, thou lovely and thou only one,
The breeze beside me, and the whispers of
The leaves do woo thee, and do speak thee love."

She felt her soul possessed; she felt her breath
    Falter and fail upon her lips; she felt
Her heart move in her as it would at death . . .
    (O Love and Death the same word doubly spelt!)

62

And love-bewildered, not a word she saith,
  But raising a pale finger which did melt
In moonlight, put it to her lips, as though
A tapered arrow to its scarlet bow.

He sighed as if to waft away the moon
  And in an instant at her couch he stood;
"The whole long night have I craved for the boon
  Of love, and longed to hide thy kiss, red-hued,
Within my lips, and yearned to hear the tune
  Of thy heart's beat on mine in amorous feud;
And I have long desired to caress
The doves that hide beneath this laciness.

My father in whose beard there was no grey
  Is gathered to his fathers; may his bones
Forever rest in peacefulness, and may
  His name be numbered with the holy ones . . .
'Tis I, his youngest, was made king today,
  Chosen over all his other sons,
And I must haste to the anointment scene;
Arise, my fair one, thou shalt be my queen!

And on the morrow when the dawn will fill
  The erst-awakened heart with thanksgiving,
The sky with splendour of a miracle,
  And dew-touched mouths of birds with songs to sing,
O, sweetheart, then assuredly they will,
  Birds will make musical our marrying
For we will vow away this night alone
Within my tent, before we seek the throne."

Lo! over the hills, and then across the plain
  A white steed races with the moon, and snorts
Scorn to his rival, while his flickering mane
  Flames a white fire as it wildly sports.
O proud is he! a king doth grasp his rein,
  And she who will be queen within the Courts
Of Solomon, doth sit upon his back!
His fleeting whiteness leaves a whitened track.

63

He took her to his tent and set for her
    Sweetness of figs and dates, and toothsomeness
Of almonds, and that palate flatterer,
    The raisin-treasuring honey-cake's caress,
And soothing dainties all devis'd for
    A princess' gum, and wine his sire did bless
When unto him was born his youngest prince,
Wine sealed in draughty cellars ever since.

And mandrakes did he give to her which stir
    Up love and tender passion, mandrakes torn
In moonlight to a murmuring of prayer.
    Ah, what sweet words upon their tongues were born,
And what forgetfulness of every care,
    Yea, even of a father gravewards borne.
For he was wise who sang with tuneful skill
That Death is strong, and Love is stronger still.

"With purple and with gold of Ophir, with
    Rare ointment and with choicest ornament
Wilt thou be placed above all others, sith
    Our stars have met within the firmament.
Our love will be a summer's midnight myth
    With which all love-talk will be redolent,
And thy name, O Shoshannah, be a charm
To make the blood of young men run more warm.

Thy smile is like the whiteness of the tusk
    Of ivory, my darling one, and thy
Sweet breath is as a waft of powdered musk
    Within a garden when a wind doth sigh.
Thy hair is like the coolness of the dusk,
    And all thy beauty is a way to vie
With beauty of the spring and make it seem
A mockery, a vanity, a dream."

What need is there of singing of their bliss?
    Or telling of true love and of its throe?
For he who is a lover knoweth this,
    And he who is none certes can not know.

64

Each star in heaven choired to every kiss
    And even the moon grew pale and wan and low,
A yellow candle melting to white dawn,
When to the city crept a caravan.

Tower and turret and dome, and fluttering
    Of flags they see; and already they hear
Triumph and trumpet and loud wassailing
    And chant of priests anointing one to bear
A crown, and then a shout: "Long live the king!"
    And sudden from the gates flash sword and spear,
And warriors cry, "He, the eldest son,
Is king! and thou—" They mock a headless one.

Yea, there was much of slaughter on that day,
    And it is writ upon the old scribe's page,
For though some few did safely fly away,
    Young warriors found death an hermitage,
And concubines were found a lusty prey . . .
    And on the spire for the ossifrage
There grinned a princely skull. Shoshannah fled
Among the pilgrims, never turned her head.

Oh, woe to fair Shoshannah, woe is her,
    And sorrow hers, and weeping without end;
Her heart it is a very sepulchre,
    And she is weary (may the Lord forfend)
Yea, weary unto death . . . . Singer, no more
    Tune thou thine harp save thou thine heart wilt rend,
But do thou hang it on the willow tree
Which weeps and let the wind lament for thee.

And none know whither she has gone; none know
    Where sad Shoshannah found her resting place:
Phylacteried and bearded men avow
    They turned askance at some strange woman's face
Nigh to the crossroads; shepherd lads tell how
    They saw a shadow move in weary pace
Within the vale; and watchers of the night
Speak of a phantom seen in full moonlight.

65

None know her death. Inquire of the sky
    If thou wouldst seek to find the how and where;
Make question of the knowing birds who fly
    Singing their secrets into hidden air;
Or ask it of the rose's guilty dye;
    Or pluck it from the spotted leopard's lair;
Or from a brook's dull brooding monotone,
For these may make an answer, these alone.

Yea, even to this day, the singing tongue
    Takes up the parable in Galilee,
And tells to listening lovers how the young
    Shoshannah, she who was a princess, she
Who had been queen had not the wicked wrung
    Her dearest one from her, how lonesomely
Her spirit wanders in the valley, and
Calls blessings on the lovers of the land.

And the enamoured ones who walk in cool
    And fragrant orchards which are Paradise,
Praising the midnight, and the beautiful
    Things of the midnight, oft-times hear faint cries,
Echoes of wailing, plaintive and most cruel,
    Drop down from the high mountains and the skies,
And find themselves still staring, even at dawn,
Upon a white moon on white Lebanon.

JONAH

Within the whale's belly
Good Jonah at home
Ate fish made of jelly
And drank frothy foam.

O, all the whale swallowed
Stood him in good stead,
From coral he hollowed
A table and bed.

66

The lobsters which wandered
Beneath the whale's nose
Beheld pincers sundered
To hang Jonah's clothes.

A mermaiden chatted
With Jonah, who found
Her rushes she matted
For slippery ground.

On the heart of the whale, he
Carefully stuck
The round leaf of lily
And made him a clock.

O Jonah, the wizard,
O Jonah, the free'd,
Did drape the whale's gizzard
With fragrant seaweed.

A pearl from an oyster
Brought light out of shade.
O how they did roister,
Did Jonah and maid!

Until the Lord wished him
Back to his host,
And whale-gullet dished him
Up on a rough coast.

ARITHMETIC

The leper counts his sores;
The emperor his flags;
The hunchback weighs his hunch;
The beggar tells his rags;
By candlelight the miser drops
His worn coins into bags.

A wise man on a knoll
Numbers the stars on high;
He names the lowest star,
Then climbs up the sky;
And if he does not fall asleep,
He ends with a long sigh.

For he cannot compute
The stars, before the dawn
Comes poking from the east
A mischievous sun.
Proving in his arithmetic
Totality is One.

MANUSCRIPT: THIRTEENTH CENTURY

Who has not heard of Blanche the beautiful,
    Envied of every proud and ermined dame,
Of whom the tall knight in the castle-hall,
    Yea, and the blond page at the chessmen's game,
Speak with a sigh that makes each syllable
    An adoration of her candid fame?
Where is the youth whose banner vaunts no trace
    Of the high lady of the ineffable face?

The jongleur juggled the rhymed line in her praise;
　　The sculptor carved her in a gothic trance;
The scribe illumined with some bible phrase
　　The pale madonna of her countenance;
The stained-glass window and the sunset rays
　　Blazoned her in a tale of old romance;
And boys ensorceled with an ancient spell
　　Flattered their loves with Blanche as parable.

Joy was there in that southern land of sun,
　　Where foreign knights, sojourning in their tents
Dreamed of the lady, jousted for and won,
　　Amid the strife of trumpeted tournaments.
Others there were of no such benison
　　Seeing that on their shields there were no dents,
Enamoured chivalry, that pale-faced came
　　To breathe upon the rose her brief white name.

These christened lilies after her in vain;
　　In vain these whetted sword-points for the thrust;
For journey home may each, from thrall to thane,
　　No joust will be; the coat of mail may rust;
The knight may chafe; the charger shake his mane
　　Eager to snort at blood and valiant dust;
Cobwebs may grow a pennon to the lance,
　　Fair Blanche regards these dons and lords askance.

Albeit within the heart of every youth
　　There sat a bright-hued perroquet that cried
Her name again and again, she showed no ruth
　　Unto these bridegrooms suing for a bride.
Her love it was suborned, suborned in sooth
　　By the grand gallantry, the comely pride,
The manner brave and courteously bland
　　Of Roland, robber and outlaw of the land.

Who fares through tenebrous forests of Boisvert
　　Leading his horse through moonlit paths, he may
Discover the couchant leopard in his lair
　　When of a sudden, a mask will bid him stay,

69

Ordering his ducats or his prayer.
        Shall he, then, lift a dagger for the fray
When Roland, who dubs corpses with his sword,
        Utters the swift behest, the short grim word?

Roland the robber-chief! his swarthy crew!
        Their very mention breeds a pious curse!
He halts the rich-apparelled retinue
        And sends them home, as poor as pilgrimers.
He pries the coffers of the trembling Jew;
        He slits the byzants from the bishop's purse;
He hunts the royal deer; he laughs to scorn
        The surly provosts of the lords high-born.

Mysterious is love; no wizards know
        Its secrets; no astrologers can read
Its purport in the stars, of weal or woe;
        The sages are confounded in their creed
Before this matter, and before this throe
        The doctors of the schools are not agreed.
Wherefore unriddle shall none why the pale dove
        Betook her to the falcon of her love.

The arrow fleeting to the casement brought
        His messages to her; they met at dusk.
Only the stars can tell the trysting-spot,
        The wind betray it with the smell of musk;
April beheld them in some garden-plot,
        October wandering through the golden bosk
Treading the booty of the pilfered year;
        And no December unto them was drear.

When the sun pressed warm kisses on her eyes
        She woke for the fulfilment of a dream,
The whole long day the horloge of her sighs
        Awaited the sun's last and vanquished gleam,
An oriflamme abandoning the skies.
        The whole long day her heart had love for theme
And love for memory, and love for words
        Of song that blossomed from the throats of birds.

70

Alas, that lovers never will be loath
    To fling their vows to all the winds that pass,
To be oblivious to the triple oath,
    Perjure the largess of their love, alas!
Many the testaments Sire Roland quoth
    And many the hesperidan promises
He lavished as he held her in embrace
    And kisses took the pallor fom her face.

O, that which must be, in the end will be!
    The churl who brought fair Blanche her scarlet shame
And caused a twittering at her purity
    And made a byword of her sullied fame
Is fleeted hence, is gone forever. He
    Laughs with his cronies at her mentioned name
And by the fire in the forest den
    Raises guffaws among his uncouth men.

Staid gossips whisper of the wedded maid;
    Good mothers bid their daughters have a care,
Merchants some time forget their talk of trade;
    Rude villeins glimpse her, and they stop to stare
Seeing how that her loveliness did fade
    And how her beauty is no longer fair;
For Blanche pined daily for the sight of him,
    His souriant face, his body tall and slim.

Daily she rises, weeping, from her bed;
    And steps upon the fennel-scented floor
Seeking the arrow that has never fled:
    Ye sparrows privy to all secret lore
Some solace bring to the uncomforted,
    Ease me my bosom of its bleeding core
Banish my sorrow, sparrows, for love's sake.
    Where does he bide for when I lie awake?

Surely he is not quarry to the king?
    O little minions of the air, tell me
He does not lie beneath the roots of Spring;
    He is not dead, he wants no threnody

71

And no worms sew his body while ye sing?
　　Adorn this truth with all your melody;
And if you cannot say this thing is so,
　　Cease you your chirping that I may not know.

She said: This world is very anguish; life
　　Grows keen and bitter at its mouldy root;
The moon to me is an assassin's knife;
　　The sun hangs in the sky, an empty fruit;
Sorrow, alas, has taken me to wife,
　　And all my pride is trodden underfoot!
O heart, forego, then, and forsake, forget,
　　The petty passion and the paltry fret.

Unto the Lord through cells untapestried
　　Daily she prayed in Latin monotones,
Dropping each bead after each hesitant bead
　　Punctilious of tierce, sext, prime, and nones.
Devotional, her tender knees did bleed,
　　Her hungered flesh clave to her very bones,
So that it was a spirit that did fix
　　Its palms in prayer before the crucifix.

Said Sister Agathe: She has forgotten him,
　　She paints the azure robe of heaven's queen,
Said Sister Therese: She tells of seraphim
　　Flaming through dreams. Said Sister Celestine:
Most piously doth she intone the hymn.
　　They knew not, these white nuns, the forest green
That quivered before her eyes, the roses red
　　Ensanguining the missal that she read.

Guard your soul in your scabbard, Roland; live
　　Vigilant as the vulture, look to yourself!
The guerdon on your head retributive
　　Breeds many a traitor titillant for pelf.
Fates may be hopping through a witch's sieve;
　　Treachery may be whispered by the elf;
Murder may lurk in hidden paths; and death
　　Be borne upon justiciary breath.

72

Roland the robber-chief—he is betrayed!
    He contemplates his dungeon's scurrying mice.
Now may the castillan stay unafraid,
    The usurer uncheated of his price,
No more will merchant-princes be waylaid,
    Nor mints ransacked. He will not harass twice
Domains whose carpenters do now prepare
    A pedestal for him on empty air.

It is not holy hour, no holy day;
    That belfry clamours forth its ominous noise,
Viaticum for the unsacred way
    That leads to sorrow deep-dyed and no joys.
The peers have spoken; the bishop has his say;
    The scaffold rises; virtue regains its poise,
And while the sexton digs the profane tomb
    The heralds trumpet forth a festal doom.

Rumbles the death-cart over the cobbled street;
    Sire Roland and the hangman bandy jests;
The clerics prophesy the nether heat;
    The good wives sigh and heave their heavy breasts;
The dogs bark at the prospect of dead meat;
    The urchins thumb their noses; all the guests
Attendant on this true morality,
    Sagely discourse the varlet and his fee.

The dark steed halts before the convent-gate;
    Such the indulgence that old sanction grants
To felons doomed about to hang in state,
    That ere the good nuns sing the godspeed chants
The wine-filled goblet and the bread on plate
    May give an easement to his fleshly wants.
Along the convent-walk the sisters go
    Singing the benediction of his woe.

Marvel of marvels in the annals writ!
    It was fair Blanche who bore the proffered wine,
It was her pale white hand that unsealed it
    And it was she who did incarnadine

The goblet dulling the imbiber's wit,
    Yea, dulling better than the hempen line.
Sire Roland scarcely quaffs the tinctured cup
    When lo! to God he gives his spirit up.

He lies upon the death-cart's broken boards,
    Uncognizant of any further dearth,
Forgetful of the bandit's buried hoards,
    Aloof from sorrow, and disdaining mirth,
Slain better than by headsman's two-edged swords,
    Awaiting only a cool bed in earth.
There is upon the mouth that open gapes
    A potency, forsooth, not crushed from grapes.

Old sisters mumble now: Fair Blanche it was
    Who at the midnight from the garden tore
The herbs malevolent and the poisonous grass;
    Fair Blanche who made a dust of hellebore
And powdered roots against the heathen brass,
    Initiate in worse than devil's lore,
The brain-touched Blanche who sang her screech-owl tune
    Plucking mandragora in the light o' the moon.

Was it in wrath she mixed the baneful draught
    For that she might wreak vengeance? Did she crave
Such retribution from her pestilled craft?
    Hatred unlooses tongues of men to rave;
Venom doth render its dread victims daft—
    Was it through these she so despatched the knave,
Sending his spirit volent to atone
    Before the Lord, before the heavenly throne?

Or was it, as divining poets tell,
    Apothecary passion that thus brewed
The potion reeling towards the bourne of hell,
    The drink mortific? Was it love that rued
To see him pendent from the fifty ell?
    Unpollen the rose, unbeard the lion's brood
Pluck out the stars; forage the eagle's nest,
    Sooner do these, than search the secret breast.

74

The bitter gouts have granted him reprieve;
  The rope is cheated by the mordant juice;
The friar shuts his book; the burghers leave;
  The gallows creak in the wind; the swinging noose
Upholds no corpse; the executioners grieve;
  The hangman scowls at the enforced truce;
Bereft of carrion for their ravenous maws
  The crows afflict the heavens with their caws.

SONG OF SWEET DISHES

Pharaoh was plagued with lice and frogs,
Pests visited upon his head.
His death makes bright the synagogues
Wherefore we eat unleavened bread.

Foul Haman swung from a gallows-tree!
May all such end in similar fashion
Therefore in Israel, jubilee;
We munch our *haman-taschen.*

Now what shall we eat, what shall we gobble
What toothsome dish shall we prepare
When Adolph wretchedly will hobble
From scaffolding upon thin air?

GETZEL GELT

A tradesman Getzel Gelt would be,
He went into the field
With barrow and with scissors, and
He clipped the flowers: he wheeled

75

The barrow to his father's barn,
He shook the barnyard bell.
Cried he: A farthing for a whiff,
A penny for a smell.

Now every youngster in the town
Turned up a hungry nose
For scent of daisy, dandelion,
Cowslip and dogrose.

In vain their famished nostrils sniffed
The unperfumed air
For every little smell they paid
The small coins they could spare

To Getzel Gelt who watched the door
And let no youngsters pass
Within his flowerly barn, unpaid.
The poor, they could smell grass.

But Kalman, with the big nose says:
I have a right to smell.
The flowers belong to heaven, and
Our Getzel—shakes a bell.

We will not pay for what is God's,
For every flower that blows,
No youngster shall so filch from me
The pleasures of my nose.

He planned a plan; then every boy
Went out and caught a bee
And brought it to this Getzel's barn,
They buzzed out joyously;

They settled on the flowers; they
Hummed songs of paradise,
They sucked the honey from the cups
And tears from Getzel's eyes.

He wants no flowers; he wants no coins,
He wants no stinging bees,
Our Getzel only wants to be
Left in penniless peace.

So sing the song of victory
Shake Getzel's barnyard bell
For those who fought, and stingingly
Won liberty a smell.

CALENDAR

Behold the months each in their season:
Showers and blossoms perfume *Nissan*.
The tree a sage, the flower a seer
Make holy gestures in the month of *Iyar*.
Forget not too, the days of *Sivan*
When thunder and Torah came from heaven;
Nor the sky polished as with pumice
Radiant with the sun of *Tammuz*.
Howbeit in the month of *Av*
Consider no flowers, but think of
Messiah somewhere in a cell; ill;
Then be consoled by clovered *Ellul*.
The wet wind rushed with a swish, raw
Upon the leaves of autumn's *Tishri*.
Haybarrow, harvest-rain and thresh-van
Stalk slowly through the month of *Heshvan*,
Through barn and granary the whistle of
The last fall wind sings loud in *Kislev*.
But oak log and warm hearth will save us
From the keen blasts of winter *Tevus*.
At long last, bloodroot, tongue-of-adder
Peer from the thawing snow of *Ader*.

77

BALDHEAD ELISHA

Baldhead! Baldhead!
The little children mocked
As surly Elisha
Through the town stalked.

Baldhead! Cleancrown!
Smoothpate! Noodlenude!
The little children twittered
The little children mewed.

The prophet Elisha
He turned in his wrath
And cursed the urchins
With a terrible oath.

Whereupon there sallied
Bears from their grots
Who tore to giblets
Forty-two tots!

Such was the horrible
Vengeance that bears
Wreaked for the honour
Of forty-two hairs!

CONCERNING FOUR STRANGE SONS

Concerning four strange sons, the Torah wrote:
The sage, the simpleton, the knavish lout,
And the poor yokel whence no speech will out.

He is the wise one, who, most curious,
Queries his sire: Why these laws for us?
Answer him therefore so and such and thus.

What is the yokel's query and demand?
Merely, what is this? Make him understand
The miracles that lit the Egyptian land.

What does the wicked son, the Rasha, want?
An answer for his every profane taunt?
Make his speech dull, and render his teeth blunt!

And as for the meek dolt, the narrow brow,
Untroubled by questions,—begin, then, thou
And make it clear to him, the when and how.

RADICAL POEMS

1932-1938

DIARY OF ABRAHAM SEGAL, POET

7:15—He rises.

No cock rings matins of the dawn for me;
No morn, in russet mantle clad,
Reddens my window-pane; no melodye
Maken the smalle fowles nigh my bed.

The lark at heaven's gate may sing, may sing,
And Phoebus may arise;
And little birds make a sweet jargoning;
And shepherds pipe their pastoral minstrelsies;
All these things well may be; my slug-a-bed ears
Hear them not; nor see them my bronze eyes.

No triple braggadocio of the cock,
But the alarum of a dollar clock,
Ten sonorous riveters at heaven's gate;
Steel udders rattled by milkmen; horns
Cheerily rouse me on my Monday morns.

Is it a wonder then, that in my dreams,
My five o'clock dreams, my boon-companions are
Ogres in planes, ranunculi in ships,
Thin witches mounting escalators, imps
Hopping from telephones, and negresses
Lipping spirituals into radios?
Is it a wonder that these *cauchemars* stamp
With elves on girders i' the light of the moon,
Or with wild worshippers before a mazda lamp?

So have
They clipped the wings
Of fiery seraphim,
And made of them,—ye angels, weep!—
Dusters.

82

*8:15—He travels on the street-car, and reads over a neighbour's
    shoulder.*

Communists ask for more bank holidays.
A broken heart is glued by so much. Ex-
Champion scores k.o. on his wife. No sex
Appeal say critics of two bankrupt plays.
Actress weds crown-prince. Zulu bob new craze.
Bootleg kills ten. Tenor smokes only Rex.
Girl dances hula robed in cancelled cheques.
Convicted murderess weeps: The woman pays.
Champagne bath brings eczema. New gang wars
Disturb police. Explorer still alive.
XY declares YX controls chain stores.
Screen star makes seventh matrimonial dive.
Upholster Spanish throne. Man seeks divorce
Because his wife (continued on page five).

8:45—He considers the factory hands.

What a piece of work is man! the paragon
Of animals! the beauty of the world!
So Dr. Aesculapius Pavlov
Dissects cadavers, and reports as follows:
Fats in this human paragon, enough
For so much soap; for so much writing, lead;
Two thousand match-heads from his phosphorus;
A nail from his iron, medium-sized head;
Magnesium—one full-sized powder, plus;
Whitewash enough for one coop, board and crack;
Sufficient arsenic to leave them dead,
The fleas upon a bitch's front and back;
In fine, each worth a dollar, dames or gents,—
In U.S. money, eighty-seven cents.

9:05—He yawns; and regards the slogans on the office walls.

Blessed the men this day,
Whether at death or birth,
Who own good sites, for they
Shall inherit the earth.
The Lord in silence works
Towards mysterious ends.
The same omniscience lurks
In dividends.
Open, ye gates, before
The man who gets or gives!
Open, thrice-padlocked door,—
Executives!

Scorn not the profiteer,
Minor or major; priest,
Bard, speculative seer,
Moneytheist.
Initiative—this was,
Is, and will be our foil.
Consider the bloom which does
Not spin, nor toil.

In sacred stocks, O Lord,
Impound us; bind our wounds
For sweet sake of Thy word,
In hallowed bonds!

11:30—He receives a visitor.

Milady Schwartz, beloved of the boss,
Married with documents, parturitive,
Into the office waddles, makes a pause
To note the pimply girls, her choice, still live;
Then sweetly coos to hubby dearest, pats
The proud oasis of his glabrous head,
And with her pendulous chins, and gold teeth, smiles
Amorously at the giver of her bread.
He is too busy signing cheques, post-dated.

84

Milady Schwartz, (oh, no, she is no snob)
Speaks to the staff: The season is belated.
Her husband works too hard. You'd never think
So fine a soul would take to cloaks and suits,
Competing with such thieves as Levy, Inc.
But she does not complain. We all must suffer
For those the higher things life has to offer.
Does Mr. Abram Segal still write verses?
It must be wonderful. She envies him.
She wishes she could make up rhymes. She nurses
Feelings unuttered, smitten by lockjaw.
(Moi, j'ai Apollon sur les bouts de mes dix doigts . . .)
Of course she loves art. She goes to lectures.
But yesterday she heard a recitation
About the patter of a babe's pink toes.
He should have heard it, should the poet, Abe.
Also, she is a member of a club
Occasionally addressed by local bards.
(A teaspoonful of art, before and after cards.)
Milady Schwartz, aware she is confiding
Beyond the limits of her dignity;
She must not talk so much about herself.
Are we all happy at our several jobs?
Wages are low, but hope eternal bobs
Upwards; and money, after all, is pelf.
Moreover, so many poor people go
Looking for work, tramping their both legs lame,
It is a pity, a disgrace, a shame!
Why only last week she was overjoyed
To go to the Grand Ball, Chez Madame Lloyd,
And dance all night for the poor unemployed.
Milady Schwartz utters her shrill goodbyes,
Lets love domestic issue from her eyes,
And from her plump hand, jewelled with costly warts,
Wafts kisses. Exit Lady Schwartz.

12:20—He worships at the North-Eastern.

In one-armed restaurants where Cretan floors
Mosaically crawl towards Alpine walls,
The human soul, like a brave leopard, roars,
Like a young lion, *de profundis,* calls:
Waiter, a plate of beans.
Waiter, some coffee and toast.
Waiter, inform the Lord, our Host.
Snappy, I says what I means!
From behind the marble lichen
Providence thunders: Clean the kitchen.
The customer pays the pale cashier.
The Angel punches the register:
    A soul ate here.

12:20-12:45—He reads his pocket edition of Shakespeare;
and luxuriously thinks.

Beneath this fretted roof, the knave, swag-bellied,
Struts him before his calibans i' the sun,
Gloats o'er his shillings, byzants, ducats, smiles
At gaunt clerks, their nockandros flat on stools,
With borrowed quills in hired tomes accounting
His profits, his sweet profit, sweet sweet profit.
The villain smiles: if fools be fools, why, let them,
If sweat on their lips is nectar, here's a health!
They wake to toil? They sleep to dream of toiling?
Be their days long upon this earth.
Aye, but these have immortal yearnings. So.
The brimstone brabble of divines looks to't,
Granting the widow her fond spouse in heaven,
The maimed celestial wings, the dumb a harp,
The starved, ethereal guts . . . But mark, these dudgeons,
Even these blocks, these stones, these honoured men,
Quick at such pleasures metaphysical,
Seeking the grosser lust, the grander passion.
They clink their canakins in pot-houses,
And swollen with wine, they mouth brave oaths and cry:

86

Out with your fee-fi-fum of ichor blood!
A fico for your flibbertigibbet god!
Then staggering in dark lanes, their bodkins raised,
They hail a perfumed placket, and drool, "Chuck,
Let me lie in thy lap, Ophelia."

6:30—He eats at the family-board.

Because to Him in prayershawl, he prays,
My father's God absolves his cares and carks;
My wedded sister likes no empty phrase,
Her spaniel brings her cash, not learned barks.
My brother in his bed-room den displays
The dark capacious beard of Herr Karl Marx;
My uncle scorns them all; my uncle says
Herzl will turn the Jews, now moles, to larks;
My cousin, amiable, believes them both,
Serving a beard of Herzlian-Marxian growth.
And as for me, unlike the ancient bards,
My idols have been shattered into shards.

7:15—He contemplates his contemporaries.

La chair est triste, hélas, et j'ai lu tous les livres.
An octopus of many tentacles,
Boredom, enjoins the slow heart, the dead pulse,
With north as drab as south, and south as dull
As the gray east, the west unbeautiful,
Where shall I go? What pathway shall I choose?
Where shall I point the nozzles of my shoes?
Around the corner is a cinema,
Where heroines squeak, "Oh," and knaves gasp "Ah. . ."
Where paupers get their feet numb, buttocks callous,
Watching wealth serve a grand vicarious phallus,
Therefore, my soul, not there! A pool-room? No.
A dance-hall? No. A lecturer? No! no!
My friends? My bitter friends, at loggerheads,
The blackshirts, the bluestockings, and the reds,
Evoke from me the vast abysmal yawn:

87

The poet, with the unmowed cranial lawn
(And Shakespeare, he was bald! . . .) the theolog
Anent the sure uncleanliness of hog;
The dandy, boasting of his latest moll;
The lawyer, and his case; the radical
Pounding upon an unprovisioned table
Rendering it, not Canada, unstable—
All, in the end, despite their savage feuds,—
Italic voices uttering platitudes,
So Segal, undernourished, surfeited,
Wearied but sleepless, sick at heart, abashed,
Giving his anguish voice, cries: Life is dead
Echo, and letters—macaronics washed
From distant shores upon a rocky bed.

9:00—He communes with Nature.

Within the meadow on the mountain-top
Abe Segal and his sweetheart lie. Lover,
Sweet is the comradeship of grass, the crop
Being mown, the hay dry, dry the clover;
And sweet the fiddling of the crickets, dear
The bird-song for a prothalamium.
They see again, his eyes which once were blear.
His heart gets speech, and is no longer dumb.
Before the glass o' the moon, no longer high,·
Abe Segal nattily adjusts his tie.
Gone the insistence of inveterate clocks;
The heart at last can flutter from its bars.
Upon the mountain-top, Abe Segal walks,
Hums old-time songs, of old-time poets talks,
Brilliant his shoes with dew, his hair with stars. . . .

88

SOIRÉE OF VELVEL KLEINBURGER

In back-room dens of delicatessen stores,
In curtained parlours of garrulous barber-shops,
While the rest of the world most comfortably snores
On mattresses, or on more fleshly props,
My brother Velvel vigils in the night,
Not as he did last night with two French whores,
But with a deck of cards that once were white.

He sees three wan ghosts, as the thick smoke fades,
Dealing him clubs, and diamonds, hearts and spades.

His fingers, pricked with a tailor's needle, draw
The well-thumbed cards; while Hope weighs down his jaw.

O for the ten spade in its proper place,
  Followed by knave in linen lace,
    The queen with her gaunt face,
      The king and mace,
        The ace!

Then Velvel adds a foot-note to his hoax:
I will not have your wherefores and your buts;
For I am for the Joker and his jokes;
I laugh at your alases and tut-tuts,
My days, they vanish into circular smokes,
My life lies on a tray of cigarette-butts.

For it is easy to send pulpit wind
From bellies sumptuously lined;
Easy to praise the sleep of the righteous, when
The righteous sleep on cushions ten,
And having risen from a well-fed wife
Easy it is to give advice on life.

But you who upon sated palates clack a moral,
And pick a sermon from between your teeth,
Tell me with what bay, tell me with what laurel

Shall I entwine the heaven-praising wreath,
I, with whom Deity sets out to quarrel?

But, prithee, wherefore these thumbed cards?

O do not make a pack of cards your thesis
And frame no lesson on a house of cards
Where diamonds go lustreless, and hearts go broken
And clubs do batter the skull to little shards,
And where, because the spade is trump
One must perforce kiss Satan's rump.

For I have heard these things from teachers
With dirty beards and hungry features.

Now, after days in dusty factories,
Among machines that manufacture madness
I have no stomach for these subtleties
About rewards and everlasting gladness;
And having met your over-rated dawns,
Together with milkmen watering their milk,
And having trickled sweat, according to a scale of wages,
Sewing buttons to warm the navels of your business sages,
I have brought home at dusk,
My several bones, my much-flailed husk.

> My meals are grand,
> When supper comes
> I feed on canned
> Aquariums.
>
> The salmon dies.
> The evening waits
> As I catch flies
> From unwashed plates.
>
> And my true love,
> She combs and combs,
> The lice from off
> My children's domes.

Such is the idyll of my life.
But I will yet achieve
An easier living and less scrawny wife
And not forever will the foreman have
The aces up his sleeve,
But some day I will place the lucky bet.
(Ho! Ho! the social revolutions on a table of roulette!)

Alas, that Velvel's sigh makes eddies in the smoke.
For what's the use?
While the pale faces grin, his brow is hot;
He grasps a deuce . . .

A nicotined hand beyond the smoke sweeps off the pot.

O good my brother, should one come to you
And knock upon the door at mid of night
And show you, writ in scripture, black on white,
That this is no way for a man to do?—
What a pale laughter from these ghosts, and "Who
Are you, my saint, to show us what is right?

Make a fifth hand, and we will be contrite;
Shuffle the cards, be sociable, Reb. Jew."

My brother's gesture snaps; *I spoke.*
His cheeks seek refuge in his mouth.
His nostrils puff superior smoke.
His lips are brown with drouth.

> Hum a hymn of sixpence,
> A tableful of cards
> Fingers slowly shuffling
> Ambiguous rewards.
> When the deck is opened
> The pauper once more gave
> His foes the kings and aces
> And took himself the knave.

Once more he cuts the cards, and dreams his dream;
A Rolls-Royce hums within his brain;

Before it stands a chauffeur, tipping his hat,
"You say that it will rain, Sir; it will rain!"
Upon his fingers diamonds gleam,
His wife wears gowns of ultra-Paris fashion,
And she boasts jewels as large as wondrous eyes
The eyes of Og, the giant-king of Bashan.

So Velvel dreams; dreaming, he rises, and
Buttons his coat, coughs in his raised lapel,
Gropes his way home; he rings a raucous bell.

OF DAUMIERS A PORTFOLIO

HIS LORDSHIP

Who remembers not this eminently capable man,
Magician of costumes; factotum: changer of roles?
How, in his youth, he gowned himself: a lawyer:
And with cold logic proved contiguous the poles . . .
How, later, having wedded a legal fiction,
His wife: the Corporation: endowed him, debtor;
Whereat he stayed, in gratitude, for all time faithful,
Except when other corporations endowed him better . . .
Again, having eloquently defended on the hustings
The chastity of three deflowered regimes—
Behold him in overalls, among the paupers!
I am the toiler's friend! He smiles; he beams.
On to the bench he goes now, gifted maestro;
Before him walks a crier, and he cries:
Silence! The Honourable Mr. Justice Hogarth,
Arriving in robes judicial, his new disguise!

SENTENCE

These robbers filched electricity:
This is a crime to property!
In jail for one month let them be,
To privately own—their privacy.

A SONG OF THREE DEGREES

The prisoner confessed most willingly.
Of his own free will he confessed, my Lord.
There were no threats, no, nor cajolery.
I say this on my good policeman's word.
The bruises on his face? The bruises? They're
The sure stigmata of a contrite course:
Behold you, too, how penitence doth stare
Out of a black eye, coloured with remorse.
I swear there was no use of physical force.

PROSECUTOR

Holy, holy, holy,
Consider the prosecutor;
Who failing arguments acute
Finds arguments acuter.

PUBLIC UTILITY

The pimp, he pays his fine and costs,
Which monies go to stock
The Treasury which builds more streets
For streetwalkers to walk.
The wench, alas, must earn her fine.
So back to her tenement,
This civil servant toils and spins;
She keeps the Government.

LA GLORIEUSE INCERTITUDE

The law is certain; and the law is clear.
Having invoked Justinian, exorcised
That Pothier of the tomes where s is f,
The five good judges of the higher court,
Each conning the same gospel, toothlessly
Splutter their wisdom on the *fleur de lys*.
Two greybeards, cutting syllogistic dolls,
Issue their answer: unambiguous *Yea*.
Two others, scissoring a similar script,
With many curlecued wherefores, shape their *Nay*.
The fifth, a younger sage, and nimbler, skips
Trippingly on his hypothetic way
To halt him, cutely, pendent in mid-air.
The law is certain; and the law is clear.

SLEUTH

Dizzy amidst a whorl of fingerprints;
Playing ballistics; learned; nobody's fool;
Reading from unseen ink invisible hints;
Look! A detective of the modern school.
By sniffing, he could trace a noxious wind.
He solved *The Mystery of the Door Ajar;*
In pride, he framed his cases,—even pinned
A rap of arson on a falling star.
So trained, and so instructed, no surprise
Startled his rapt admirers when he found—
Because in Hull, tears shone in a servant's eyes
And at Quebec, a swabbing sailor groaned,
A man on relief at Hochelaga wept—
The province by sedition swept.

94

GUARDIAN OF THE LAW

How have you become not that which once you were,
Brass-buttoned blue-serged hero of my youth!
I laid me down, when six, to sleep untroubled
By dreams of ogres, fearsome and uncouth,
Or sound of robbers whispering in the dark;
And this, because you walked the street and park.
A prober of door-knobs, peerer into glass-fronts,
From curb to curb escorter of the blind,
Friendly your smile to me that day I wandered
Around the corner and wept, and could not find
The way back to the apron of my home.

You held me, dried my tears, and wiped my nose—
(Your uniform smelled like my own father's clothes)—
You led me, and I followed, like a mouse,
Until I suddenly ran, to recognize my house!
And now have I seen you in your colour, slave,
Paid hater of your kin!
Against the unarmed and helpless, mightily brave
Mightily noble—for a fin!
For I have seen you grin
Outside the factory where my father is
A spool for a spool of thread
Yes, seen you grin, and strike my father's friend
With baton on the head!
So do you earn your bread,
And butter,
And good red jam well-bled!

CORRIGENDUM

Now finally, by way of corrigendum:
Judges they be, not only solemn, but wise
To whom their justice is no thing of trade.
The law requests I make this fair addendum.
It is made.

95

BLUEPRINT FOR A MONUMENT OF WAR

Instructions to the stenographer:

Address: The Board for Monuments of War
The thirteenth residence, Rue de la Mort;
If within five days not delivered on the chairman's desk,
Return to My Self, Esq.

Copy for Mr. Algernon B. Brown—
Look up the who's who for the alphabet,
Trailing his name, like the train of milady's gown.
(This is the man who sold the soldiers shoes—
Aye, what a host of feet there marched then, wet!
Now is he rated pillar of the town,
Sits with his footwear—first-class—on the desk,
Puffs at his pipe, is sad about the war,
And plans great honour for the boots that walk no more . . .)

Also a copy for Sir Alfred Poyns.
(General of the Army—he survived!
Great man! The hour struck. He girded his loins.
And with the arrival of slaughter, he arrived.
His ghost now pens his memoirs, to narrate
His epic of indomitable will
His saga, both of destiny and fate,
How he was bravely timid, shrewdly rash,
And how he bought—attend the bargain, and thrill!
The salient for ten thousand lives, cold cash . . .)

Omit not, please, Rev. Smith and Rabbi Cohen,
The one in his temple, t'other in his church,
Twin footstools, burnished, of the heavenly throne.
These men know monuments; it is their perch.
They also know, as they have always known
Infallibly what side the Lord was on.

Address him—lest we forget—the editor:
Mustering infantry in pica;

96

zooming in paragraphs;
Throwing his word-grenades;
featly bombarding
Big Bertha headlines on the metropolis.
Advancing with slogans;
retreating with epigrams;
Fighting courageously;
bugling the call;—
All
On the map that hangs upon his office wall!

(His essays did prelude obituaries.
Hinc illae lachrymae, this blueprint packet:
The editorial we; the obit; the *hic jacet.*)

Epistle and Enclosure:

The blueprint's clear, and all who skip may see:
Gathered the unseamed flesh, the jagged bone
Of the eclectic anonymity,
The valiant alias, the brave unknown.
Dig, then, the grave, as deep as spade will go—
Who lived in a trench, may in a trench lie dead.
Lift up the hero, minus nose, thumb, toe,
And crypt the treaty underneath his head.
So is it wiser. Parchment will preserve
Mortality from the immortal worm.
The monument? 'Tis simple, but 'twill serve:
To wit: a stone, a cairn, cemented, firm.
The corpse, perforce such sure impedimentum
Never to rise. *Exegi monumentum!*

Memorials need mnemonics. Surely, then,
Our pawn, the unknown soldierman, yclept
Andrew Angelo Francois Xavier Sam
Stanislaus Thomas Abraham
Jones
(God rest his bones)
Deserves some chiselling, grandiloquent and apt!

97

So be it.
Who shall gainsay that on a tombstone, Latin
Is for the great departed
A winding sheet of satin?
Wherefore, Horatius Flaccus, who fought and ran away
And therefore lived to fashion many a martial lay,
Be with us now.
Dvlce et decorvm est pro patria mori
(What is more beautiful than dying? Think,
More beautiful than flowering into flesh,
Than gaining glory in indelible ink
Upon an archive page, and what more noble
Than being consumed by scientific stink?

Nothing; unless for some wild slogan's sake
To hang in barbed wire i' the light o' the moon.
And hear the thunder roll, the thunder break,
And watch the issuing guts until you swoon . . .)

Mors et fvgacem perseqvitvr virvm

And if, among the number of men, there be
Some men whom Death has skipped—
Why, gentlemen, your duty is most clear:
Conscript, conscript.

Virtvs reclvdens immeritis mori
Coelvm, negata temptat iter via

(Behold my brother, sans both legs
A military loss
However, now he ambulates
On a Victoria Cross.)

P.S.
If you desire English text, then go
To Rupert Brooke whose bugles always blow;
Or Mr. Tennyson
Who will tell any son
Of battle's benison!

98

P.P.S.
Appendix for the Pious—Isaiah, chapter sixty-seven.

And it shall come to pass that the king's high counsellor, desiring honourable mention in a footnote of the chronicles, shall stand up upon a balcony and he shall shout: They hold me in derision.

The alien three oceans beyond us holds me in derision.

Wherefore you shall be amazed, you shall stand confused, you shall not know when or how. It shall be a thing you have not heard.

But the emissaries of the whetted tongue shall go forth to the market-places, and shall stand them up upon a chariot, and shall pound upon their chests, groaning; Honour, honour.

Until you too shall rise, shaking your fists, and crying with a loud voice: We shall not be held in derision.

You shall journey long distances to lands in a picture-book.

Your farewells shall be full of glory; paid speakers will laud you.

The manufactories of bunting shall do much trade; the writers of martial musick shall win them renown.

The speeches shall be uttered, the bugles shall be blown, and the kisses wafted

And you shall go the long way over many seas.

This also I know, that the high-counsellor and his brother the swordsmith will rub their hands, warm at the prospect of seven fat years

And will hasten to their secret chambers, there to calculate calculations.

And you shall journey great distances to lands in a picture-book,

And shall discover yourselves in the midst of a strange people, who have not ever lifted a little finger against you, or said a short word ill of you. And you shall array yourselves, each against the other

And the voice of the captain shall thunder, and it shall rain brimstone.

For many days you shall rest in the watery pit

Until your feet shall be swollen, and you shall remember with great longing a pair of slippers and a chair.

Vermin shall crawl about you, the louse shall move in on you

And you shall curse your fingers because they are few.

99

Worse than the great noise of the instruments of war shall be the
terrible silence

When you shall bethink yourself of kith and kin, and of the king's
counsellor

Causing himself to be regarded full-face and in profile.

The generals shall be bathed in lotions, the captains shall be
perfumed with myrrh

And you, son of man, shall own mud as your breastplate, and mire
as your armour.

The battle shall rage, and men with strange devices shall signal to
one another

Signals of victory, honour, and inches of land.

Until both you and the alien shall be weary, and the counsellors
weary of profit.

Peace shall be heard in the land, but who shall hear it? Truce shall
be called in the land, who shall hearken unto it?

For your brothers shall lie in foreign fields, where the crow may
bring them the tiding, and the worm whisper the news.

OF CASTLES IN SPAIN

TO ONE GONE TO THE WARS

For S. H. A.

Unworthiest crony of my grammar days,
 Expectorator in learning's cuspidor,
Forsaking the scholar's for the gamin's ways,
 The gates of knowledge for the cubicular door,

How you have shamed me, me the noble talker,
 The polisher of phrases, stainer of verbs,
Who daily for a price serve hind and hawker,
 Earning my Sabbath meat, my daily herbs.

'Tis you who do confound the lupine jaw
    And stand protective of my days and works,
As in the street-fight you maintain the law
    And I in an armchair—weigh and measure Marx.

Alas, that fettered and bound by virtues long since rusty,
I must, for spouse and son,
Withhold, as is befitting any prison trusty,
My personal succour and my uniformed aid,
And from the barracks watch the barricade—
Offering you, meek sacrifice, unvaliant gift,
My non-liturgic prayer:
For that your aim be sure,
Your bullet swift
Unperilous your air, your trenches dry,
Your courage unattainted by defeat,
Your courage high.

TOREADOR

Unfurl the scarlet banner, Toreador,
Take up your stance;
Let, then, the bull bicornate for the gore,
Snorting, advance,
To meet your clean thrust, bringing to his knees
The taurine beast.
Let banner upon blood proclaim the peace
Of bull, deceased.

SONNET WITHOUT MUSIC

Upon the piazza, haemophilic dons
delicately lift their sherry in the sun.

Having recovered confiscated land,
and his expropriated smile redeemed,
the magnate, too, has doff'd his socialized face.
He beams a jocund aftermath to bombs.

Also, the priest,—alas, for so much bloodshed!—
cups plumpish hand to catch uncatechized belch.

The iron heel grows rusty in the nape
of peasant feeding with the earthworm—but
beware aristocrat, Don Pelph, beware!
The peon soon will stir, will rise, will stand,
breathe Hunger's foetid breath, lift arm, clench fist,
and heil you to the fascist realm of death!

BARRICADE SMITH: HIS SPEECHES

OF VIOLENCE

What does the word mean: *Violence*?
         Are we not content?
Do not our coupons fall, like manna, from the bonds?
Are we not all well-fed?
         Save for twelve months of Lent?
Is it not slander to aver the Boss absconds
With all the embezzled dollars in his delicate hand?
Is there not heard a sound
Of belching in the land?

Who, then, would speak of violence, uncouth and impolite?
Surely not we, the meek, the docile, the none-too-bright!
The askers with cap-in-hand, the rebels, Emily Post
Who know too well our place, our manners, and our host!

Wherefore, though wages slither, and upward soar the rates,
Not we will be the churls rudely to doubt that boast
Of Labour and Capital, that Siamese twin alright,
One of whom eats, the other defecates.

The Board of Directors sits
And cudgels its salaried wits:—

102

At cost of life and limb
Show profits, and still be
Unviolent as a hymn.

They syncopate your groans
on gramaphones;
Your muscles throb in their Rolls-Royce;
They triturate your sweat in cocktail-shakers.

But they are not violent, for violence is wicked;
And worse than that—I shudder to say the word,
That fell indictment—
It simply is not cricket!

Go therefore, tell your wives that the breadbox must stay breadless,
The rent unpaid, the stove unheated, you enslaved;
Because you *must* be above *all* things, well-behaved.
And having uttered these heroic words, slink hence
Into some unleased corner, and there vanish—
But not with any violence.

OF DAWN AND ITS BREAKING

Where will you be
When the password is said and the news is extra'd abroad,
And the placard is raised, and the billboard lifted on high,
And the radio network announces its improvised decree:
You are free?
Where will it find you, that great genesis?
Preparing your lips for a kiss?
Waiting the call of next in a barber-shop?
Rapt with the ticker's euphony?
Or practising some negroid hop?
Where will you be?
When the news is bruited by the auto horn?
Holding a pair of aces back to back?
Paring a toe-nail, cutting out a corn?
Or reading, with de-trousered back,
Hearst's tabloid, previously torn?

103

Or will you be—O would that you should be!—
Among those valiant ones returning to their
    homes
        To tell
Their daughters and their sons to tell posterity
How they did on that day,
If not create new heaven, at least abolish hell.

OF THE CLIENTS OF BARNUM

Clients of Barnum, yours no even break!
The maestros have you, have you on the hip!
They gloat: they hold you ready for the take:
And you, O rube, fall smacko for the gyp!

Sucker, you stand no choice; the cars are nicked,
The factory, believe you me, is one clip joint;
The sadness is you know not you are licked,
Come from the cleaners, you have missed the point.

Buffalo'd, taken for a ride, you gape;
Say dirty work at the cross-roads, but can not
Articulate its manner, form or shape.

For deadheads, here where X proclaims the spot,
Enters Politico, and p.d.q.—
To tell you what a lovely land is ours;
With him, Kid Pedagogue, the champ who slew
All challenging low wages and long hours;
Also Don Pulpiteer, to promise you,
Not earthly dwellings—no—celestial bowers!
Is it not time

Before they shove you on an unemployment shelf,
Or freeze you in a pension-frigidaire,
That you do get
Wise to yourself?

OF PSALMODY IN THE TEMPLE

They do lie heavily upon me, these
Sores of the spirit, failings of the flesh!
Wherefore, O triply-purgatoried soul,
Scram;
And chastened O my body,
Take it on the lam—
To the colossal, suprasuper hideout, blow,
To the lotiferous movie-show!

There I do sit me down in thick upholstery;
I do not want.
A tale is prepared before me: heroine enters,
Slim; and a villain, gaunt:
Also a well-groomed esquire saying I love you—
Fade out, fade in;
Shots of a lot of legs, and a couple of stooges,
Close-up, a grin.
The decent, the fair, win prizes; the wicked
Their just desserts.
The prince weds Cinderella, and virtue triumphs
Until it hurts.

O these felicitous endings, sweet finales,
They comfort me—
O bodies' beatitude, O soul's salvation,
Where this can be!
Most surely I shall dwell in this great temple
And take my bliss
Forever out of scenes which end forever
In an eight-foot kiss.

OF FAITH, HOPE, AND CHARITY

Beware,—spiritual humankind,—
Faith, contraceptive of the mind;
And hope, cheap aphrodisiac,
Supplying potency its lack;
And also that smug lechery
Barren and sterile charity.

OF BEAUTY

Seeing that planets move by dynamos,
And even the sun's a burnished well-oiled spring,
What glory is there, say, in being a rose
And why should skylarks still desire to sing,
Singing, and no men hear, men standing close
Over some sleek, mechanic and vociferous thing?

For these there is one beauty; put it on a table:
A loaf of bread, some salt, a vegetable.

OF POESY

Bard, paying your rental of the ivory tower,
With the old coin of hoarded metaphor,
Abandon now the turret where you cower;
Descend the winding staircase; and let your
Speech be, not of the thrush's note, long sour,
But of the Real, alive upon a floor.

Let Keats forget his father's stables, smelling
The mythical odour of the asphodel;
Let Wordsworth clutch his sensitive bosom, leaping
When he beholds a rainbow he can sell:
Let butler Tennyson pour out old vintage
For the good knights at Arthur's King Hotel.

But you, O streamlined laureate,
What's Hecuba to you?
How long will you yet bind your fate
With stars archaic and with obsolete dew?

Go out upon a roof, and laud the moon!
Your words are sweet and flattering, as if
The moon were a good corpse, a threnoided stiff!
O idiot bard, O frenzied loon,
Such words to blow
Upon that smooth hydraulic dynamo!

For soon, O sooner than the laurel grows—
Will come to you, superior of the mass,
The foreman Death,
To push you into one of many rows
And bodily have you manufacture grass,—
Of your sweet immortality, true token,
Wage of the foreman Death
His time-clock, broken.

OF SOPORIFICS

These be repasts lethean of your kind:
the tabloid whispering, the penny sheet
shouting the scoop that even the richest meet
with mesalliance, murder, maddened mind;
the sermon showing corpses wined and dined;
the radio hour and its jovial bleat;
the circus come to town, a breadless feat;
two weeks of grace for fifty weeks of grind.
These are the brews that are allowed to mull
in crucibles of bone one would call sane;
these are concoctions patented to dull
the too-keen edge of the too-querulous brain,
persuading the cockerel dung is beautiful,
and the bespatted, spit is only rain.

OF SHIRTS AND POLICIES OF STATE

A shirt! a shirt! a kingdom for a shirt!
Open your paper; bargains, if you please!
A principality goes for less than dirt,
The palmiest state for any pied chemise.
A red blouse buys the franchise of the czar;
The brown habergeon claims an Arian realm;
Where once were candid togas, blackshirts are;
Shirtless is but mahatma at his helm.

107

Wherefore, O Machiavel,
Get you a rag, a shoulder-strap or a brassiere,
And be it but of the right proper hue
And kings will come in trembling and in fear
And peoples, hoarsely obedient, will come to you!
Make haste; and use dispatch!
The shirts of the spectrum governance the world!
Get yourself, therefore, while you can, a patch
Of rainbow silk, of motley linen, and
Declare another philosophic shirt unfurled!

OF THE LILY WHICH TOILS NOT

You, Tillie the Toiler and Winnie the Worker, consider
This fabulous lily—and her milk-fed pride,—
She toils not, no, and neither does she spin!
O not like yours her most egregious skin,
Her epidermis gilt-edged, bonded hide!

For she has been a child most delicate,
Bathed in milk, filched from the wild goat's haunt;
She has thrived, has grown, has come to man's estate,—
She is the season's worthiest debutante!
Her grandfather sold cheap gawds in quantity;
Non-lilies in their hundreds toiled for them.
Now, dough is no consideration, see,—
The girl must have her court and diadem.

Call the reporters, call the photographers!
Here, for The Sportsman, a snap of Lilia
Patting the groomed posterior of a horse;
And for The Social Star,
Lily and jaguar.
And please, good fellow, print this one apart,—
(It goes to show our hot-house Lily has
Not only a big bosom, but a heart.)
Photo of limousine, and background-slums,
Lily dispensing to the poor unmentioned sums,

108

Already titled for the typesetter:
Deb and debtor.
Isn't that cute?
Also do not forget to comment on the style of her spring-suit.
Have a drink; drink hearty;
Here are passes to the party.

And what a party! *Outré, a l'outrance!*
Strawberries from the Himalayas, and
Fowl hatched somewhere in some uncharted land
And other tidbits, costly all, and all
Prepared by (trumpets!) Oscar Cinq of France.

The wine, the flowers, the music, and the guests!
The liquor gurgled of Napoleon's wars,
The hired jester made financial jests,
The slick musicians juggled their music scores,
While dignified doormen guarded all the doors
Permitting only the *distingué* who
Could swear he never laced up his own shoe.

Tillie, it was a glorious sight to see!
Tails and white ties, and gowns, and naked backs;
Chrysanthemums, pink, brought from beyond the sea,
Tinted, by artists, with bright blues and blacks,—
And brooding, like a spirit,
Over the champagne flood that never once did ebb,
Lily the Deb!

Of course, I did not see it all myself;
Sadly, I lacked, what millionaires call pelf,
And so I must, in honesty, relate,
That Barry Cade-Smythe did not crash the gate.
But Barricade Smith did love her from afar,
Watched her, in due time, go upon a cruise
And come back, headlined in the nation's news,
As wife of the tenth cousin of the Czar.
Whom, in due time, she buried. No one needs
To be reminded of that tragic cut
Of her Paris widow's weeds.

109

That season over, with the coming of the spring
And dividends blossoming on many a bank,
She wedded, being now a lady of rank,
A closer relative of a deposed king,
Whom, in due course,
She did divorce,
And sent him packing, with a little tip,
Two million dollars, and a discarded ship.

And still to-day, Tillie, if you have the time,
And Winnie, if you care, you may,
Ahunting go to Africa, or climb
Some hills Helvetian, yodelling, and find
Lily at play;
Or on the Riviera, or shooting birds of clay,—

Perhaps, however, you cannot get away.

HATH NOT A JEW...

... Hath not a Jew eyes? hath not a Jew hands, organs, dimensions, senses, affections, passions? fed with the same food, hurt with the same weapons.... If you prick us, do we not bleed? if you tickle us, do we not laugh? if you poison us, do we not die? ...

—MERCHANT OF VENICE

AVE ATQUE VALE

LAUNCELOT:
If thou comest with me to an alehouse, so.
If not thou are an Hebrew and a Jew, and not
worthy the name of Christian.
                    —*TWO GENTLEMEN OF VERONA*

No churl am I to carp at the goodly feres
In the Mermaid Tavern, quaffing the lusty toast;
Myself twanged Hebrew to right English cheers,
Though now I do bid farewell to mine host;

And not, in sooth, for that I am a wight
Of sober mien and melancholy way,
Drinking my water in sips, in life's despite
Changing heigh-nonny-no to lack-a-day,—

But that that parfait jolly company
That roistered in my salad days, calls me—
O sages of Sura, Pumbeditha's wise,
Drawers of elephants through needle's eyes!

To you I turn, and eke to Jabna-town,
Which brave ben-Zakkai, rising from a coffin,
Saved from the claws of Titus, when Titus' heart did soften
Towards the town of scholars, towards the lean Reb Zadoc,
Swallowing his fig that tumbled down
His throat, transparent and ascetic.

Not merely rabbins of the whetted brain,
Not solely jousters of the supple thumb,
But brawny men, who featly did maintain
The Talmud a pie, and argument a plum:

Abbaya and Rabba, most obstreperous twins,
In dialectic spittle washing away their sins;
The smiling Kahana; Shammai in a mope;
Hillel instructing an obtuse Ethiop;
Finding for vermin dietetic uses,
Reb Meir and his se'en score ten excuses;

112

Ambiguous Resh Lakish, gladiator,
A hearty glutton, and a staunch debater;
Obese Reb Paupa, whose belly so did wax
It sheltered a camel, hump, and load of flax;
That consummate apocalyptic liar,
Bar Huna, more mendacious than a friar;
Uncouth Akiva; cobbler Jochanan;
Achair who quoted Greek; that witty man
Yitschok who most hilariously conjectured
What Adam wrought alone before God lectured;
And Abba Saul, plying his adamant trade,
Murmuring jests at each throw of the spade.

Howbeit I do not scorn the gloomier sages,
The fasters, mortifiers of the flesh,
Who wept for the sins of past and future ages,
And being skinny, slid through Satan's mesh:
Reb Judah, undefiled, who did disdain
Anatomy below the brain,
Or he who even in his sleep
Taught his penitence to weep,—
Howbeit I love these men at distances
And choose sodality with the sprightlier few,

When he forsakes you, Shakespeare, for a space,
Or you Kit Marlowe of the four good lines,
Or Jonson, you, your sack, your muscadine, your wines,
This Jew
Betakes him to no pharisaic crew . . . .

CHILDE HAROLD'S PILGRIMAGE

Of yore yclept in old Judaea Zvi;
Cognomen'd Cerf where Latin speech is carolled;
Dubbed Hirsch, a transient, in wild Allmany;
For sweet conformity now appellated Harold,—

Always and ever,
Whether in caftan robed, or in tuxedo slicked,
Whether of bearded chin, or of the jowls shaved blue,
Always and ever have I been the Jew
Bewildered, and a man who has been tricked,
Examining
A passport of a polyglot decision—
To Esperanto from the earliest rune—
Where cancellation frowns away permission,
And turning in despair
To seek an audience with the consul of the moon.

For they have all been shut, and barred, and triple-locked,
The gates of refuge, the asylum doors;
And in no place beneath the sun may I—
On pilgrimage towards my own wide tomb—
Sit down to rest my bones, and count my sores.
Save near thy shimmering horizon, Madagascar!
Where in the sickly heat of noon I may
Bloom tropical, and rot, and happily melt away.

Aye, but thy fell is somewhat safe in Muscovy!
Quoth Kamenev to me.
And truth it is, as all the world avows:
Provided
I cast off my divine impedimenta,
And leave my household gods in the customs house.

And there is also Palestine, my own,
Land of my fathers, cradle of my birth,
Whither I may return, king to his throne,
By showing the doorman, Mr. Harold's worth
Several thousand pounds (and not by loan!)
Redemption for the pawned and promised earth!

O mummied Pharaoh in thy pyramid,
Consider now the schemes thy wizards schemed
Against those shrewd proliferous Israelites!
Son of Hamdatha, though the witless Mede
Did gibbet thee, behold thy inventions deemed

114

Wisdom itself by many worthy wights.
Rejoice, Judaeophobes,
The brew you brewed and cellared is not flat!
See, in the air, mad Antiochus, the
Inimitate image of thy frenzy, and
Lean Torquemada, look about thee, and grow fat.

  Sieg heil!
Behold, against the sun, familiar blot:
A cross with claws!
Hearken
The mustached homily, the megaphoned hymn:
Attila's laws!
He likes me not.
He does not like my blood in state unspilled;
Pronounces me begotten of canaille
Talmudic, biblic riff-raff, and polluted
Blood of the prophets, and their Marxian guild.
The sage has elocuted.
Not blue my eyes, ergo, I am ill-bred;
My head is short, wherefore, I am too long
By a head!
Tow hair on Teuton skull—this is the token
By which to take the measure of the strong.
The seer has spoken.

So sound the trumpet!
And join, ye burghers, in the ditty that the sick Horst Wessel
Wrote for his strumpet!
O fellowman—forgive the archaic word!—
Break now your sullen silence, and expound
Wherefore you deem me that foul mote in your eye,
That bone in your throat, that ugly scab, that plague,
That in your gospels you so character
Me and my kin, consanguine and allied?
Is it my wealth you envy, my wine-goblet,
My candlesticks, my spattered gaberdine?
Why, take them; all my goods and chattels—yours.
Take them, I shall not so much as say O,
And let there be an end. The scowl persists.

It is my thoughts, then, that you do begrudge me?
Good; I'll expunge them! I will bid my brain
Henceforth to cease, go dry, be petrified,
And as it was in my mother's womb, remain.
Cousin, will that be pleasing to you? No?
You are not pleased at all. Pray do not tell me,
I will myself unfathom the dark reason—
My father's heresy, his obstinate creed?
That is the sword between us? Bring it down.
I pledge you for the sake of peace, that I
Will be your most observing true marrano
That ever bent the knee to several gods.
Not so, you say, for being a generous mind
You will forgive the false. What is it, then,
That ghostly thing that stalks between us, and
Confounds our discourse into babel speech?
I am too forward; wherever you seek me not
There you do find me, always, big in your sight.
That, too, good brother, is no difficult matter—
For I will dwarf myself, and live in a hut
Upon the outskirts of nowhere, receive no mail,
And speak so low that only God shall hear me!
So, surely shall we be as bosom-friends.
I stray; I grope; I have not read your mind.
Perhaps I am a man of surly manners,
Lacking in grace, aloof, impolitic,
To wit, an alien? And *that* is false.
For on occasion and in divers lands
I have sojourned, set up abode with you,
Drank the same drinks, partook of the same food,
Applauded the same music, uttered the
Very same language, thought a similar thought,—
And still you have sneered *foreigner,* and still
Your hate was great, as reasonless hatred is.

Stranger and foeman, I know well your wish!
My blood, my blood! Shall I, then, sever a vein,
Drain off an artery, open the valves
Of my much too-Semitic heart, and be

That blond cadaver pleasing to your eye?
Have I not well conjectured? Is not your mind
Now laid on the table, pointed, like a dagger?

In such sad plight, in such sore case,
My sire would turn his bearded face
Upwards, and, fast or festive day,
Would don his prayershawl, and pray.
To him in converse with his God,
The wicked king was less than sod,
And all his machinations were
Less than the yelpings of a cur.
For as my father prayed, he heard
The promise of the holy word,
And felt them watching over him,
The furious fiery seraphim.

My father is gathered to his fathers, God rest his wraith!
And his son
Is a pauper in spirit, a beggar in piety,
Cut off without a penny's worth of faith.

Esau, my kinsman, would, in like event,
Devise a different answer for the foe;
And let the argumentative bullet dent
The heart of the tyrant, let the steel blade show
The poor mortality of the heaven-sent,
And let the assassin's bomb, vociferous, throw
Defiance to the oppressor,
Booming *No!*

Alas, for me that in my ears there sounds
Always the sixth thunder of Sinai.

What, now, for me to do?
Gulp down some poisoned brew?
Or from some twentieth storey take
My ignominious exit? Make,
Above this disappearing Jew,
Three bubbles burst upon the lake?

117

Or dance from a rope upon the air
Over an overturned chair?

No, not for such ignoble end
From Ur of the Chaldees have I the long way come;
Not for such purpose low
Have I endured cruel Time, its pandemonium,
Its lunatic changes, its capricious play;
And surely not that I might at long last
Vanish
Have my feet crossed these many frontiers, and
My brain devised its thoughts.
'Tis not in me to unsheathe an avenging sword;
I cannot don phylactery to pray;
Weaponless, blessed with no works, and much abhorred,
This only is mine wherewith to face the horde:
The frozen patience waiting for its day,
The stance long-suffering, the stoic word,
The bright empirics that knows well that the
Night of the *cauchemar* comes and goes away,—
A baleful wind, a baneful nebula, over
A saecular imperturbability.

PORTRAITS OF A MINYAN

LANDLORD

He is a learned man, adept
    At softening the rigid.
Purblind, he scans the *rashi* script,
    His very nose is digit.

He justifies his point of view
    With verses pedagogic;
His thumb is double-jointed through
    Stressing a doubtful logic.

He quotes the Commentaries, yea,
      To *Tau* from *Aleph,*—
But none the less, his tenants pay,
      Or meet the bailiff.

PINTELE YID

Agnostic, he would never tire
      To cauterize the orthodox;
But he is here, by paradox,
      To say the *Kaddish* for his sire.

REB ABRAHAM

Reb Abraham, the jolly,
Avowed the gloomy face
Unpardonable folly,
Unworthy of his race.

When God is served in revel
By all his joyous Jews,
(He says) the surly devil
Stands gloomy at the news.

Reb Abraham loved Torah,
If followed by a feast:
A *milah*-banquet, or a
Schnapps to drink, at least.

On Sabbath-nights, declaring
God's praises, who did cram
The onion and the herring?
Fat-cheeked Reb Abraham.

On Ninth of *Ab,* who aided
The youngsters in their game
Of throwing burrs, as they did,
In wailing beards? The same.

And who on *Purim* came in
To help the urchins, when
They rattled at foul Haman?
Reb Abraham again.

On all feasts of rejoicing
Reb Abraham's thick soles
Stamped pious metres, voicing
Laudation of the scrolls.

Averring that in heaven
One more Jew had been crowned,
Reb Abraham drank even
On cemetery-ground.

And at Messiah's greeting,
Reb Abraham's set plan
Is to make goodly eating
Of roast leviathan.

When God is served in revel
By all His joyous Jews,
(He says) the surly devil
Stands gloomy at the news.

SHADCHAN

Cupid in a caftan
   Slowly scrutinizes
Virgins and rich widows,
   And other lesser prizes.

Cupid strokes his chin, and
   Values legs at so much,
So much for straight noses,
   Cupid pays love homage.

What's a squinted eye, or
   What's a halting stutter,
When her father offers
   More than bread and butter?

120

Cupid whets his arrows—
    Golden, golden rocket!
Aims, not at the bosom,
    Aims them at the pocket.

Cupid in a caftan
    Disregards the flowery
Speech of moon-mad lovers.
    Cupid talks of dowry.

SOPHIST

When will there be another such brain?
Never; unless he rise again,
Unless Reb Simcha rise once more
To juggle syllogistic lore.

One placed a pin upon a page
Of Talmud print, whereat the sage
Declared what holy word was writ
Two hundred pages under it!

That skull replete with *pilpul* tricks
Has long returned to its matrix,
Where worms split hair, where Death confutes
The hope the all-too-hopeful moots.

But I think that in Paradise
Reb Simcha, with his twinkling eyes,
Interprets, in some song-spared nook,
To God the meaning of His book.

READER OF THE SCROLL

Divinely he sang the scriptured note;
He twisted sound, intoned the symbol,
Made music sally, slow or nimble,
From out his heart and through his throat.

121

For in a single breath to hiss
The ten outrageous names of those
Who on the Persian gallows rose—
Oh, this was pleasure, joyance this!

SWEET SINGER

O what would David say,
Young David in the fields,
Singing in Bethlehem,
Were he to hear this day
Old Mendel slowly hum
His sweetest songs,
Old Mendel, who being poor,
Cannot through charity
Atone his wrongs,
And being ignorant,
Cannot in learned wise
Win Paradise,
Old Mendel who begs Heaven as his alms
By iterating and re-iterating psalms?

JUNK-DEALER

All week his figure mottles
    The city lanes,
Hawking his rags and bottles
    In quaint refrains.

But on the High, the Holy
    Days, he is lord;
And being lord, earth wholly,
    Gladly is abhorred.

While litanies are clamoured,
    His loud voice brags
A Hebrew most ungrammared.
    He sells God rags.

HIS WAS AN OPEN HEART

His was an open heart, a lavish hand,
His table ever set for any guest:
A rabbi passing from a foreign land,
A holy man, a beggar, all found rest
Beneath his roof; even a Gentile saw
A welcome at the door, a face that smiled.
The chillest heart beneath his warmth would thaw.
And for these deeds, God blessed him that he saw
The cradle never emptied of its child.

AND THE MAN MOSES WAS MEEK

This little Jew
Homunculus
Found four ells too
Capacious.

He never spoke,
Save in his prayer;
He bore his yoke
As it were air.

He knew not sin.
He even blessed
The spider in
His corner-nest.

The meek may trust
That in his tomb
He will turn dust
To save some room.

GREETING ON THIS DAY

i

Lest grief clean out the sockets of your eyes,
Lest anguish purge your heart of happiness,
Lest you go shaking fists at passive skies,
And mounting blasphemies in your distress,

Be silent. Sorrow is a leper; shun
The presence of his frosted phantom. Plant
Small stones for eyes so that no tears may run;
And underneath your ribs set adamant.

ii

O Chronicler, pull down the heavy tome;
  Open a blank page, fashion a pen from bone;
Dip it in skulls where blood is ink; inscribe
The welcome Jews received on coming home.

Omit your adjectives, sad Jeremiah,
Spare you your adverbs; let your phrases house
No too-protesting tenant of despair;
And if the meagre tale brings no Messiah,
Messiah is a short conspiracy
  Of throat and air.

iii

Why do I weight my words with things irrelevant?
  O Safed, Safed,
Though never have I left my northern snows,
Nor ever boarded ship for Palestine,
Your memory anoints my brain a shrine,
Your white roofs poetize my prose,
Your halidom is mine.
Your streets, terraced and curved and narrow,
I climbed in my youth, attending on your sages,

124

I sat at the feet of Rabbi Joseph Caro,
I turned the musty and snuff-tinctured pages
Of mystic books bewildering my little pate,
And with Reb Isaac Luria, surnamed the Pard,
Who rose on Friday twilights to become God's ward
I ate, and blessed the single plate.
I followed them, I loved them, sage and saint,
Graybeard in caftan, juggling the when and why,
Ascetic rubbing a microscopic taint,
Scholar on whose neat earlocks piety ascended
In spiral to the sky—
I followed them, for better or for worse,
Even as now I follow this impromptu hearse.

iv

The ghosts of Hebron lift their coffinlids
    And throw the shards from off their eyes.
Spectres of Talpioth arise.
The cemetery sighs.
Even as unrest scurries in these skulls,
So are there those tonight
Who toss upon a bed where terror falls,
Where falls the rodent fright,
Who rise from off their couches, try the door,
Stare out of windows, see the moon drip gore,
Light up a candle, set it near the bed,
Mumble a Moslem prayer, lie up all night,
And wait, recumbent, for the ceiling to grow white.

v

The white doves flutter
From the roofs
Where stones did utter
Dark reproofs.

That these pale pigeons
Be alarmed

Guerilla legions
Have been armed.

Effendi, Mufti,
Holy ones—
They are not thrifty
With their stones.

This is the manner
Doves take flight:
The sky a banner
Blue and white.

vi

O who is this, rising from the Sharon, bearing a basket of grapes,
   vaunting the golden apples? And who is he, that other one,
   following behind a plough, breaking the soil, as hard as the heart
   of Pharaoh?

If this be a Jew, indeed, where is the crook of his spine; and the
   quiver of lip, where?
Behold his knees are not callous through kneeling; he is proud,
   he is erect.
There is in his eyes no fear, in his mind no memory of faggots.
And these are not words wherewith one tells a Jew.

Truly this is such an one; he has left his hump in Ashkinaz; in
   Sphorad his maimed limb; beyond the seas his terror he has
   abandoned.
He has said to the sun, Thou art my father that gives me strength;
   and to the cloud, Thou art my mother suckling me thy milk.

The sign of his father is on his brow, and the breath of his mother
   renders him fragrant. No legion affrights him, no flame in the
   dark, no sword in the sun. For a thousand shall come upon him,
   and a thousand be carried away.

A son has returned to her that bare him; at her hearth
   he grows comely; he is goodly to behold.
Behind the bony cage there beats the bird of joy;
   within the golden cup is wine that overflows.

126

vii

We are a people of peace. Shall I then say,
Showing the whites of my eyes upraised to you,
"Forgive them, Lord, they know not what they do?"
Not so, not so; no peace can be until
Sleek Syrian landlord and fanatic priest,
The greater and the lesser lice have creased
Their paunches to a pellicle,
No peace to them—the bandits battening on blood!
No peace!
Rather the dagger to the hilt,
The bullet to the heart,
The gallows built,
And the ignoble cart!

viii

To them no peace, but unto you, O fellaheen,
   O workers in the smithy of the sun,
Dupes of ventriloquists who belch the Unseen,
Good men deluded by the Evil One;
I, the son of a worker, and a worker myself,
I, who have known the sweat that salts the lip,
The blister on the palm, the aching hip,
I offer you companionship,
Saying:

ix

Accursed he who mouths a scarlet threat!
Who lets new blood before the old congeals,
Who makes of carcasses his festal meals,
And who declares that he will not forget!

The muezzin upon the minaret
Announces dawn once more; the Moslem kneels;
Elation lifts the Jew from off his heels;
Izak and Ishmael are cousins met.
No desert cries encircle Omar's dome,

No tear erodes the Wall of ancient pain;
Once more may brothers dwell in peace at home;
Though blood was spattered, it has left no stain;
The greeting on this day is loud Shalom!
The white doves settle on the roofs again.

SONNET IN TIME OF AFFLICTION

The word of grace is flung from foreign thrones
And strangers lord it in the ruling-hall;
The shield of David rusts upon the wall;
The lion of Judah seeks to roar, and groans . . .
Where are the brave, the mighty? They are bones.
Bar Cochba's star has suffered its last fall.
On holy places profane spiders crawl;
The jackal leaves foul marks on temple-stones.
Ah, woe, to us, that we, the sons of peace,
Must turn our sharpened scythes to scimitars,
Must lift the hammer of the Maccabees,
Blood soak the land, make mockery of stars . . .
And woe to me, who am not one of these,
Who languish here beneath these northern stars . . . .

OUT OF THE PULVER AND THE
POLISHED LENS

i

The paunchy sons of Abraham
Spit on the maculate streets of Amsterdam,
Showing Spinoza, Baruch *alias* Benedict,
He and his God are under interdict.

Ah, what theology there is in spatted spittle,
And in anathema what sacred prose
Winnowing the fact from the suppose!
Indeed, what better than these two things can whittle

The scabrous heresies of Yahweh's foes,
Informing the breast where Satan gloats and crows
That saving it leave false doctrine, jot and tittle,
No vigilant thumb will leave its orthodox nose?
What better than ram's horn blown,
And candles blown out by maledictory breath,
Can bring the wanderer back to his very own,
The infidel back to his faith?

Nothing, unless it be that from the ghetto
A soldier of God advance to teach the creed,
Using as rod the irrefutable stiletto.

ii

Uriel da Costa
Flightily ranted
Heresies one day,
Next day recanted.

Rabbi and bishop,
Each vies to smuggle
Soul of da Costa
Out of its struggle.

Confessional hears his
Glib paternoster;
Synagogue sees his
Penitent posture.

What is the end of
This catechism?
Bullet brings dogma
That suffers no schism.

iii

Malevolent scorpions befoul thy chambers,
O my heart; they scurry across its floor,
Leaving the slimy vestiges of doubt.

129

Banish memento of the vermin; let
No scripture on the wall affright you; no
Ghost of da Costa; no, nor any threat.
Ignore, O heart, even as didst ignore
The bribe of florins jingling in the purse.

iv

Jehovah is factotum of the rabbis;
And Christ endures diurnal Calvary;
Polyglot God is exiled to the churches;
Synods tell God to be or not to be.

The Lord within his vacuum of heaven
Discourses his domestic policies,
With angels who break off their loud hosannas
To help him phrase infallible decrees.

Soul of Spinoza, Baruch Spinoza bids you,
Forsake the god suspended in mid-air,
Seek you that other Law, and let Jehovah
Play his game of celestial solitaire.

v

Reducing providence to theorems, the horrible atheist compiled
such lore that proved, like proving two and two make four, that in
the crown of God we all are gems. From glass and dust of glass he
brought to light, out of the pulver and the polished lens, the prism
and the flying mote; and hence the infinitesimal and infinite.
Is it a marvel, then, that he forsook the abracadabra of the
synagogue, and holding with timelessness a duologue, deciphered a
new scripture in the book? Is it a marvel that he left old fraud for
passion intellectual of God?

vi

Unto the crown of bone cry *Suzerain!*
Do genuflect before the jewelled brain!
Lavish the homage of the vassal; let

The blood grow heady with strong epithet;
O cirque of the Cabbalist! O proud skull!
Of alchemy. O crucible!
Sanctum sanctorum; grottoed hermitage
Where sits the bearded sage!
O golden bowl of Koheleth! and of fate
O hourglass within the pate!
Circling, O planet in the occiput!
O Macrocosm, sinew-shut!
Yea, and having uttered this loud *Te Deum*
Ye have been singularly dumb.

vii

I am weak before the wind; before the sun
    I faint; I lose my strength;
I am utterly vanquished by a star;
    I go to my knees, at length

Before the song of a bird; before
    The breath of spring or fall
I am lost; before these miracles
    I am nothing at all.

viii

Lord, accept my hallelujahs; look not askance at these my petty
words; unto perfection a fragment makes its prayer.

For thou art the world, and I am part thereof; thou art the blossom
and I its fluttering petal.

I behold thee in all things, and in all things: lo, it is myself; I look
into the pupil of thine eye, it is my very countenance I see.

Thy glory fills the earth; it is the earth; the noise of the deep, the
moving of many waters, is it not thy voice aloud, O Lord, aloud that
all may hear?

The wind through the almond-trees spreads the fragrance of thy
robes; the turtle-dove twittering utters diminutives of thy love; at the
rising of the sun I behold thy countenance.

Yea, and in the crescent moon, thy little finger's finger-nail.

If I ascend up into heaven, thou art there; If I make my bed in hell, behold thou art there.

Thou art everywhere; a pillar to thy sanctuary is every blade of grass.

Wherefore I said to the wicked, Go to the ant, thou sluggard, seek thou an audience with God.

On the swift wings of a star, even on the numb legs of a snail, thou dost move, O Lord.

A babe in swaddling clothes laughs at the sunbeams on the door's lintel; the sucklings play with thee; with thee Kopernik holds communion through a lens.

I am thy son, O Lord, and brother to all that lives am I.

The flowers of the field, they are kith and kin to me; the lily my sister, the rose is my blood and flesh.

Even as the stars in the firmament move, so does my inward heart, and even as the moon draws the tides in the bay, so does it the blood in my veins.

For thou art the world, and I am part thereof;

Howbeit, even in dust I am resurrected; and even in decay I live again.

ix

Think of Spinoza, then, not as you think
Of Shabbathai Zvi who for a time of life
Took to himself the Torah for a wife,
And underneath the silken canopy
Made public: Thou art hallowed unto me.

Think of Spinoza, rather, plucking tulips
Within the garden of Mynheer, forgetting
Dutchmen and Rabbins, and consumptive fretting,
Plucking his tulips in the Holland sun,
Remembering the thought of the Adored,
Spinoza, gathering flowers for the One,
The ever-unwedded lover of the Lord.

132

TALISMAN IN SEVEN SHREDS

SYLLOGISM

If golem is the effigy of man,
and man the simulacrum of the Lord,
the sequitur—I blanch to mouth the word,
the blasphemous equation framed to span
chasm between the Lord and Caliban!
Such is the logic that befouls the bird,
bemires the stars, reduces to the absurd,
the godhead on the heavenly Divan.
Kismet, Ananke, Golem, these are one:
implacable automata no mortal
swerves from their single purpose in the sun,
driving the human through a mouldy portal.
Implore the golem to undo the done;
the golem will emit an idiot's chortle.

EMBRYO OF DUSTS

Geographers may mark Prague on the map
as a right Christian city: friars may
seek to bring Hebrews to unhallowed clay,
or suckle them upon a Catholic pap;
Johann Silvester in his scarlet cap,
and aproned Havlicek, the butcher, may,
whether it is a Jew or swine they flay,
convince themselves Jehovah takes a nap.
In vain: He sleeps not, neither does He drowse,
custodian of Israel; He entrusts
unto a guided nit-wit his chief house;
therefore Reb Jacob Loew essays to rouse
the name ineffable, maieutically thrusts
the golem from his embryo of dusts.

133

TETRAGRAMMATON

What scrofulous ashes upon sack-cloth, what
gaunt fasts, what scourges, yea, what Zohar's spark,
what candles nibbling se'en wounds in the dark,
have filched the logos from the polyglot?
Phylactery on brow in lieu of thought,
rabbi, communing with the hierarch,
unto what portents have you gasped, hark! hark!
and added at the last th' ineffable jot?
On parchment in the mouth of golem, it,
the tetragrammaton was placed, his ward!
A golem held the Lord's name, even as spit.
And now it is gone, O rabbi, it is marred,
(upon what margin shall I find it writ?)
it is fled, and remains the golem's shard.

FONS VITAE

Mud and mire of Moldau, that was the sperm
that nurtured him, while rabbi and sextons three
beheld that which before was not, to be—
life sanguine behind scabrous epiderm.
Ibn Gabirol, some say, did once affirm
the font of life; Maimonides fed a wee
homunculus in a jar, a dwarf which he
created. These, then, knew the pristine germ.
Sanctum sanctorum! how can I ever pry
behind the mystic chromosome? Grasp you,
even as Tycho Brahe, by raking the sky?
Can you be fashioned from the alembic's spue?
Can grace after meat in terms of x and y
suggest the dark formula, the vital cue?

134

ENIGMA

Solve me this riddle: Rumours are bruited
the Jews spit venom on the holy rood;
leagued with the devil and his horned brood
they prick the wafer, and pollute the bread.
Pestilence on the waters do they spread,
and Christian infants are their drink and food;
the rumours being such, so grows the feud
even the palest Slovene blood boils red.
How, then, and wherefore, despite barbaric wrath,
does Jacob swallow sword and fire-brand
to outlive every Judeophobic froth?
Is it the finger of the Lord's right hand?
Or is the golem saviour, this rude goth
whose earthy paw is like a magic wand?

GUIDE TO THE PERPLEXED

The paleface mutters; Lord God is a myth;
do you your genuflexions to the Rose.
Be merry, eat and drink, the large paunch crows,
the worms adore a man of guts and pith.
Voices: He is the Anvil and the Smith.
He is comminglement of yeas and noes.
He died, and then trisected He arose.
The Rock of Ages is a monolith.
The kennels of the hounds of God are full—
Aye, what a baying at the moon is there!
What, then, is good and true and beautiful?
The tongue is bitter when it must declare:
matter is chaos, mind is chasm, fool,
the work of golems stalking in nightmare . . . .

IMMORTAL YEARNINGS

*To sleep, perchance to dream. Where there is smoke
there is fire. Death does not end the act.*
With these neat phrases leap a cataract?
With similar bywords to unyoke the yoke?
There is no witch of En-dor to invoke
asking dead spirits to pronounce the fact.
No subtleties, no flattery, no tact,
can make the virgin doff her triple cloak.
Ask the golem? O, he will answer yes,
It suits the golem to disclose it so.
But I will take a prong in hand, and go
over old graves and test their hollowness:
be it the spirit or the dust I hoe
only at doomsday's sunrise will I know.

DESIGN FOR MEDIAEVAL TAPESTRY

Somewhere a hungry muzzle rooted.
The frogs among the sedges croaked.
Into the night a screech-owl hooted.

A clawed mouse squeaked and struggled, choked.
The wind pushed antlers through the bushes.
Terror stalked through the forest, cloaked.

Was it a robber broke the bushes?
Was it a knight in armoured thews,
Walking in mud, and bending rushes?

Was it a provost seeking Jews?
The Hebrews shivered; their teeth rattled;
Their beards glittered with gelid dews.

136

Gulped they their groans, for silence tattled;
They crushed their sighs, for quiet heard;
They had their thoughts on Israel battled

By pagan and by Christian horde.
They moved their lips in pious anguish.
They made no sound. They never stirred.

REB ZADOC HAS MEMORIES

Reb Zadoc's brain is a German town:
Hermits come from lonely grottos
Preaching the right for Jews to drown;

Soldiers who vaunt their holy mottos
Stroking the cross that is a sword;
Barons plotting in cabal sottos;

A lady spitting on the abhorred.
The market-place and faggot-fire—
A hangman burning God's true word;

A clean-shaved traitor-Jew; a friar
Dropping his beads upon his paunch;
The heavens speared by a Gothic spire;

The Judengasse and its stench
Rising from dark and guarded alleys
Where Jew is neighboured to harlot-wench

Perforce ecclesiastic malice;
The exile-booths of Jacob where
Fat burghers come to pawn a chalice

While whistling a Jew-hating air;
Peasants regarding Jews and seeking
The hooves, the tail, the horn-crowned hair;

And target for a muddy streaking,
The yellow badge upon the breast,
The vengeance of a papal wreaking;

137

The imposts paid for this fine crest;
Gay bailiffs serving writs of seizure;
Even the town fool and his jest—

Stroking his beard with slowly leisure,
A beard that was but merely down,
Rubbing his palms with gloating pleasure.

Counting fictitious crown after crown.
Reb Zadoc's brain is a torture-dungeon;
Reb Zadoc's brain is a German town.

REB DANIEL SHOCHET REFLECTS

The toad seeks out its mud; the mouse discovers
The nibbled hole; the sparrow owns its nest;
About the blind mole earthy shelter hovers.

The louse avows the head where it is guest;
Even the roach calls some dark fent his dwelling.
But Israel owns a sepulchre, at best.

NAHUM-THIS-ALSO-IS-FOR-THE-GOOD PONDERS

The wrath of God is just. His punishment
Is most desirable. The flesh of Jacob
Implores the scourge. For this was Israel meant.

Below we have no life. But we will wake up
Beyond, where popes will lave our feet, where princes
Will heed our insignificantest hiccup.

The sins of Israel only blood-shed rinses.
We teach endurance. Lo, we are not spent.
We die, we live; at once we are three tenses.

Our skeletons are bibles; flesh is rent
Only to prove a thesis, stamp a moral.
The rack prepared: for this was Israel meant.

ISAIAH EPICURE AVERS

Seek reasons; rifle your theology;
Philosophize; expend your dialectic;
Decipher and translate God's diary;

Discover causes, primal and eclectic;
I cannot; all I know is this:
That pain doth render flesh most sore and hectic;

That lance-points prick; that scorched bones hiss;
That thumbscrews agonize, and that a martyr
Is mad if he considers these things bliss.

JOB REVILES

God is grown ancient. He no longer hears.
He has been deafened by his perfect thunders.
With clouds for cotton he has stopped his ears.

The Lord is purblind; and his heaven sunders
Him from the peccadillos of this earth.
He meditates his youth; he dreams; he wonders.

His cherubs have acquired beards and girth.
They cannot move to do his bidding. Even
The angels yawn. Satan preserves his mirth.

How long, O Lord, will Israel's heart be riven?
How long will we cry to a dotard God
To let us keep the breath that He has given?

How long will you sit on your throne, and nod?

139

JUDITH MAKES COMPARISONS

Judith had heard a troubadour
Singing beneath a castle-turret
Of truth, chivalry, and honour,
Of virtue, and of gallant merit,—
Judith had heard a troubadour
Lauding the parfait knightly spirit,
Singing beneath the ivied wall.
The cross-marked varlet Judith wrestled
Was not like these at all, at all . . . .

EZEKIEL THE SIMPLE OPINES

If we will fast for forty days; if we
Will read the psalms thrice over; if we offer
To God some blossom-bursting litany,

And to the poor a portion of the coffer;
If we don sack-cloth, and let ashes rain
Upon our heads, despite the boor and scoffer,

Certes, these things will never be again.

SOLOMON TALMUDI CONSIDERS HIS LIFE

Rather that these blood-thirsty pious vandals,
Bearing sable in heart, and gules on arm,
Had made me ready for the cerement-candles,

Than that they should have taken my one charm
Against mortality, my exegesis:
The script that gave the maggot the alarm.

Jews would have crumpled Rashi's simple thesis
On reading this, and Ibn Ezra's version;
Maimonides they would have torn to pieces.

140

For here, in black and white, by God's conversion,
I had plucked secrets from the pentateuch,
And gathered strange arcana from dispersion,

The essence and quintessence of the book!
Green immortality smiled out its promise—
I hung my gaberdine on heaven's hook.

Refuting Duns, and aquinatic Thomas,
Confounding Moslems, proving the one creed
A simple sentence broken by no commas,

I thought to win myself eternal meed,
I thought to move the soul with sacred lever
And lift the heart to God in very deed.

Ah, woe is me, and to my own endeavour,
That on that day they burned my manuscript,
And lost my name, for certain, and for ever!

SIMEON TAKES HINTS FROM HIS ENVIRONS

Heaven is God's grimace at us on high.
This land is a cathedral; speech, its sermon.
The moon is a rude gargoyle in the sky.

The leaves rustle. Come, who will now determine
Whether this be the wind, or priestly robes.
The frogs croak out ecclesiastic German,

Whereby our slavish ears have punctured lobes.
The stars are mass-lamps on a lofty altar;
Even the angels are Judaeophobes.

There is one path; in it I shall not falter.
Let me rush to the bosom of the state
And church, grasp lawyer-code and monkish psalter,

And being Christianus Simeon, late
Of Jewry, have much comfort and salvation—
Salvation in this life, at any rate.

ESTHER HEARS ECHOES OF HIS VOICE

How sweetly did he sing grace after meals!
He now is silent. He has fed on sorrow.
He lies where he is spurned by faithless heels.

His voice was honey. Lovers well might borrow
Warmth from his words. His words were musical,
Making the night so sweet, so sweet the morrow!

Can I forget the tremors of his call?
Can *kiddush* benediction be forgotten?
His blood is spilled like wine. The earth is sharp with gall.

As soothing as the promises begotten
Of penitence and love; as lovely as
The turtle-dove; as soft as snow in cotton,

Whether he lulled a child or crooned the laws,
And sacred as the eighteen prayers, so even
His voice. His voice was so. His voice that was . . . .

The burgher sleeps beside his wife, and dreams
Of human venery, and Hebrew quarry.
His sleep contrives him many little schemes.

There will be Jews, dead, moribund and gory;
There will be booty; there will be dark maids,
And there will be a right good spicy story . . . .

The moon has left her vigil. Lucifer fades.
Whither shall we betake ourselves, O Father?
Whither to flee? And where to find our aids?

The wrath of people is like foam and lather,
Risen against us.Wherefore, Lord, and why?
The winds assemble; the cold and hot winds gather

To scatter us. They do not heed our cry.
The sun rises and leaps the red horizon,
And like a bloodhound swoops across the sky.

142

HAGGADAH

ETCHING

The sky is dotted like th' unleavened bread,
The moon a golden platter in the sky.
Old midget Jews, with meditated tread,
Hands clasped behind, and body stooped ahead,
Creep from the synagogue and stare on high
Upon a golden platter in a dotted sky.

ONCE IN A YEAR

Once in a year this comes to pass:
My father is a king in a black skull cap,
My mother is a queen in a brown perruque,
A princess my sister, a lovely lass,
My brother a prince, and I a duke.

Silver and plate, and fine cut-glass
Brought from the cupboards that hid them till now
Banquet King David's true lineage here.
Once in a year this comes to pass,
Once in a long unroyal year.

BLACK DECALOGUE

Compute the plagues; your little finger dip
In spittle of the grape, and at each pest
Shake off the drop with the vindictive zest:
Thus first: the Nile—a gash; then frogs that skip
Upon the princess' coverlet; the rip
Made by dark nails that seek the itching guest;
The plague of murrained carcasses; the pest;
Full boils that stud the Ethiop, leg to lip.
The guerdon of hot hail, the fists of God;
The swarm of locusts nibbling Egypt clean;

Thick darkness oozing from out Moses' rod;
And first-born slain, the mighty and the mean;
Compute these plagues that fell on Egypt's sod,
Then add: In Goshen these were never seen.

THE BITTER DISH

This is the bread of our affliction, this
The symbol of the clay that built Ramses,
And that horseradish-root of bitterness,
And you, my brethren, yea,
You are the afflicted, the embittered, and the clay.

SONG

Fill the silver goblet;
Make open the door-way;
Let there be no sob; let
Elijah come our way.

And let him come singing,
Announcing as nigh a
Redemption, and drinking
The health of Messiah!

CHAD GADYAH

This is a curious plot
Devised for eager riddling;
My father had a kidling
For two good *zuzim* bought.

Graymalkin ate it; and
A dog munched sleek Graymalkin,
Whereat a Rod did stalk in
Beating his reprimand

144

Upon the Dog's spine. Came
Red Fire, and did sputter
His wrath on Rod; came Water
And sizzling, quenched the flame.

And down a bovine throat
Went Water, which throat, tickled
By pious *Shochet,* trickled
Red blood upon his coat.

The Angel of Death flew
And smote the *Shochet*; whereat
The Lord gave him his merit—
The Lord the Angel slew.

In that strange portal whence
All things come, they re-enter;
Of all things God is centre,
God is circumference.

This is a curious plot
Devised for eager riddling;
My father had a kidling
For two good *zuzim* bought.

THE STILL SMALL VOICE

The candles splutter; and the kettle hums;
The heirloomed clock enumerates the tribes,
Upon the wine-stained table-cloth lie crumbs
Of *matzoh* whose wide scattering describes
Jews driven in far lands upon this earth.

The kettle hums; the candles splutter; and
Winds whispering from shutters tell re-birth
Of beauty rising in an eastern land,
Of paschal sheep driven in cloudy droves;
Of almond-blossoms colouring the breeze;
Of vineyards upon verdant terraces;

145

Of golden globes in orient orange-groves.
And those assembled at the table dream
Of small schemes that an April wind doth scheme,
And cry from out the sleep assailing them:
Jerusalem, next year! Next year, Jerusalem!

REB LEVI YITSCHOK TALKS TO GOD

Reb Levi Yitschok, crony of the Lord,
Familiar of heaven, broods these days.
His heart erupts in sighs. He will have a word
At last, with Him of the mysterious ways.

He will go to the synagogue of Berditchev,
And there sieve out his plaints in a dolorous sieve.

Rebono shel Olam—he begins—
Who helps you count our little sins?
Whosoever it be, saving Your grace,
I would declare before his face,
He knows no ethics,
No, nor arithmetics.

For if from punishments we judge the sins,
Thy midget Hebrews, even when they snore,
Are most malefic djinns,
And wicked to the core of their heart's core;
Not so didst thou consider them,
Thy favourite sons of yore.
How long wilt thou ordain it, Lord, how long
Will Satan fill his mickle-mouth with mirth,
Beholding him free, the knave who earned the thong,
And Israel made the buttocks of the earth?

The moon grinned from the window-pane; a cat
Standing upon a gable, humped and spat;

146

Somewhere a loud mouse nibbled at a board,
A spider wove a niche in the House of the Lord.

Reb Levi Yitschok talking to himself,
Addressed his infant arguments to God:
Why hast thou scattered him like biblic dust,
To make a union with unhallowed sod,
Building him temples underneath a mound,
Compatriot of the worm in rain-soaked ground?

The lion of Judah! no such parable
Is on my lips; no lion, nor lion's whelp,
But a poor bag o'bones goat which seeks thy help,
A scrawny goat, its rebel horns both broken,
Its beard uncouthly plucked, its tongue so dumbly lolling
Even its melancholy ma-a- remains unspoken.

The candles flicker,
And peeping through the windows, the winds snicker.
The mice digest some holy rune,
And gossip of the cheeses of the moon....

Where is the trumpeted Messiah? Where
The wine long-soured into vinegar?
Have cobwebs stifled his mighty shofar? Have
Chilblains weakened his ass's one good hoof?

So all night long Reb Levi Yitschok talked,
Preparing words on which the Lord might brood.
How long did even angels guard a feud?
When would malign Satanas be unfrocked?
Why were the tortured by their echoes mocked?
Who put Death in his ever-ravenous mood?
Good men groaned: Hunger; bad men belched of food;
Wherefore? And why? Reb Levi Yitschok talked . . .
Vociferous was he in his monologue.
He raged, he wept. He suddenly went mild
Begging the Lord to lead him through the fog;
Reb Levi Yitschok, an ever-querulous child,
Sitting on God's knees in the synagogue,
Unanswered even when the sunrise smiled.

147

PLUMAGED PROXY

O rooster, circled over my brother's head,
If you had foresight you would see a beard
Pluck little feathers from your neck, a blade
Slit open your alarum, and a thumb
Press down your gullet, rendering it dumb.
My brother sends you to a land of shade,
Hebraically curses your new home,
And sets his sins upon your ruddy comb,
Atonement for the gifts of Satan's trade.
O rooster in a vortex of repentance,
Proxy of my little brother's soul,
You speed into a land where death pays toll;
Where no sun rises to evoke a crow
    You go.
Be you not lonesome. I will send you thither
Each year a new companion for each year
My brother lets his peccadilloes wither.
Be you intrepid, therefore; do not fear.
May six score roosters in the course of time
Be cooped with you upon your nether stage.
And may my brother live to a ripe age.

DANCE CHASSIDIC

Twist each side-curl; form the symbol
Of a quaver; comb the beard;
Let the prayer make all toes nimble . . .
The Lord loved and the Lord feared
In your attitude, the pendules dangled
Ecstatically, defiantly the fingers snapped,—
In such wise is cursed Satan to be wrangled,
In such the Chassid to be rapt.

148

Let the Rebbe take the mantled Scroll;
You, Chassidim, lift your caftans, dance;
Circle the Torah and rejoice the soul,
Look God-wards and He will not look askance.

Let this be humility;
Back bent in the pious reel,
Head inclined imploringly,
And palms upward in appeal.

And let this be pride;
Beard pointed upward, eyes aflame like *yahrzeit* lamps,
And right hand stretched as if it held God's left hand in it,
Marching as into Paradise, while each foot stamps,
Crushing Eternity into a dusty minute . . .

Thus let the soul be cast from pride, gesticulating
Into humility, and from humility
Into the pride divine, so alternating
Until pride and humility be one,
Until above the Jews, above the Scroll, above the Cherubim,
There broods the Immanence of Him . . . .

PREACHER

He quoted *midrash* and the psalms;
    He fancied parables;
He wept; he smote his anguished palms;
    He hushed his voice in spells;
He urged the rich to lavish alms
    To save them from their hells.

His eyes were pellets set between
    The sling of bare cheek-bones;
His index-finger, long and lean
    Shook to accusing tones;

His Adam's apple could be seen
   Gulping down godly groans.

Who froze the eager blood to curds?
   Who melted adamant?
Who wrought up tears? Who conjured words
   Wherewith to cavil cant?
Who called his audiences herds?
   Who phrased the subtle taunt?

And at his speech the old Jews wept;
   With prayer-shawls they dried
Their tears; the women overleapt
   Decorum, and they cried;
And every little urchin kept
   Near to his father's side . . .

They wept, and they repented while
   Gehenna crackled from
His lips, and Satan spread his guile,
   And scourges made a hum;
They wept, and they repented while
   His terrors struck them dumb.

SCRIBE

The black phylacteries about his arm
Impress the first initial of God's name
Upon the skin, encircled by this charm.
The Sheen of Shaddai intricately drawn
Into the flesh sets bone and blood aflame.
The heart beats out the tetragrammaton.

Let heathenesse seek refuge in its steel;
Let pagandom invest its coat of mail;
This prayer-shawl is armour to this Jew!

150

Satan endures its pendules as a flail;
Demons are frightened by its white and blue;
And Lilith knows a hauberk she can not undo.

His eyes are two black blots of ink.
The thin hairs of his beard
Are symbols of the script revered;
His broad brow is the margin of a parchment page,
Clean for the commentaries of age.

Having shaped a chapter of the Holy Writ,
Having reached the name of God,
Let no hair fallen from his beard unhallow it.
Let no imp alcoved in a finger nail
Play his unsacred fraud.
Therefore let living water wash his right hand clean,
Drowning the satans on his palm, unseen and seen.

And after three score years and ten,
He will have raised three pentateuchs
Aloft to be the praise of men;
His eyes will then be water, his bones hooks.
His fingers will not write again.

He will descend unto that other ark
Which has no curtains save an empty shroud.
And there the slimy exegetes will mark
Exegesis upon the parchment-browed.

But the true essence, joyous as a lark,
Will settle on God's wrist, devoutly proud!

151

SACRED ENOUGH YOU ARE

Sacred enough you are.
Why should I praise
You, make you holier
Than is the case?
One does not wear
Phylacteries
On Sabbath days.

SONNETS SEMITIC

i

Would that three centuries past had seen us born!
When gallants brought a continent on a chart
To turreted ladies waiting their return.
Then had my gifts in truth declared my heart!
From foreign coasts, over tempestuous seas,
I would have brought a gold-caged parrakeet;
Gems from some painted tribe; the Sultan's keys;
Bright coronets; and placed them at your feet.
Yea, on the high seas raised a sombre flag,
And singed unwelcome beards, and made for shore
With precious stones, and coins in many a bag
To proffer you. These deeds accomplished, or
I would have been a humble thin-voiced Jew
Hawking old clo'es in ghetto lanes, for you.

ii

These northern stars are scarabs in my eyes.
Not any longer can I suffer them.
I will to Palestine. We will arise
And seek the towers of Jerusalem.

152

Make ready to board ship. Say farewells. Con
Your Hebrew primer; supple be your tongue
To speak the crisp words baked beneath the sun,
The sinuous phrases by the sweet-singer sung.
At last, my bride, in our estate you'll wear
Sweet orange-blossoms in an orange grove.
There will be white doves fluttering in the air,
And in the meadows our contented drove,
Sheep on the hills, and in the trees, my love,
There will be sparrows twittering *Mazel Tov.*

iii

Upon a time there lived a dwarf, a Jew.
His shelter was a thatch, a beard his clothes.
He loved God, and feared women. When he knew
A girl was at his hut, he thumbed his nose.
One night the moon turned *shadchen.* In its glow
The dwarf beheld a girl, a maid, a lass . . .
He had no name for her. He said, Oh. Oh.
He knelt and kissed her toes upon the grass.
The dowry that she gave him were the stars,—
Only he must go get these stars himself.
The bridegroom took a flower—gold was scarce—
And made a ring. The cantor was an elf.
O, there were nectar-cups, and there was laughter!
The dwarf and wife lived happily ever after . . .

iv

I shall not bear much burden when I cross
My father's threshold to our common door;
Only some odds I would not count as loss,
Only some ends old days can not ignore:
The prayer-shawl my mother cast upon
My shoulders, blessing Israel with a man;
Phylacteries my father gave his son;
The bible over which my young eyes ran;
And Talmud huge, once shield from heathen stones.

153

I bring these as mementos; also, verse
Scribbled in rhymes that memory condones,
And a capacious though still empty purse.
For your old age I keep a psalter-book
From which to read on Sabbaths, in perruque.

v

Now we will suffer loss of memory;
We will forget the tongue our mothers knew;
We will munch ham, and guzzle milk thereto,
And this on hallowed fast-days, purposely . . .
Abe will elude his base-nativity.
The kike will be a phantom; we will rue
Our bearded ancestry, my nasal cue,
And like the Gentiles we will strive to be.
Our recompense—emancipation-day.
We will have friend where once we had a foe.
Impugning epithets will glance astray.
To Gentile parties we will proudly go;
And Christians, anecdoting us, will say:
"Mr. and Mrs. Klein—the Jews, you know. . . ."

FOR THE LEADER—WITH STRING MUSIC

SONG OF TOYS AND TRINKETS

What toys shall I buy my little lad?
No urchin's bauble, and no waif's doodad;

No little brass cannon; no sorcerer's dress;
Not these shall I buy my blessedness.

He shall not play at run-sheep-run,
At leapfrog, or with badge and gun,

154

But he shall have his daily sport—
Fearless,—with them of the evil sort.

So shall he whip with pendules eight
Imps that for small boys lie in wait.

His *grager* shall make terrible sound
The name of Haman to confound.

He shall don *tallis*; Satan's host
Shall flee his footsteps, crying: Ghost!

No ball and bat, but palmleaf and
Citron will grace his pious hand.

Phylacteries shall be the reins
With which he'll ride through God's sweet lanes.

A little *zaddik!* men will say,
Seeing my little boy at play.

SONG OF EXCLAMATIONS

May the sun wash your eyes; may you
Rise to the crow of *cu-cu-ru*.

Let piety and Chassidim
Teach your small voice the *bam-bim-bim*.

May cantors, singing the Lord's law,
Rejoice you with their *tra-la-la*.

Never let my glad Yankele
Wearily utter *eh-beh-meh!*

May pity sit in your heart, and note
Even the *maa* of the gloomy goat.

In days to come may ecstasy
Dance on your lips its *ai-ai-ai*.

But never, never let sorrow say
Its doleful *oi,* its whimpering *weh.*

SONG TO BE SUNG AT DAWN

Heigh ho! the rooster crows!
The rooster crows upon the thatch;
A dog leaps up to pull at a latch;
The dew is on the rose.
The daisies open; they shine like money;
The bees are busy gathering honey;
The pigeons hop on their toes.
The birds chirp underneath the eaves;
They sing from their nests among the leaves;
The sun is in the skies!
The barn is bright; the meadow sunny;
The sun smiles into every cranny.
A little boy rubs his eyes,—
A little boy rubs his eyes and nose,
And says his *Modeh Ani.*

MARKET SONG

Plump pigeons, who will buy?
Plump pigeons, and fat doves?
Come, gossips, hurry nigh;
Shake purses, hearty loves,
    And buy my doves.

Oh, cheap at any price,
A most delicious morsel,
Made ready in a trice!
Take home a feathered parcel,
    A dainty morsel.

Wives, do you love your men?
Set love upon a plate.
A good bird is worth ten

Grown bony in a crate.
  Wives, do not wait!

Go feel them, look at them—
Their breasts, their bright pink eyes!
You buy the like of them
Elsewhere, and at my price,
  My petty price?

Unknot your kerchiefs, then,
Shake out your coins, my loves,—
Buy now, you know not when
You will catch such fat doves,
  Such doves again.

COUNTING-OUT RHYME

Orange, citron, fig and date,
While the fruit buds, we stand and wait;
Flower on branch, and grape on vine,
One of us soon will leave the line.
Blossoms burst, the fruit will swell,
Who it will be, one can not tell.
Almond, raisin, olive, plum.
The word is hush, the sign is mum.
Oh, the sun shone, Oh, the wind blew,
The apple fell to this little Jew.

OF KITH AND KIN

HEIRLOOM

My father bequeathed me no wide estates;
No keys and ledgers were my heritage;
Only some holy books with *yahrzeit* dates
Writ mournfully upon a blank front page—

157

Books of the Baal Shem Tov, and of his wonders;
Pamphlets upon the devil and his crew;
Prayers against road demons, witches, thunders;
And sundry other tomes for a good Jew.

Beautiful: though no pictures on them, save
The scorpion crawling on a printed track;
The Virgin floating on a scriptural wave,
Square letters twinkling in the Zodiac.

The snuff left on this page, now brown and old,
The tallow stains of midnight liturgy—
These are my coat of arms, and these unfold
My noble lineage, my proud ancestry!

And my tears, too, have stained this heirloomed ground,
When reading in these treatises some weird
Miracle, I turned a leaf and found
A white hair fallen from my father's beard.

BESTIARY

God breathe a blessing on
His small bones, every one!
The little lad, who stalks
The bible's plains and rocks
To hunt in grammar'd woods
Strange litters and wild broods;
The little lad who seeks
Beast-muzzles and bird-beaks
In cave and den and crypt,
In copse of holy script;
The little lad who looks
For quarry in holy books.

Before his eyes is born
The elusive unicorn;
There, scampering, arrive
The golden mice, the five;

Also, in antic shape,
Gay peacock and glum ape.

He hears a snort of wrath:
The fiery behemoth;
And then on biblic breeze
The crocodile's sneeze.
He sees the lion eat
Straw, and from the teat
Of tigress a young lamb
Suckling, like whelp nigh dam.

Hard by, as fleet as wind
They pass, the roe and hind,
Bravely, and with no risk,
He holds the basilisk,
Pygarg and cockatrice.
And there, most forest-wise
Among the bestiaries
The little hunter eyes
Him crawling at his leisure:
The beast Nebuchadnezzar.

MOURNERS

O, when they laved my uncle's limbs
My aunt wept bitter and long:
Who will now show my little son
The right from the wrong?
And who will sing for my delight
The holy Sabbath's song?

O, when they dug my uncle's grave,
My little cousins cried:
Who will now tell us tales about
A princess and her pride?
And who will give us pennies to
Save for a lovely bride?

Even the sparrows on the roof
Twittered their sorrow, too:
Oh, never will be thrown to us
The breadcrumbs soaked in dew;
For men have nailed him in a box,
That good little Jew.

GIFT

I will make him a little red sack
    For treasure untold,
With a velvet front and a satin back,
    And braided with gold,
    His *tfillin* to hold.

I will stitch it with letters of flame,
    With square characters:
His name, and his father's name;
    And beneath it some terse
    Scriptural verse.

Yea, singing the sweet liturgy,
    He'll snare its gold cord,
Remembering me, even me,
    In the breath of his word,
    In the sight of the Lord.

OF SUNDRY FOLK

INTO THE TOWN OF CHELM

On a little brown pony, a little boy rides
Over cobblestone roads through strange countrysides;
He rides to and fro, and he rides up and down,
Asks milkmaids and blacksmiths how far 'tis to town,
    To topsy-turvy town.

160

His grandfather told him that would he be wise
He must see the fool's town with his very own eyes;
See Jews catch the moon in a bucket for cheese,
And find the next night that moon stuck in the trees—
    That moon stuck in the trees.

See the simpleton settling high matters of state;
The rabbi a-scratching his dubious pate,
Watch the baker knead rolls out of dough made of lime,
Since it never turned sour, and kept a long time,
    Because it kept a long time.

And hear the philosopher in the town-hall
Drone nothing is nothing, and that is all;
And also the poet who bawled out a song
Which proved that the heat stretched the summer day long,
    Did stretch the summer day long.

So into the hamlet the little boy rides—
Oh, even his pony is holding its sides!
The little boy smiles to the Jews of the realm,
Nods right and nods left to the burghers of Chelm,
    The simple burghers of Chelm.

JONAH KATZ

Jonah Katz
Was quaint and queer;
Some called him bard,
Some called him seer.

His phrases mad,
His speech absurd,
Who will explain
Me his occult word?

For he did speak
Strangely of these:
Bears with berets,
Goats with goatees,

Apes in aprons,
In cowslips cows,
Foxes in foxgloves,
In samite sows.

Why did he dress
In robes the rabbit?
Why did his beasts
Don bystic habit?

Jonah Katz:
Was he a seer?
A poet? Sage?
Or only queer?

BANDIT

There was a Jewish bandit who lived in a wood,
He never did much evil, nor ever did much good,
For he would halt a merchant, quivering to his toes,
And in a gruff voice whisper: *You'll pay through the nose.*
And then he'd search his person, having bid him pray,
And snatch his broken snuff-box, and sneeze himself away.

A DEED OF DARING

This is a tale of a deed of daring:
How Samson got the rabbi a herring,
The rabbi who ate for his Sabbath supper
A herring's parts, lower, middle, and upper.

So Samson the brave, his pennies sparing,
Into the market went wayfaring,
And bought, and got, and brought the herring:
This is a tale of a deed of daring.

BIOGRAPHY

A little Jew lived in a little straw hut;
There was thatch on his roof; on his floors there was not;
There was smoke in his chimney, and sun on his cot;
  But
There was nothing in his pot.

So, hungry and little in a world that was wide,
He tried to get used to not eating; he tried
The first day, the second. "A habit!" he cried.
  Then sighed.
And thus the little Jew died.

DOCTOR DWARF

Into his beard he laughs at the
Musty apothecaries;
A doctor, and no quack is he,
He learns his lore from fairies.

And if there is an ill for which
He knows no herb himself,
He goes not to the broomstick witch,
He hies him to the elf.

Is there a little boy who's ill?
A little lad who's hurt?
He gives him an almond for a pill,
A raisin for dessert.

He takes the blindman from his hut
To see the moon i' the sky.
"A ladder!" the blind man cries, "to cut
Two slices of that pie!"

A lover pined away for love,
He could not dine nor sup;
Until the wise man poured for him
Dew from a buttercup.

There was a hunchback in our town.
He was so hunched, was he,
That when he looked up he still looked down.
Now he's as straight as me.

With a pine needle and some hay
He sewed my cousin's stitches;
Oh, it was such a sunny day
When he broke my brother's crutches!

He lived on the hill; and in his time
One never moaned in pain
For longer than it takes to climb
The hill, and down again.

OF KINGS AND BEGGARS

BALLAD OF THE DANCING BEAR

i

Fat grows Stanislaus, *Pan,* whose
Hamlets teem with busy Jews,

Arguing about one topic:
Thrift of rouble, thrift of kopek;

Tailors, sitting on their shins,
Cutting cloth, and spitting pins;

Bakers kneading their thumbs callous,
Fashioning gigantic *chalos;*

Butchers cutting kosher meat;
Millers raising ghosts of wheat;

Cobbler, praying for bad weather,
Spitting on his polished leather;

Pieman selling children sweets;
Potters hawking in the streets;

Gossips vending Sabbath candles,
Wrapped in paper and in scandals;

Binders gluing holy books,
Liturgies and pentateuchs;

Merchants, or in Slav or jargon,
Driving each his petty bargain.

ii

They were rich then, were they not,
With such commerce polyglot?

If full moons are yellow cheeses,
If blessed herbs can cure diseases,

If Pan Stanislaus is lean,
Or sheep crafty, or swine clean,

If good words can come from witches,
They, assuredly, had riches!

iii

Poor they were, a town of paupers:
Ants rewarded like grasshoppers;

Huts, whose windows storm-abused,
Let in hunger to its roost;

Walls where spider webs were swinging
To the tune of strong winds singing;

Roofs with dried and meagre thatch,
Doors without a knob or latch;

Stool and bed and table broken,
Witness misery outspoken;

165

And bare pantries where the mice,
Every day starved at least thrice.

iv

For, as all their commerce waxes,
Lo, it wanes beneath hard taxes,

Tax on birth and tax on death,
Tax on gone and coming breath,

Filling Pan Stanislaus' coffers
With the wealth the impost offers,

Keeping him in meats and wines,
Not to speak of concubines,

For the music of gold roubles,
Tintinnabulates his troubles.

Thus, Pan Stanislaus grows fat,
Swilling strong ale from a vat.

v

At the sight of churlish Jew
Thaddeus priest retched forth his spew.

He abhorred the tribe of Moses;
Barbs in his heart were their hooked noses.

So he rummaged the whole Bible,
Seeking some new spicy libel.

Telling beads, he mouthed curses
That the Lord increase their hearses.

Oh, to sprinkle holy water
On their foul skins—or to slaughter,

Sweep them out like filthy maggots,
Make them crackle on dry faggots,

166

And as finis to his work,
Ease their whines with fat of pork.

vi

Filaments of evil slip
From the holy spiderlip.

Pan Stanislaus guzzling beer,
Piously inclines his ear:

In our midst there is a people
That thumbs noses at our steeple,

That, though seeming poor, has riches,
Hid in cracks and profane niches,

Stuffed with feathers in their cushions,
Polish coins and German groshens,

And old deeds from peasant-debtors,
Pressed among their sacred letters.

Railing ever at Christ-Jesus,
Every Jew as rich as Croesus,—

Sire, their purses are too heavy;
May your Lordship please to levy

Taxes on the Hebrew scoffers
To replenish Caesar's coffers.

Tax the cradle, tax the coffin;
Jews are never taxed too often.

Therefore, let them be beholden
To their Lord with many a gulden.

Let the folk whose life besmirches
Us, erect our ruined churches.

So, while each Jew weeps his dirge, he
Helps to feed God's favourite clergy.

Be it that they will not pay,
Let them further on their way,

Bearing on unbaptized legs,
All their holy thingumjigs.

Pan Stanislaus yawned, and drank,
Drank and yawned, his vile mouth stank;

Ho, he said, and *hum,* he said,
Scratched his fumed and dizzying head,

Wiped back each mustachio,
And then hiccupped: Be it so.

vii

When the crier cried the news
To the hamletful of Jews,

They were nibbling each his crumb,
They were smitten dumb.

But they donned no sackcloth, for
Sackcloth were the clothes they wore.

They poured ashes on their heads;
Fasted; they ate Sorrow's breads.

And to live through these grim threats,
They bribed God with epithets.

viii

In the castle-tower, she
Sings her sorrow wistfully,

Paulinka, the princess, sings
Valiant but uncouth things:

Giants slain by manikins;
Beanstalks climbed by crippled shins;

Ogres discomfited by maimed
Knights that in an hour are famed;

Lions bearded in their dens
By an outcast pauper-prince;

Hunchback troubadours who wed
Princesses of royal blood;

Kingdoms in remote lands won
By a disinherited son;

Imps in pandemonium
Cowering before Tom Thumb.

In the tower alone, she sings
Of God's ill unfavoured things.

Paulinka forgets her maim
Singing; she, alas, is lame.

From her couch she sadly watches
Days that amble by on crutches.

Old wives say it was a witch,
Sired of demon, dam'd of bitch,

Cursed her with an evil spell.
(May she shrivel up in hell.)

Pan Stanislaus sent for sages;
Tartar quacks and eastern mages,

Doctors bearing bitter potions,
Broths and brews and mystic lotions;

Monk and priest and sorcerer,
All came kneeling unto her.

Vain the prayers; frustrate the brews;
The incantation of small use;

Fickle the astrolabe; the wise
Mutter, yet she can not rise.

Upon her couch she sits and sings
Of the Lord's unfavoured things.

ix

Lustier was the village dog
Than the Jews in the synagogue.

All were sore perplexed, save Motka,
Blithe as if he had drunk vodka,

And not carried on his shoulders
Water-pails as large as boulders.

His eyes were like dots of flame,
The iotas of God's name.

Flourishes on holy script:
Hairs with which his chin was tipped.

On his brow the *tfillin* set
Seemed a Hebrew coronet.

Tzizith danced against his legs,
Jubilant with caftan-rags.

It was rumoured he was one
For whom God preserved the sun.

Thus in some way, rather subtle,
It was manifest to Mottel

That the Lord could not reject,
Nay, nor scorn His Hebrew sect.

x

Jews do now prepare to wend
Their long way to the world's end.

170

Hope grows great, like three-day yeast,
In the heart of Thaddeus priest.

Motka peddles joy; no worries
Come to mar his witty stories.

In the castle-tower, the
Princess sings most wistfully.

Stanislaus the baron nuzzles
Foaming beer-mugs; as he guzzles

A thought pierces through his skull,
A thought torturesomely droll:

"Bring me to my banquet-table,
Come this night, a Hebrew able

To hop sprightly, to amuse
Stanislaus well rid of Jews."

xi

Jews, cease lamentation; throttle
Sorrow; I will dance, says Mottel.

Lords and barons, dukes and pans,
Seated on their silk divans,

At the banquet-feast prepare
To see Motka dance in air.

Barons slap their Christian thighs
As they see tall Motka rise,

Dancing, waving paws in air,
A pathetic Hebrew bear,

Flaunting his ungrizzly beard,
Ignorant of knaves who jeered.

A huge moujik cracks his whip
Loudly to make Mottel skip.

The bear leaps, he hops, he prances,
Tzizith flutter as he dances.

Drummers, drum; and fiddlers, fiddle!
Make a music for the Zhid'l!

Happy as a bloated louse,
The fat baron Stanislaus

Swills his beer, and munches pork
While he keeps time with his fork.

Motka leaps, he pirouettes,
Gasps and gambols, Motka sweats.

With God's praises on his lips
Motka capersomely skips.

Barons pat their shaking paunches,
Motka rises on his haunches,

Leaps and dances; when behold!
By his rhythms so cajoled,

Even servants drop their plates,
Drop the ducal delicates;

Guardian-varlets leave their stances
And leap into Mottel's dances.

Yea, the butler breaks his bottle
As he strives to out-do Mottel.

Lo! the Pan, sucking a bone,
Suddenly forsakes his throne,

With him in the circle hop
All the lords; they cannot stop.

Drummers, drum! and fiddlers, fiddle!
Make a music for the Zhid'l.

For from off her couch she rises,
Paulinka the princess, rises,

No more a bed-ridden cripple,—
Tall, her lovely limbs most supple,

Rises, trips toward him, halts,
And takes Motka for a waltz!

xii

In the hamlet busy Jews
Ply their trades in wonted use.

Thaddeus priest now tells his beads,
While his stone heart bleeds, and bleeds.

Paulinka the princess sings
Of God's unforsaken things.

In Pan Stanislaus's throat
Overbrimming bumpers float.

Motka sells his crystal waters,
Earning dowries for his daughters.

And God in His heaven hums,
Twiddling His contented thumbs.

BALLAD FOR UNFORTUNATE ONES

The benison of health will yet be theirs!
The pale wan creatures crawling in the sun
Toward heaven upon much bespatted stairs,
And at the door left shamed, abashed, undone,
Will yet be without blemish, everyone.
Then will the stars sing sweet songs of degrees,

And the moon drum a measure, and the seas
Beat psalms, and birds make music in the air;
O, then will beast and man go to their knees
Before Messiah on his dappled mare.

The blind man will know whither his foot fares,
His eyes will hail the gold coin of the moon;
The hunchback will stand poplar-straight; the heirs
Of beggars will go shod in velvet shoon.
The poor men will know bounty; the ill, boon.
Thieves will make end to thefts; the dumb will cease
Their gesturing; the mad, their fantasies.
What now is foul, will then be turned to fair.
The lame will hang their crutches upon trees,
And run towards Messiah on his mare.

Do saints hawk miracles, like bargain-wares?
Do men, possessed, no longer foam, and swoon?
Do sorrows crawl back to their lizard lairs?
The ram's horn jubilant will trumpet soon.
For when the deafmen can return a tune,
And journeymen can sing their mysteries,
And healing come to leper's sores,—when these
Wonders and signs proclaim all men's welfare,
Then will be heard a neighing on the breeze:
For the Messiah rides his dappled mare.

Pauper, and man unfortunate, know this:
When at each hearth there is a meed of bliss,
When mighty man grants mean man brother's care,
When the full pot doth boil, the kettle hiss,
Then only will Messiah ride his mare.

KING ELIMELECH

King Elimelech—
A dent in his crown,
A twist in his sceptre—
Limps through the town.

174

He hawks little trinkets,
He cries his small wares;
He gets him a table
At all the town fairs.

"Ho, goodman, will you buy
A patched purple robe,
Aristocrat garters,
My last wizard's globe?

"Farthings buy medals;
A penny will buy
My most potent signet,
My bright heraldry.

"Yea, I will barter
This throne whence I rule
For a much more cosy
Artisan's stool."

The pedigreed peddler
Flaunts his strange goods,
But yokel and bumpkin
Chaffer for foods.

Such gauds are costly—
The peasant folk say—
With straws and pebbles
Let children play.

Alas, these are hard times,
When even a crowned head
Can not get his daily
Butter and bread.

If kings will not hunger,
Then let them all fast!
So said King Eli-
Melech the Last.

KING DALFIN

King Dalfin sat on his throne, the size of a thimble,
  And waved a hairpin, his wand.
The guardsmen about him clashed cymbal on sounding cymbal.
  Music: was the King's command.

Then suddenly swift between two notes, the midget
  Emperor vanished, was gone;
Quoth his chamberlain, wisely, though somewhat in a fidget:
  He will be back anon.

Anon! Anon! There was no king returning.
  The chamberlain was shot
For not deserving the hire that he was earning.
  The vizier then was brought

Into the court, and on a charge of treason
  He was dispatched.
Ten egg-shaped skulls were then lopped ere their season
  For the dread plot they hatched.

Then, high and low, the sages with their glasses
  Looked for their little king.
Failing, they were, for the crime of being asses,
  All hung from one big string.

Throughout the realm, fleet couriers sought the tiny
  Rex Imperator; in vain.
'Twas said that a vulture fly had dropped him in the briny
  Sea, off the coast of Spain.

Now, where was the King? He turned up a week later;
  He could not catch the gale
Of the cymbal-music, so hid him in the crater
  Of the cymbalist's fingernail.

P.S.
  The cymbalist was hanged for a knave and traitor.

176

WANDERING BEGGAR

Who envies not this beggar, who
Sits in the sunny market place,
Shaking the pebbles from his shoe,
Knotting again his torn shoe-lace?

From daisied path, from dusty road,
From cobbled ways, and country lanes
Hither he hops from his abode
In gypsy wagons and huckster wains.

Come, children of the town, and hear
What tales this jolly traveller brings,
What coloured tiding he doth bear,
What foreign-sounding songs he sings.

Though it be true that in his purse
A small green penny sleeps alone,
And in his sack, two crusty loaves,
One mouldy, and one hard as stone,—

Consider but the towns he saw,
The curious hamlets, the queer inns!
The road his realm, a song his law
And he an incognito prince!

Who wants for burgher's clothes? Do not
This beggar's tatters sweetly smell
Of sleeping in a grassy spot,
Of lazing in a fragrant dell?

And what the sight of gold coin to
One who has lately gazed upon
The kingdom of the small red Jew,
The turbulent Sambation?

OF HOLY VESSELS

BAAL SHEM TOV

Be his memory forever green and rich,
Like moss upon a stone at a brook's edge,
That rabbi of infants, man of children's love,
Greybeard and leader of tots, the Baal Shem Tov!
Who hearing a child's song float on sunlit air
Heard far more piety than in a prayer
That issued from ten synagogal throats;
Who seeing an urchin bring a starved mare oats,
Beheld that godliness which can break bars
Of heaven padlocked with its studded stars;
The Baal Shem Tov, who better than liturgy
Loved speech with teamsters and with gypsies! Be
His memory ever splendid like a jewel,
His, who bore children on his back to school
And with a trick to silence their small grief
Crossed many a stream upon a handkerchief.
Oh, be there ever pure minds and bright eyes,
Homage of children ever, eulogies
Of little folk so that the humble fame
Of the Baal Shem, the Master of the Name,
May be forever green and fresh and rich
Like moss upon a stone at a brook's edge.

ELIJAH

Elijah in a long beard
With a little staff
Hobbles through the market
And makes the children laugh.

He crows like a rooster,
He dances like a bear,
While the long-faced rabbis
Drop their jaws to stare.

178

He tosses his skullcap
To urchin and tot,
And catches it neatly
Right on his bald spot.

And he can tell stories
Of lovers who elope;
And terrible adventures
With cardinal and pope.

Without a single pinch, and
Without a blow or cuff,
We learned from him the *Aleph,*
We learned from him the *Tauph*.

Between the benedictions
We would play leapfrog—
O, this was a wonderful
Synagogue!

He can make a whistle
From a gander's quill;
He can make a mountain
Out of a molehill.

Oh, he is a great man!
Wished he, he could whoop
The moon down from heaven,
And roll it like a hoop;

Wished he, he could gather
The stars from the skies,
And juggle them like marbles
Before our very eyes.

CANTOR

They quacked and they cackled,
The geese and the hens,
As they laid their eggs in
Their coops and their pens.

Now eggs, half-a-dozen
Lie smoothly in
A grandma's basket,
Fresh from the bin.

She wheezes, she cackles,
She shuffles her legs:
In a hamlet of paupers
Not one soul eats eggs.

O what will she do? Put
Her teeth on a shelf?
The eggs will grow stale, save
She eat them herself.

With portly belly
A cantor comes;
Through musical nostrils
He sweetly hums.

Towards the good grandma
He goes and he picks
The eggs in the sunlight.
He buys all six.

And the jubilant grandma
When she sold these eggs,
Juggled her sixpence
And tossed her legs!

O what an eggnog
That cantor swilled,
And O how sweetly
He carolled and trilled!

The hen, too, seeing,
Her eggs well-used,
Cackled a *kdusha*
From her *Mizrach* roost.

SCHOLAR

A goat a scholar,
A goat a sage,
That ate *gemara*
From a grassy page!

Hot for wisdom
His dry mouth lipped
The small green mosses,—
His *rashi* script.

For higher lore
He chewed red clover;
He conned his Torah
Over and over.

And when his throat
Went dry on this book,
He ran and drank from
A garrulous brook.

Then up on his two
Hind legs stood he
And scratched his horns
Against a tree.

And crooned a *mishna*
In a voice most weird,
And nodded his wise pate,
And shook his beard.

Upon my word,
A learned one!
A scholar out of
Babylon!

THE VENERABLE BEE

The *shamash* of the glade,
The venerable bee,
In caftan bright arrayed,
Hums honeyed liturgy.

He brushes off the dust
From sacred leaves; he frees
With but a single thrust
The arks of chalices.

The convoluted rose
Is *torah* scroll to him:
He reads, with index-nose,
Of bee-like seraphim.

Tendril and bud he sees
To signify God's yoke
In green phylacteries
For all his kindred folk.

Gay fields and flowered walks,
His many-coloured home,
Will scent his *besomim* box,
His fragrant honeycomb.

Blessed is that happy one.
Who from a sylvan pew
Attends his *kiddush* on
A flowercup of dew.

REV OWL

Erudite, solemn,
The pious bird
Sits on a tree,
His *shtreimel* furred.

The owl, chief rabbi
Of the woods,
In moonlight ponders
Worldly goods.

With many a legal
To who? To wit?:
He nightly parses
Holy writ.

And then tears gizzards
Of captured fowl
To find them kosher
For an owl.

OF NOTHING AT ALL: ORDERS

Muffle the wind;
Silence the clock;
Muzzle the mice;
Curb the small talk;
Cure the hinge-squeak;
Banish the thunder.
Let me sit silent,
Let me wonder.

THE HITLERIAD

i

Heil heavenly muse, since also thou must be
Like my song's theme, a sieg-heil'd deity,
Be with me now, but not as once, for song:
Not odes do I indite, indicting Wrong!
Be with me, for I fall from grace to sin,
Spurning this day thy proffered hippocrene,
To taste the poison'd lager of Berlin!

Happier would I be with other themes—
(Who rallies nightmares when he could have dreams?)
With other themes, and subjects more august—
Adolf I sing but only since I must.
I must! Shall I continue the sweet words
That praise the blossoming flowers, the blossoming birds,
While, afar off, I hear the stamping herds?
Shall I, within my ivory tower, sit
And play the solitaire of rhyme and wit,
While Indignation pounds upon the door,
And Pity sobs, until she sobs no more,
And, in the woods, there yelp the hounds of war?

I am the grandson of the prophets! I
Shall not seal lips against iniquity.
Let anger take me in its grasp; let hate,
Hatred of evil prompt me, and dictate!
And let the world see that swastika-stain,
That heart, where no blood is, but high octane,
That little brain—
So that once seen the freak be known again!

Oh, even as his truncheon'd crimes are wrought,
And while the spilt blood is still body-hot,
And even as his doom still seems in doubt,
Let deeds unspeakable be spoken out.
Wherefore, O Muse, I do invoke thy aid,
Not for the light and sweetness of the trade,
But seeing I draw a true bill of the Goth,
For the full fire of thy heavenly wrath!

186

Aid me, and in good time, for as I talk
The knave goes one step nearer to the dock;
And even as triumphant cannon boom
He marches on his victories—to doom!

ii

See him, at last, the culprit twelve men damn.
Is this the face that launched the master-race
And burned the topless towers of Rotterdam?
Why, it's a face like any other face
Among a sea of faces in a mob—
A peasant's face, an agent's face, no face
At all, no face but vegetarian blob!
The skin's a skin on eggs and turnips fed,
The forehead villainous low, the eyes deepset—
The pervert big eyes of the thwarted bed—
And that mustache, the symbol of the clown
Made emperor, and playing imperial pranks—
Is this the mustache that brought Europe down,
And rolled it flat beneath a thousand tanks?

iii

Judge not the man for his face
Out of Neanderthal!
'Tis true 'tis commonplace,
Mediocral,
But the evil of the race
Informs that skull!

You ask, is paragon'd
The Nordic in this thrall?
Why, chivalry's not found
In him at all!
And he's the beast not blond,
Nor is he tall.

His strength is as the strength
Of ten, and ten times ten;

187

For through him, magnified
Smallness comes to our ken—
The total bigness of
All little men.

iv

The dossier, then; the facts, the untampered text:
Let *this* world know him, ere he goes to the next!
Where was he born? (Born is the word that I
Use, seeing *littered* is not poesy.)
Where was he born? In Braunau at the Inn—
And Austria paid for that original sin!—
Born to a father, old and over-wined
Who had he slept one night, had saved mankind!
At first hight Shicklgruber—'what a name
To herald through the mighty trump of fame'—
Heil Shicklgruber! Shicklgruber, heil!
Methinks this lacks the true imperial style,
And certainly no poet's nor mob's tongue
Could shake from shekel-shackle-gruber—song!
The gods are kind. His father changed his name,
And saved, at least the Shicklgrubers' shame.
Soon he removed to Linz. Now, note this well,
This was the town where Rilke wove his spell,
Where Rilke dreamed the beautiful and good—
And on this *boden,* Hitler dreamed of *blut!*
His teachers have since died; and fortunate they
Who else had died ten deaths to see the day
The dunce of the corner corner better men,
And great wealth his who could not count to ten!
Doctrine he spurned, and scholarship despised:
Let others win the palms so meanly prized—
The teacher's apple and the fiat lux—
Sheepskin for sheep, and for the bookworm books.
Let others learn to love their fellowmen;
He had no fellow, neither now, nor then.
Let others learn to love their neighbours. He
Hated his father and all Linz-ery

188

(Forgive the young: he'd see his hate untwined
To take in, generously, all humankind.)
Wherefore, uncouth, untutored, unconcerned,
He left his school most thoroughly unlearned,
Fit for the plough—before it, not behind!—
And as time proved, the premier German mind!

v

But did he not in art show promise, such
As to forgive, if not all ignorance, much?
He did; the first of many promises
Still unfulfilled, most tolerable, this:
He drew a line, it was not crooked, so
He thought that he was Michelangelo!
Yet is it true that in due time, he would
Incarnadine him murals with much blood;
To Europe's marbled treasures adding his
Ruins out-ruining Acropolis;
Yes, with a continent for easel, he
Would yet show vicious virtuosity,
Would yet achieve the opus of his dream,
The classic painting, masterpiece supreme:
The Reich's *Last Supper* (out of stolen pots)
With quislings six, and six iscariots!

Meanwhile he dreamed, and dreaming saw himself
Rich and esteemed on many a library shelf,
In many paintings hanging from a wall,
(This hanging theme, is it prophetical?)
And *Hitler fecit, pinxit Hitler* was
The only Latin of his final class.
He comes before his betters to stand test:
Is this an artist, for he is ill-dressed?
Is he to paint, because he cannot write?
We believe his linens would look better—white!
And for the first time Adolf's judged aright.

vi

Here stutters biography. The scribes conflict
In qualifying Vienna's derelict:
Was he a bricklayer, as some aver,
A paperhanger, or a carpenter?
The witnesses ignore.
It seems, in any case,—symbolic thing!—
He always worked on scaffolding.
Some others say—on oath—he had no trade,
Blame his survival on the public aid.
He slept, they say, in flophouses; he wore
Castoff; he ate handouts at the door;
('Tis no disgrace. Disgraceful only is
Ignoring in others one's own miseries.)
He fed on alms, these say. 'Twas Jewish food.
Hate knows no firmer ground than gratitude.

vii

And then there came—blow, trumpets; drummers, drum!—
The apocalypse, the pandemonium,
The war the Kaiser from his shrivelled hand
Let fall upon the European land.
Mark well, O men, the manner of our man:
He who not once in his entire life-span
Was either by sympathy or sorrow swept,
Heard of the carnage imminent—and wept!
He wept—but let us his own words employ:
"I fell on my knees, I wept, I wept for joy!"

Now this was the stuff of which a soldier's made!
But after four years, where is Adolf's braid?
Where are his medals? His promotions, where?
He had none; could it be he'd failed to dare?
Or could it be the brave of the front-line
Too often showed the salient his spine,
And chose too often duties, unsung, drear—
But safe—"to bring dispatches to the rear"?
O could it be that this was, after all,

190

How Adolf humbly stayed a corporal?
Alas, that then the untaught General Staff
Knew *intuition* as an epitaph,
And did not, as in later times, bestow
On this non-sense its generalissimo!

viii

Why, even in his private little war,
His march on Munich, when for the first time
This painter showed his phobia of red,
It was old Ludendorff, the warrior,
Still battling Foch, but now in pantomime,
Who marched breast forward, while—while Adolf fled,
Fled, with the fleeing of his own brave words,
Fled, fell on his face, and not upon his spear,
Got up, and fled, a rabbit to its hutch.
Such was the hero, flashing others' swords!
Such was the leader, leading bouts with beer!
Such was the puttering-out of the Great Putsch!

ix

Let it be said of Hitler, then, that he
Had courage, when he had a guarantee;
He risked, when primed assurance smiled; he dared
When the positions had been well-prepared.
He sought the German power—but no haste:
The dotard Hindenburg would see him placed.
He marched across the Rhine; yet it was plain
A bullet would have marched him back again.
He coveted the Czech-land; yet he waited
Until that prize was generously donated.
Circumspect, cautious, of an humble air—
Until he found he could afford to dare.
Then, summoning the pensioned warriors,
Then, even then, he followed his true course,
Mounting no charger, but a Trojan horse!

x

So, you may say, he was a miracle
Of bold persuasion and of iron will—
And sure he needs no courage who has skill!
What skill? And what persuasion? Skill to use
Hatred as bomb, and rhetoric as fuse?
Persuasion to persuade the Swabian mind
It was the unwhipped cream of humankind?
A bag of tricks, a mountebank's recipes,
Fit only for the half-mentalities
By birth and training sedulously bred
To swap, for circuses, their daily bread.
Consider with what petty bribes these were
Perverted from both Kant's and Goethe's lore,
Pure Reason bartering for Force impure,
And their Faust-soul betraying for a whore!
Consider for what baubles they sold out:
The shoddy uniform; the chorus'd shout;
The bonfired books; the robot-like salutes;
The ever-marching military boots!
These, such as these, no genius, but mere quack
Could soon reduce from people to a claque,
And bid them be, enamoured and enticed,
Of crooked cross re-crucifying Christ!

xi

Go to *Mein Kampf* if you would know his trade,
And there learn how a people is unmade,
And how, with mocking pantomime,
The tyrants on its ruins climb.
There learn the rules,
(Transparent unto all, save fools)
There take the lessons from the literate boors
And learn to lead the lofty-destined Reich—
Or Barnum-Bailey tours!
Learn it from Adolf's very prosiness,
Indited by his fellow-convict, Hess,

(Though adept at the demagogic yell,
It is averred that Adolf could not spell)
Learn it from him, who, east, west, north and south,
Excelled in the loud bigness of his Mouth!

Learn
How with the double-jointed rhetoric
He turned men's minds—(and stomachs)—and the trick;
Hear him reveal the charlatan's technique:
The prearranged ad-libs, the advised shriek,
The spontaneities prepared, the stance
Best suited for prophetic eloquence,
The iterated and ecstatic prose,
And above all, the pose, the Wagnerian pose!
And hear him brief his wisdom, brashly smooth:
"The lie, if oft repeated, is the truth!"

Read, marvelling, the slogans that did foil
The Hun intelligence; Blood, Honour, Soil:
The worship of the blood, in Arians veined,
And in all others preferably uncontained;
The practice of an Honour, modified
By the dear temperature of one's own hide;
And as for Soil, a simple ratio:
Nazis above, all others deep below!

Add then, the insured craft with which he chose
The chosen people for his choicest prose:
Here was a scapegoat to his measure made,
Big enough to inform his wild tirade
And too small to return its foe his due:
The strange ubiquitous Jew!

When could one find a better scapegoat than
The bearded Hebrew cosmopolitan,
Than this the Israelite, not far to seek,
Who was at once an alien, and weak?
Is it the rich who rouse the tribune's ire?
Some Jews are rich, and can well feed his fire.
Is it the poor, the indigent radical?

Judaea's destitution is not small.
The Jew's unsocial—he will not join in
The civic hubbub, the political din,
And also he's too forward; everywhere
Smell his ambitious presence in the air!
Pietist, he pollutes with his old creed
The pagan vigour of the German breed;
And at the same time lifts the mystic mist
From off the German mind—the atheist!
All evil from this Marxian plutocrat:
The Weimar laws, and the Versailles diktat,
The lowered standards and the rising costs,
Inflation and heat-waves, taxes and sharp frosts,
All, all achieved by the Semitic hosts.

The theorem did not matter, nor its flaws—
Sufficient to sneer "Jew" to win applause,
Yelp "Jude," and await the frenzied jeers—
And thus assure the Reich its thousand years!

So did he still the German hunger with
The ever-novel but right ancient myth,
And taught his people first to heil and hoot,
Then legislate, then doom, then persecute,
Visiting even on the blondest Jew
The crime his great-great-great-grandmother knew!

Such his persuasion, and—the authentic curse—
Such the too-soon persuaded Berliners.
(Observe the method in this madness, since
The Jew being beaten, the world did not wince,
The vogue was shown, by flesh-barometer,
He could persist, yet no great risk incur.)

xii

Yet not alone
Did Hitler do the deeds for which he must atone!
Henchmen he had,
Spirits and genii whom he did evoke
Out of the bottled Herren-volk,

194

Frustrated men, who'd tried all things, and failed,
And then determined to be jailed, or hailed!
Herr Goebbels such a one—
Club-footed, rat-faced, halitotic, the
Brave Nordic ideal, a contrario!
A kept man; eloquent, a Ph.D;
Carried no gun, forsooth; a radio
Lethal enough for him, shouting its lies,
Exploding *lebensraum* and libido;
Subtle in puncturing all human foibles
Saving his own, prolific in alibis—
Goebbels.

And such that other, Rosenberg,
The penman of the mob; had written books;
Corrected Adolf's grammar; could devise
Seventy reasons for atrocities;
Scorned pity; credited with stabbing hooks
Into the too-compassionate Christian crux;
Concocted, weekly, blood-philosophies,
To genuflect non-Arians to their knees;
Was daft about his twentieth-century spooks;
Herr Rosenberg, burdened with double shame:
A Baltic birth, and a Semitic name.

Nor was he absent, that ubiquity,
Goering, the arsonist, who loved disguise—
A uniform for every pantomime,
Including asbestos for the Reichstag crime—
Goering distinguished, mainly, by his size,
By the great girth's unrationed symmetries,
Ridiculous, in ersatz-land, sublime!
There was geheimrat who was not geheim!
Big in his own, and other people's eyes!
Loved hunting, preferably biped quarry;
Loved art, if stolen; loved imported grub;
Addicted to the narcotic and the gory;
Bore weapons (daggers); led a lion-cub;
And thought that full-face photos spread his glory.
(There is, of course, no profile to a tub.)

195

Nor yet was overlooked the fashion-plate:
Be not deceived by the manners of this fop,
His hat and gloves, his apathetic heils.
This was no dandy, but a man of wiles,
The double-swasticrossing Ribbentrop.
Think him not milksop, no, nor champagne-sop.
His morning coat was cut to the latest styles
Of armour-plate; he was the villain who smiles,
And pours the cocktails with the poison-drop.
He was the fingerman who spied the job;
The Cliveden layout was his tour-de-force,
And it was he contacted the Vichy mob,
And he who fed oats to the Trojan horse,
'Twas he, the master of the slick hobnob,
Who put in protocol the Nazi curse!

xiii

And other lesser fry there were
Who joined the Nazi exchequer,
Careerists who sought living-space
Upon the body of their race,
Each coming forward, for a price,
To sell his own especial vice:
Von Papen, spy and diplomat,
Hiding low cunning in high hat,
Giving his masters fealty
As long as they held mastery,
Reliable, whate'er might happen
To serve the good of Herr Von Papen!

And Himmler, Heinrich, mild and meek,
Most studious of the human shriek,
Inquisitive about the extent
To which men could take punishment,
Already planning for the foe
The order of the Gestapo,
Already practising to bowl
With all the heads that needs must roll,
Already forging chains and gyves

196

For the long night of the long knives,
Himmler, most self-effacing, and
Effacing others with Kultur's impartial hand.

Oily, obscene, fat as a hog,
The thick scourge of the synagogue,
The loutish uncouth pedagogue,
Streicher, brings up his hefty rear,
Among his bandit peers, a peer—
Meet now, the brothel-keeper for
The votaries of racial lore,
Who procured, by his journal's traffic
The titillation pornographic,
The lewd urge, the concupiscent thrill
By which he proved him human still.

He also stood, with beckoning claw
Holding uncandid camera—
The fawning Hoffman, who dared give
The Fuehrer his sole negative;
And he, hook-nosed, was also there,
The learned doctor Haushofer,
Expanding Hitler's empery
By dint of pure cartography:
The soldiers pluck what his school picks—
The art is geopolitics.

Nor should one fail to speak to-day
Of the besotted Robert Ley
Since drunken underneath a table
To speak himself he is unable;
Nor yet forget—alack-a-day,
Volatile Hess who flew away.

O what a crew unto their leader like!
As master mongrel, so each crawling tike,
And all the saviours of the German Reich!

xiv

Aye, were not others at that honeymoon,
Herr Strasser and his strange gregorian tune,

197

And Captain Roehm, ever in love with youth,
Best man among the paladins of truth?
Where are they now?
These knights reproachable but without fear?
O where is Shleicher's intellectual brow?
Why does not Heines, stalwart, reappear?
Where are the crows of yesteryear?

Departed, gentlemen, but without dirge.
The gallant Fuehrer had to have his purge;
These worthies, therefore, came to bitter ends:
They'd sinned the supreme sin—they were his friends!

xv

Yet not by their sole aid did Adolf rise,
His greatest help came from his enemies:
The eye-glass'd Junker looking down
Upon the upstart corporal clown;
The simple Social Democrat;
The Catholic, and concordat;
The too-shrewd plutocratic vons
Thyssen, Hugenberg and sons;
The dialectic theorist who saw the ever-thickening mist
And cheered, in hope that soon therefrom
The light, hegelian, would come;
And even Hindenburg, who in alarm,
Sold a republic for a private farm!

Each in his fashion, and for personal sake
Led Germany to Hitler's stake.
Yes, let it be told, let it be written down
How even from afar
There came the aid that burned the Republic brown;
Let it be told
How gold tycoon, how monied czar,
Reaction black, and Interest, dirty-grey
Trembled before the rumour of that plot
Plotting for Europe its Muscovian day,
And trembling, dropped more coin into the Nazi pot!

198

Let us not name the names, but let us speak
Only about munition'd dividends,
Of markets rising to an envied peak,
Of rubber's conscienceless elastic ends,
Of timely trains by fascists always mann'd,
And of umbrellas, which, alas, did leak.
Those who have memory will understand.

xvi

Who are those thousands in the goose-step march?
Athletes, said Papen, sly and arch.
Whose are those planes that through the ether race?
Commerce, said Goering, with cherubic face.
The tanks that still keep coming, on and on?
Said innocent Ley: The *Volkswagon.*
And all those lovely gases, what are they?
Said Goebbels: *Cure-alls for a better day.*

Within the chancelleries, the diplomats
Chuckled and winked behind their polished hats;
And Downing Street announced from Number Ten
The balance of power balanced once again.

xvii

There were—the decade's grace—who saw
This moulting of the moral law,
Who cried against the knaveries
Designed to please and to appease,
And such an one was he who stood
Late and alone against the flood,
The man who hated sham and cant,
Unfortunately brilliant,
Churchill, who kept our world extant!

Across the seas, still doomed to wait,
Man's conscience-made-articulate,
Roosevelt sent forth his biblic words
As he would yet send forth, for vengeance

The steel leviathans, the flaming swords,
The swift seraphic engines!

Ah, he who might have led great France
Against the brazen countenance,
Was gone from twilight into night—
The Tiger, ever-burning bright!

xviii

But was there not, to cope with this intrigue—
To keep the peace—the wise Wilsonian league?
The League of Nations—what a hope was there,
Fled with the years, vanished in spoken air!
It could have had no other fate. Alas,
Who looked, could long have seen it in the glass:
The kisses blown with weak asthmatic breath
By old men gesturing themselves to death.
Were these the men to put teeth in the law,
Who had no tooth in their collective jaw?
Were these the men that would the peace maintain
Themselves upholding only with a cane?
Could these look in the future, who could not
See without specs, and those, at home, forgot?
Most miserable world which had to lean
Upon the dotards of this dying scene!

While such as these, then, guard the public weal
And safety totters, and security
Goes palsied, doddering and down-at-heel,
While Senex drones, and all Geneva snores,
He'd be no burglar, who in such event
Did not bethink him of his burglary,
To try his key in all the tempting doors!

And Hitler read his opportunity!

200

xix

How blind these were, he thought, who did not see
The new excalibur that rose in air
That certain weapon of short victory,
Which using, even the unrash might dare
The great assault, the sudden lightning thrust!
Before this thing, defenses could not score,
And pacts were sand, and maginot were dust—
This Stuka of the fourth-dimensional war!
Let then, the old men, therefore, rack their wits,
Magniloquizing their paralysis
As if it were a tactic of Clausewitz.
From hidden hangars and fake factories
Would soon emerge the weapons of the blitz!
Then would there be, old men, a peace, the peace
That passeth boundaries!

xx

Now, the career he built on such foundations
With allies, passive, active, such as these
Is black and public on the garb of nations.
It has no secrecies.
Is there a wickedness this wicked man
Did not accomplish? An iniquity
That he did not decree?
A crime that was not indexed in his plan?
He did encompass all
The high crimes and the misdemeanours low,
Enormous, diabolical,
Lavish of suffering, and of woe
Beyond recall.

I shall not here complain that he did not
Know decency, or love, or honour, or
The other virtues surplus to the codes:
They were beyond his thought,
Here was a land his spies did not explore—
Uncharted were these roads.

xxi

But Law, uncommentaried and unburden'd Law,
The child-eye choosing between right and wrong,
The manly option made against the beast,
That, by the man so high above the throng,
That might have been expected,
That, at least!
At least! That little least was more
Than he could suffer, who despised
The norms that only weak men prized—
Not Pity, cloth by cripple spun,
Not Justice—blind—he put out both her eyes,
Nor Culture, here he cocked his gun,
Nor Worth, nor yet Humanity effete,
The weakling's meat!

Wherefore, in lieu of the illumined law
He ushered in, the better for his deeds,
The burglar's darkness and the murderer's fog.
He tore the statutes; he abjured the creeds;
He stamped on the Decalogue!

He coveted.
O what did this much-shrivelled little soul
Not covet, not lust after? Everything
That was not his:
The painter's brush, a purer genesis,
The fame of letters not won by himself,
Bismarckian role,
Power and place and pelf.

But had he merely coveted, merely bayed
At the unreachable reaches of the distant moon,
Out of his thwarting, out of hope delayed
He would have perished soon,
Heart-broken, foiled, his wrist-veins cut—
But
He also stole. He was a thief. He stole.
Even the credos of his sloganry
He piecemeal filched to make a patchwork whole.

(Forgiveable—a petty larceny!)
His depredations rose.
He robbed the rich; impartial, robbed the dole.
The folk he loved, he taxed; and those he hated
He confiscated.
The poor man for his pension-pennies sobbed.
The church he also held up for its toll.
The house of God was robbed.

Fed thus with native quarry, flesh and gore
He licked his whiskers, crouched, then stalked for more.

xxii

See, on historic film his crimes deployed,
Felonies flickering from celluloid!
And through the planes' sharp retina, behold
His victims, and their plight,
The beaten, and the ambushed, and the sold!

Austria, gay and bright and musical
Receiving in the silenced hall
The mud-bespattered guest;
And brave Bohemia—Honour's epitaph—
Broken in half,
Half blackmailed, plundered of the rest.
(Watch for the montage of accomplished guile:
As Skoda skids, the four smug men will smile.)

The scenes now change, but madness knows no halt.
Norway is sacked, and Poland's sown with salt
Explosive! Holland also visited,
    Whose dykes and Dutchmen bled.

(Montage again: the camera goes berserk
With vertical flame and towers diagonal;
Then rests to show the generals; they smirk.)

Closeup. The fascist and his rods
Flogging the Jugoslavian fading out
To Greece, her freemen broken, like her gods.

Roofs; and the Eiffel Tower's prominence—
France!
Bereft of Buonaparte
Her sated mirrors shattered, and her heart.
France, that too soon, too humble, did descend
From brightness to the dark,
Bereft of Joan of Arc,
Upon an evil day on evil hours come.
Within her conquered hall
Domremy voice is dumb.
The lesser corporal
Over prostrated France
Mimics with carpet-fretting feet
Napoleonic stance!

Look west, and see the towers of London-town
Declining, battered, but not battered down—
The burglar mounted, but he came too late:
He broke, but did not enter.
Look east, the Russian lifts avenging hands,
Waylaid, assaulted, wounded—he still stands
By dint of that unthawed triumvirate;
Cold steel, and Stalin cool, and icy Winter!

xxiii

As footnote to the headlined Terror, know
His ally fared no better than his foe.
War was a science; treaties were an art.
Wherefore, with artful pacts, he pushed the free
Contracting parties of the second part
Through slow contraction to nihility.
Met, plenipotent—farewelled, impotent,
They came as sovereigns, and as servants went.
He made of Magyarland a state in fee,
A German province out of Italy,
A dairy out of Denmark, and
An oil-well of Roumanian land.

204

And are these methods banned?
Where treaties could avail, why use the rod?
Why seek by force, what could be got by fraud?
He'd even make a ten-year truce with God!
To bear false witness was no crime. Wherefore
Upon his blood-and-soiled honour swore
He longed for peace. Was believed. And then
    prepared for war.

xxiv

Nor did he merely wage his war on Man.
Against the Lord he raised his brazen brow,
Blasphemed His name, His works, contemned His plan,
Himself a god announced, and bade men bow
Down to his image, and its feet of clay!
God's places of true worship were laid low,

And idols on the high places held their sway;
Astrologers were prophets in the land,
And mad philosophers rose to inveigh

Against the diktat of the Lord's command.
Iniquity espoused, and evil wived,
Kindliness, pity, brother-love, were banned.

The creed of the Black Forest was revived,
And ceased the ancient pieties for men.
Of manliness and godliness deprived,

The pagan, named for beasts, was born again.
The holy days were gone. The Sabbath creed
Unfit for slaves, superfluous to his reign,

Stood unobserved. The nine-month-littered breed
Traduced their parents to the Gestapo;
Adulterous, the stud-men spawned their seed.

The Madman named the Lord his personal foe.
And chained the bearers of His sacred word.
This is the sign, he shrilled: *In hoc vinco!*

205

He raised aloft the blood-stained sword;
Upon the square the heathen horde
Roared.

xxv

But not with human arrogance come I
To plead our Maker's cause, and make His cause
The mighty measure of my feeble words.
Himself, in His good time, the Lord of Hosts,
The slowness of His anger moved at last,
And His longsuffering at last forespent
Will rise, will shine, will stretch forth His right hand
And smite them down, the open impious mouth,
The tongue blaspheming, silenced, in the dust!

I come now rather as a man to men,
Seeking the justice for that voice which cries
Out of the ground, the voice of our brothers' blood!
That blood will not be still again,
Those bones unblessed will still arise,
Yes, and those living spectres, of the mind unhinged,
Will still beat at our padded memory, until
Their fate has been avenged!

xxvi

Let them come forth, those witnesses who stand
Beyond the taunt of perjury, those ghosts
In wagons sealed in a forgotten land,
Murdered; those phantoms the war-tidings boast,
Those skeletons still charred with the gestapo brand!

Let them come forth and speak, who lost their speech
Before the midnight gun-butt on the door,
The men made dumb with their last voiceless screech
In ghetto-yard, and on the Dachau floor—
Let them accuse now, who did once in vain beseech!

206

Summon them, bailiff of the dead, the ghosts
Who once were brave men stood against a wall,
Summon them, all the exsanguinated hosts,
Hero and martyr, liquidated; call,
Call forth the witnesses, the uninterred ghosts,

And let them speak. And let the dead attest
Their murder and its manner and its cause—
From shattered jaw, from perforated breast
Speak out their mauling at the bestial claws.
Speak out, or neither we, nor they, again know rest.

Let them in all their thousands speak the shame
Visited on them, and the ignoble death,
The nameless ones, and those of a great fame:
With wounded whisper and with broken breath
Speaking the things unspeakable, and the
    unspeakable name!

Then from such evidence, such witnessing,
Surely the anger of the world will burst,
Surely the wrath of nations will outfling
Against this culprit, multitude-accursed
Doom indexed by the black gloves of their reckoning!

Thief, perjurer, blasphemer, murderer,
Let him be blotted out, and all his crew.
Efface the evil; let it be no more.
Let the abomination cease; and through
Implacable Justice let emerge the world, clean, new!

Bold malefaction brought at last to bay!
Avenged the martyrs! Mankind truly purged!

Returned at last the spectres to their clay!
And over the green earth, at last emerged,
After the cock-crow of the guns, the cloudless day!

207

xxvii

And on that day as the unrighteous pass,
Unrighteousness will pass away, and men
Will see once more, as when their vision was
Illumined by the lightning strokes the ten—
Gesturing Truth ungagged will speak again,
And Man will don his godliness once more—
Then from four corners of the earth will sing
The sons of heaven, the bright freedoms four;
The field will glow again with harvesting,
And glow with argosies the deep; again
Will frolic in the ether, sunlight-blue'd—
Not the grim vulture of the brood
Its talons dripping blood,
But the bright friendly somersaulting plane
Writing against the sky
So all may read on high
Man loyal to his human brotherhood,
To human brotherhood, and to the godly reign!

POEMS

THE PSALTER OF AVRAM HAKTANI
A VOICE WAS HEARD IN RAMAH
YEHUDA HALEVI, HIS PILGRIMAGE

THE PSALTER OF AVRAM HAKTANI

PSALM I: A PSALM OF ABRAHAM, WHEN HE HEARKENED TO A VOICE, AND THERE WAS NONE

Since prophecy has vanished out of Israel,
And since the open vision is no more,
Neither a word on the high places, nor the *Urim* and *Thummim*,
Nor even a witch, foretelling, at En-dor,—
Where in these dubious days shall I take counsel?
Who is there to resolve the dark, the doubt?

O, these are the days of scorpions and of whips
When all the seers have had their eyes put out,
And all the prophets burned upon the lips!

There is noise only in the groves of Baal.
Only the painted heathen dance and sing,
With frenzied clamouring.
Among the holy ones, however, is no sound at all.

PSALM II: MASCHIL OF ABRAHAM: A PRAYER WHEN HE WAS IN THE CAVE

How is he changed, the scoffers say,
This hero of an earlier day,
Who in his youth did battle with
The wicked theologic myth;
Who daily from his pocket drew
(*Aetat.* sixteen) a writing, true,
Attested, sealed, and signed, its gist:
God swearing He did not exist;
Who in his Zion lay at ease
Concocting learned blasphemies
To hate, contemn, and ridicule
The godly reign, the godly rule.
How is he now become as one
Trembling with age before the Throne,—
This XXth century scientist,
A writer of psalms, a liturgist;

A babbling pious woman, he
Who boasted that his thoughts were free,
And who at worst did nullify
By ignorance the deity.

O Lord, in this my thirtieth year
What clever answer shall I bear
To those slick persons amongst whom
I sat, but was not in their room?
How shall I make apocalypse
Of that which rises to my lips,
And on my lips is smitten dumb:—
Elusive word, forgotten sum.

O could I for a moment spare
My eyes to them, or let them hear
The music that about me sings,
Then might they cease their twitterings.

Then might they also know, as I,
The undebatable verity,
The truth unsoiled by epigram,
The simple *I am that I am.*
But failing these powers in me, Lord,
Do Thou the deed, say Thou the word,
And with Thy sacred stratagem
Do justify my ways to them.

PSALM III: A PSALM OF ABRAHAM, WHEN HE WAS
SORE PRESSED

Would that the Lord had made me, in place of man-child, beast!
Even an ox of the field, content on grass,
On clover and cud content, had made me, made me the least
Of his creatures, one of a herd, to pass
As cattle, pastured and driven and sold and bought
To toil on ploughland or before a cart!
For easier is the yoke than the weight of thought,
Lighter the harness than the harnessed heart!

PSALM IV: A PSALM OF ABRAHAM, TOUCHING HIS GREEN PASTURES

From pastures green, whereon I lie,
Beside still waters, far from crowds,
I lift hosannahs to the sky
And hallelujahs to the clouds,

Only to see where clouds should sit,
And in that space the sky should fill,
The fierce carnivorous Messerschmidt,
The Heinkel on the kill.

They'll not be green for very long,
Those pastures of my peace, nor will
The heavens be a place for song,
Nor the still waters still.

PSALM V: A SONG OF DEGREES

Consider the son of man, how he doth get him knowledge and
    wisdom!
Not to the sorcerer does he go, nor yet to the maker of books; not
    from the gait of angels does he take example; he mimics not the
    antics of the cherubim.
The beasts of the field are his teachers; feather and fur his
    instructors, instructing him the way that he shall go therein.
Before their hooves, he sits, a disciple; to the eyrie, he climbs,
    crying, *Master, Master.*
To the ape he bows down, the ape, flinging the cocoafruit, devising
    slings.
He worships the elephant for that he has an ivory sword.
He sees the bow of the porcupine, and the arrows of his quills;
    a parable in shell the tortoise brings to him.
Even the noisome beast, whose spikenard sendeth forth the smell
    thereof, instructs him how that the enemy may be abashed.

How wonderful, therefore, is this son of man, who lets no pride
    between him and his doctors,—
Yea, at this very instant, he gapes at the eagle's talons dropping
    volcanic rock.

PSALM VI: A PSALM OF ABRAHAM, CONCERNING
THAT WHICH HE BEHELD UPON THE HEAVENLY
SCARP

And on that day, upon the heavenly scarp,
The hosannahs ceased, the hallelujahs died,
And music trembled on the silenced harp.
An angel, doffing his seraphic pride,
Wept; and his tears so bitter were, and sharp,
That where they fell, the blossoms shrivelled and died.

Another with such voice intoned the psalm
It sang forth blasphemy against the Lord.
Oh, that was a very imp in angeldom
Who, thinking evil, said no evil word—
But only pointed, at each *Te Deum*
Down to the earth, and its unspeakable horde.

The Lord looked down, and saw the cattle-cars:
Men ululating to a frozen land.
He saw a man tear at his flogged scars,
And saw a babe look for its blown-off hand.
Scholars, he saw, sniffing their bottled wars,
And doctors who had geniuses unmanned.

The gentle violinist whose fingers played
Such godly music, washing a pavement, with lye,
He saw. He heard the priest who called His aid.
He heard the agnostic's undirected cry.
Unto Him came the odour Hunger made,
And the odour of blood before it is quite dry.

The angel who wept looked into the eyes of God.
The angel who sang ceased pointing to the earth.
A little cherub who'd spied the earthly sod

Went mad, and flapped his wings in crazy mirth.
And the good Lord said nothing, but with a nod
Summoned the angels of Sodom down to earth.

PSALM VII: FOR THE CHIEF PHYSICIAN:

A song for hunters: In that wood,
That whispering jungle of the blood
Where the carnivorous midge seeks meat,
And yawns the sinuous spirochete,
And roars the small fierce unicorn,
The white-robed hunters sound the horn.
May they have goodly hunting. May
Their quarry soon be brought to bay.

PSALM VIII: PSALM OF THE FRUITFUL FIELD

A field in sunshine is a field
On which God's signature is sealed;
When clouds above the meadows go,
The heart knows peace; the birds fly low.
O field at dusk! O field at dawn!
O golden hay in the golden sun!
O field of golden fireflies
Bringing to earth the starry skies!
You touch the mind with many a gem;
Dewdrops upon the sun's laced hem;
Young dandelions with coronets;
Old ones with beards; pale violets
Sleeping on moss, like princesses;
Sweet clover, purple, odorous;
Fat bees that drowse themselves to sleep
In honey-pots that daisies keep;
Birds in the hedge; and in the ditch
Strawberries growing plump and rich.
Who clamours for a witch's brew
Potioned from hellebore and rue;
Or pagan imps of fairy band,

When merely field and meadowland
Can teach a lad that there are things
That set upon his shoulders wings?
Even a cow that lolls its tongue
Over a buttercup, swells song
In any but a devil's lung.
Even a sheep which rolls in grass
Is happier than lad or lass,
Who treads on stones in streets of brass.
Who does not love a field lacks wit,
And he were better under it!
And as for me let paradise
Set me in fields with sunny skies.
And grant my soul in after days
In clovered meadowlands to graze.

PSALM IX: A PSALM, TO BE PRESERVED AGAINST
TWO WICKED WORDS

I am not of the saints, O Lord, to wear
The broken shoes of poverty, and dance.
For I am made sick at heart with terrible fear
Seeing the poor man spurned, looked at askance,
Standing, his cap in hand, and speaking low,
And never getting his fellow's heart or ear.
O may I never beg my daily bread,
Never efface my pride, like a dirty word;
And never grovel that my little chick be fed.
Preserve me from poverty, O Lord.

Preserve me, too, and thou who knowest hearts,
Know'st this prayer does from the heart arise,
Preserve me from possessions, from the marts,
The mints, the mansions, all the worldly goods,
Debasing even the man of noblest parts.

From too much wealth that warps the very saints,
From power that ambushes the soul by stealth,
From suzerainty that fevers, and then faints:
Preserve me, Lord, from wealth.

But in Thy wisdom Thou canst so ordain
That wealth and poverty be known no more.
Then hadst Thou answered me, again and again,
Answered Thy servant, neither rich nor poor.

PSALM X: LAMED VAV: A PSALM TO UTTER IN MEMORY OF GREAT GOODNESS

Under a humble name he came to us;
Died; and left his wife executrix
Of tears, and a name for which the saints would fuss.—
I believe that he was one of the Thirty-six . . . .

PSALM XI: A PSALM OF A MIGHTY HUNTER BEFORE THE LORD

O, not for furs,
And not for feathers,
Did Chatzkel the hunter
Weather all weathers!

Neither the crow,
Nor the shy sparrow
Had fear of his bow
And rotted arrow.

A hunter he was,
Who bore no rifle
Whose snare did not kill,
Nor lariat stifle.

A dearth in the land:
Beasts die of famine—
Chatzkel the hunter
Leaves his backgammon

Traps him some wild beasts,
Keeps them in cages,

216

Until the hot sun will
Have spent its rages.

Meanwhile the tiger
Eats tiger-lilies,
And milk is fed to
The wild colt's fillies.

Upon his wrist-bone
The robin settles;
While Chatzkel crams her
With lilac petals.

And then, in the Spring-time
Chatzkel sets free
Beast and bird under
The greenwood tree.

O, what was Nimrod
Who used strength, not skill,
To quell the forest,
Compared to Chatzkel,

Chatzkel who whistled
To catch a bird;
Who hallooed, and found him
In midst of a herd?

PSALM XII: TO THE CHIEF MUSICIAN, WHO PLAYED
FOR THE DANCERS

These were the ones who thanked their God
With dancing jubilant shins:
The beggar, who for figleaf pride
Sold shoelaces and pins;
The blindman for his brotherly dog;
The cripple for his chair;
The mauled one for the blessed gasp
Of the cone of sweet kind air.

I did not see this dance, but men
Have praised its grace; yet I
Still cannot fathom how they danced,
Or why.

PSALM XIII: A SONG FOR WANDERERS

What was the song the gypsy sang
Singing to his fiddle?
The open road, and the pleasant place,
The sun that shines with a gypsy face,
The two halves of the beautiful world,
And O, himself in the middle!

What was the song the sailor sang
To the wind's soughing?
The silver on the moonlit sea,
The stars for jolly company,
The harbour pub, and the girl in port,
And O, a good wind blowing!

What was the song the weary Jew
Sang to his sorrow?
No song at all made sweet his lips,
Not of travelled roads nor travelling ships.
No song today wells from the heart
That has no morrow!

PSALM XIV: A PSALM FOR FIVE HOLY PILGRIMS,
YEA, SIX ON THE KING'S HIGHWAY

One comes:—he is a very blossoming tree—
With frankincense and perfumery:
Sweet savour for his nostril'd deity.

Another bears God trinkets, smooth and rich,
And little idols polished overmuch—
All holy objects pleasant to the touch.

218

And still another seeks the mystic word
With all the rainbows of his jewelled hoard—
His goodly proffer to the sight of the Lord.

With delicates and sweetmeats and with fruit,
Food of the blossom, eating of the root,
Comes one to flatter the taste of the Absolute.

And the fifth pilgrim trips upon the sod,
Blowing sweet music from a hollow rod:
Sounds gratifying to the ear of God.

Not sight, sound, smell, taste, touch, his freight,
One brings his heart for pawning with his fate:
He, surely, he shall come within the Gate!

PSALM XV: A PSALM OF ABRAHAM, TOUCHING THE
CROWN WITH WHICH HE WAS CROWNED ON THE
DAY OF HIS ESPOUSALS

This is the man who brought to me
The thumb-print of the Deity;
Who hung upon my hairless chest
The fringed talismanic vest;
This is the Jew who once did hem
My heart with old Jerusalem;
Who solved each letter's mystic hook
Upon the parchment Pentateuch,
And poured me out the *kiddush*-wine,
Sparkling with all the clandestine
Eye-winks of angels; this is he
Who made my youth worth memory.
Most fitting is it, then, that this
Old Rabbi, Eden-bent, should now
Sanctify our marriage-vow.

PSALM XVI: TO THE CHIEF SCRIBE, A PSALM OF
ABRAHAM, IN THE DAY OF THE GLADNESS OF HIS
HEART

Prepare the inks, the red, the green, the black;
Thicken the paints, the purple and the gold;
Make smooth the goatskin; fatten each wry crack;
Wash out the clotted brush, and shape some old
And many-flourished symbol in its track.

Take hold your quill, meticulously cleanse
Its point, and thinly trace the guiding line;
Affix to your left eye the perfect lens,
Then write in the square letter, black and fine,
To wit: *That love will never wander hence.*

And unto this last final verse,
Add my name, and add hers.

PSALM XVII: FOR THE BRIDEGROOM COMING OUT
OF HIS CHAMBER, A SONG

The young men with the sparse beards laud the bride;
"She puts no rouges to her lips; no small
Black beauty spots upon her cheeks; no pall
Of perfumed dust upon her neck; no dyed
Resplendence on her lovely head; no pride
Of henna on her finger-nails at all;
Yet is she very beautiful withal,
Most beautiful and yet not beautified."
The long-haired virgins musically doff
Their silence, and around the bridegroom wheel,
Singing his bride and all the seven days' love
That will be hers anon, the nuptial weal
That he will serve; in evidence whereof
He breaks the wineglass underneath his heel.

PSALM XVIII: FOR THE BRIDE, A SONG, TO BE SUNG BY VIRGINS

She has laved her body in living water. She
    Has touched no food all day. She is most pale.
Her face is white. That she lives one can see
    Only by the quivering of her veil.

The vile tongue falters; it can bear no tale.
    Speak of the dove, if you will speak of her.
She is a flower. She is flower-frail.
    Regard her. She is virgin. She is pure.

PSALM XIX: A BENEDICTION

    O bridegroom eager for the bride,
    O white-veiled bride,
May love be on your pillow; may
    The quiet turtledove preside
Your sweet consortments night and day;
May the months be fat for you; bask
    In the sun; love in the moon; let bread
    Be never wanting from your table,
      Wine from your cask,
      Warmth from your bed.
O let the almond flourish on your tree,
O let the grape grow big, and full of juice
    And of the perfect shape:
Let nine months grow diffuse, and wax and grow diffuse,
    And let the first-born be.

PSALM XX: A PSALM OF ABRAHAM, WHICH HE MADE AT THE FEAST

Bring on the rich, the golden-dotted soup;
Set down the viands, odorous of spice;
Let the plate steam with capons; fetch the pies;
And tender chicken to this fragrant group.

Forget not, prithee, the replenished fish
Smacking of sea and land and heaven; fill
Each plate to a most toothsome pinnacle;
Make a small Lebanon of every dish.

The pickled tongue must find its place; the roast,
Sending enticements to the nostrils, must
Show promise of soft meat and tasty crust;—
O cooks, belittle not the bridegroom-host!

Unseal the bottles of grandfather's day;
And empty them into the goblets; then
Empty the goblets to be filled again;
Let wine say what dry tongues can never say.

When clean bones and dry flasks will be the trace,
The only trace that here has been a feast,
Then let each voice find its own strength increased
To laud the Lord with a well-chanted grace!

PSALM XXI: A BENEDICTION FOR THE NEW MOON

Elder, behold the Shunamite, the rumour of her face,
And young man, know, the mirror of thy love!

Praise ye, therefore, the moon: each after his own fashion!
Sing ye a song:
The warrior for the brass buckler of David;
The learned man in his tent
For the bright candle smiling on his book.
Before that newly-minted coin
Rub, O little merchantman, thy joyous palms!

For the weaver of your tides,
Sing, O mariners, shuttlers of ships!
Praise it, O hunters, the hind you cannot stalk!

Lift up your heels; lift up your eyes to see,
Each after his own fashion, the seal of God
Impressed upon His open writ!

PSALM XXII: A PRAYER OF ABRAHAM, AGAINST MADNESS

Lord, for the days allotted me,
Preserve me whole, preserve me hale!
Spare me the scourge of surgery.
Let not my blood nor members fail.

But if Thy will is otherwise,
And I am chosen such an one
For maiming and for maladies
So be it; and Thy will be done.

Palsy the keepers of the house;
And of the strongmen take Thy toll.
Break down the twigs; break down the boughs.
But touch not, Lord, the golden bowl!

O, I have seen these touched ones—
Their fallow looks, their barren eyes—
For whom have perished all the suns
And vanished all fertilities;

Who, docile, sit within their cells
Like weeds, within a stagnant pool.
I have seen also their fierce hells,
Their flight from echo, their fight with ghoul.

Behold him scrabbling on the door!
His spittle falls upon his beard,
As, cowering, he whines before
The voices and the visions, feared.

Not these can serve Thee. Lord, if such
The stumbling that awaits my path—
Grant me Thy grace, thy mortal touch,
The full death-quiver of Thy wrath!

PSALM XXIII: A PSALM OF JUSTICE, AND ITS SCALES

One day the signal shall be given me;
I shall break in and enter heaven, and,
Remembering who, below, held upper hand,
And who was trodden into misery,—
I shall seek out the abominable scales
On which the heavenly justice is mis-weighed.
I know I am no master of the trade,
Can neither mend nor make, clumsy with nails,
No artisan,—yet am I so forespoken,
Determined so against the automaton,
That I must tamper with it, tree and token,
Break bolts, undo its markings, one by one,
And leave those scales so gloriously broken,
That ever thereafter justice shall be done!

PSALM XXIV: SHIGGAION OF ABRAHAM WHICH
HE SANG UNTO THE LORD

O incognito god, anonymous lord,
with what name shall I call you? Where shall I
discover the syllable, the mystic word
that shall evoke you from eternity?
Is that sweet sound a heart makes, clocking life,
Your appellation? Is the noise of thunder, it?
Is it the hush of peace, the sound of strife?

I have no title for your glorious throne,
and for your presence not a golden word,—
only that wanting you, by that alone
I do evoke you, knowing I am heard.

PSALM XXV: TO THE PROPHETS, MINOR AND MAJOR, A PSALM OR SONG

They are upon us, the prophets, minor and major!
Madame Yolanda rubs the foggy crystal.
She peers, she ponders, the future does engage her;
She sees the *Fuehrer* purged by Nazi pistol.

Sir Aries Virgo, astrology-professor,
Regards the stars, and prophesies five truces.
Herr Otto Shprinzen, of the same guild, a guesser,
From the same stars the contrary deduces.

They too have thoughts, those scriptural inspectors;
They count the verses, the hapaxlegomena,
By means of esoterical detectors
Foretell next year's right-guaranteed phenomena.

Ides is foretold, and doomsday, and God's thunders.
January greets the unseen with a seer.
Augurs prognosticate, from signs and wonders,
Many a cradle, yea, and many a bier.

These, then, the soothsayers, and this their season:
But where, O where is that inspired peasant,
That prophet, not of the remote occasion,
But who will explicate the folded present?

PSALM XXVI: TO THE CHIEF MUSICIAN, A PSALM OF ISRAEL, TO BRING TO REMEMBRANCE

By the rivers of Babylon, there we sat down, we wept
When we remembered Zion,—
O they are many that have had our tears!
The alluvium of Nilus is still fat
With the tender little bones of our firstborn,
And Tiber is still yellow like our badge.
Shall one forget the bears, and the Jews like bears
That danced on the shores of the savage Vistula?

225

Forget the crystal streams of castled Spain
So many fires failed to boil to salt?
Forget the Rhine? O Rhenish wines are sharp.
The subtle salt of blood gives them their sharpness.

Gather them up, O Lord, these many rivers,
And dry them in the furnace of Thy wrath!
Let them not be remembered! Let them be
So many soon-to-be forgotten clouds
Dropping their rain
Upon the waters of Thy favourite Jordan!

PSALM XXVII: A PSALM TO TEACH HUMILITY

O sign and wonder of the barnyard, more
beautiful than the pheasant, more melodious
than nightingale! O creature marvellous!

Prophet of sunrise, and foreteller of times!
Vizier of the constellations! Sage,
red-bearded, scarlet-turbaned, in whose brain
the stars lie scattered like well-scattered grain!

Calligraphist upon the barnyard page!
Five-noted balladist! Crower of rhymes!

O morning-glory mouth, O throat of dew,
announcing the out-faring of the blue,
the greying and the going of the night,
the coming on,
the imminent coming of the dawn,
the coming of the kinsman, the brightly-plumaged sun!

O creature marvellous—and O blessed Creator,
Who givest to the rooster wit
to know the movements of the turning day,
to understand, to herald it,
better than I, who neither sing nor crow
and of the sun's goings and comings nothing know.

226

PSALM XXVIII: A PSALM OR PRAYER — PRAYING
HIS PORTION WITH BEASTS

The better to understand Thy ways,
Divinity I would divine,
Let me companion all my days
The more-than-human beasts of Thine;

The sheep whose little woolly throat
Taught the child Isaac sacrifice;
The dove returning to Noah's boat,
Sprigless, and with tearful eyes;

The ass instructing Balaam
The discourse of inspired minds;
And David's lost and bleating lamb,
And Solomon's fleet lovely hinds;

Enfold me in their fold, and let
Me learn their mystic parables—
Of food that desert ravens set,
And of the lion's honeyed fells.

Above all, teach me blessedness
Of him, Azazel, that dear goat,
Sent forth into the wilderness
To hallow it with one sad note.

PSALM XXIX: TO THE CHIEF MUSICIAN, A PSALM
OF THE BRATZLAVER, A PARABLE

An aged king, his brittle shins in hose,
Spoonfed, dribbling over a purple bib,
Upon a time and at a banquet board
Raised bony palm, and stayed the resined bows,
And hushed the drums, and stilled the cornet's chord.
Then caused to issue from his seventh rib
These toothless words:
                    Thane of four graveyard ells,

Soon shall you mark me, vassal of the worm.
The eager belfry waits to cluck its bells;
The royal sexton, palsied and infirm,
Lets rust grow on his spade, moss on my tomb.
Wherefore, my son, my immortality,
Ascend my throne; don crown; let cannon boom!
For though from my high tower in the sky
My rheumy eyes have seen your star and doom,
Be of good cheer, of noble temper be;
And never let a baneful wind blow dust
Between yourself and your felicity . . . .

PSALM XXX: TO THE CHIEF MUSICIAN, A PSALM OF
THE BRATZLAVER, WHICH HE WROTE DOWN AS
THE STAMMERER SPOKE

At unprehensile Time, all fingers clutch.
Can it be counted on an abacus?
Or weighed on scales, most delicate to the touch?
Or measured with rods? What Mathematicus
Can speak thereof, save as a net on the brain,
A web some much-afflated spider weaves
On which hang chronicles, like drops of rain?
That, and no more, the quarry he retrieves.
But, truly, in what smithy is it forged?
In what alembic brewed? By what bird hatched?
I, but a stammerer, by the spirit urged,
Having approached that Door, found it unlatched,
Say Time is vacuum, save it be compact
Of men's deeds imitating godly act.

228

PSALM XXXI: TO THE CHIEF MUSICIAN, A PSALM OF THE BRATZLAVER, TOUCHING A GOOD GARDENER

i

It was a green, a many-meadowed county!
Orchards there were, heavy with fruitage; and
Blossom and bud and benison and bounty

Filled with good odour that luxurious land.
Stained with crushed grass, an old and earthy yeoman
Sceptred that green demesne with pruning wand.

ii

Suddenly came the chariots of the foeman;
Suddenly vanished that good gardener,—
Ruled in the land, three companies of bowmen.

One company polluted its sweet air,
Another rendered its ripe fruitage bitter;
A third made foul its beauty which was fair.

People of starving sparrows, loud their twitter!
Wherefore I did bespeak a neighbouring folk:
Behold your kin devoured by a wolf's litter,

Release their land, unburden them their yoke
Or similar evil may transgress your borders!

iii

Now, though they made them ready, as I spoke,
In tippling and in gluttonish disorders
They tarried on their march, until one day
As they descried the invaders' spectral warders,

Their flagons soured, their viands did decay,
And odour and taste did utterly forsake them.
Then in their sore distress, they sought to pray.

O but my ungraped water did so slake them!
My poor dry crust did such rich taste afford!
They ate, they drank, they slept, and none could wake them.

iv

Wherefore, alone, I mingled with the horde,
And unknown walked in many public places.
God save me from the ugly words I heard!

And from those gates, beset by wrothful faces
Where Bribery stretched its hand, and turned its head!
And from quick Lust, and his two-score grimaces!

Salute them, now, three companies of dread:
Filth, in its dun array, the clean taste killing;
Embattled Bribery, with stealthy tread
Advancing on the vanquished, all too-willing
To barter visions for a piece of gold;
And legioned Lust, at its foul buckets swilling . . .

v

They did salute them, did my henchmen bold,
With many a sword, and many an eager arrow,
And driven was the foe from wood and wold.

Then did we come upon him, in a narrow
Streetyard, followed by children, and a cur,—
We brought him fruit, high-piled in a barrow,
Gift for a king,—for that good gardener.

PSALM XXXII: A SONG THAT THE SHIPS OF JAFFA
DID SING IN THE NIGHT

The ship leaves Jaffa, treasure in its hold:
Figs, coronets of sweetness; sweeter dates;
Citrons, like perfume phials, packed in crates;
Boxed oranges, the scented globes of gold;

230

Grape clusters, and wine bottles, dusty, old;
Sweet almonds, toothsomest of delicates;
Bleeding golgothas of red pomegranates;
All smooth and fresh; and innocent of mould.
And Torah scrolls penned by some scribe, now dead,
And pray'r-shawls woven in an eastern loom,
And palm-leaves shipped to the Uncomforted,
And candlesticks to light some Sabbath gloom.
And little sacks of holy earth to spread
Under a pious skull in a far tomb . . . .

PSALM XXXIII: A PSALM, FORBIDDEN TO COHANIM

Who coming from the synagogue
On Sabbath eves to always find
The sacred Sabbath triple sign—
The burnished candle on the cloth,
The white bread still unbroken, and
The beaker full of hallowed wine,—
Now on this Friday evening waits
For no such signs. His voice is stilled.
There is no soft tread at the door.
The bread is baked, unbroken, and
The beaker is not even filled.

The candles flicker on the floor.

PSALM XXXIV: A PSALM OF ABRAHAM, TO BE
WRITTEN DOWN AND LEFT ON THE TOMB OF
RASHI

Now, in this terrible tumultuous night,
When roars the metal beast, the steel bird screams,
And images of God, for fraud or fright,
Cannot discern what is from that which seems,—
I, in bewilderment, remember you,
Mild pedagogue, who took me, young and raw,
And led me, verse by verse, and clue by clue,
Mounting the spiral splendid staircase of the Law,—

231

You, Rabbi Solomon bar Isaac, known
Rashi, incomparable exegete,
Who did sustain my body and my bone
With drink talmudic and with biblic meat,—
Simple, and for a child were they, your words,
Bringing into the silent wooded script,
Texts that came twittering, like learned birds,
Describing mightily the nondescript.
Not these can I forget, nor him ignore,
That old archaic Frank expounding lore
From his Hebraic crypt.

Nothing was difficult, O Master, then,
No query but it had an answer, clear,—
But now though I am grown, a man of men,
The books all read, the places seen, the dear
Too personal heart endured all things, there is
Much that I cannot grasp, and much that goes amiss,
And much that is a mystery that even the old Gaul,
Nor Onkelus, nor Jonathan, can lucidate at all.

Yours were such days, great rabbi, like these days,
When blood was spilled upon the public ways,
And lives were stifled for the glut of gore,
As they marched on, those murderous four,
Hunger and hate and pestilence and war!
              Wherefore, O *Parshandatha* of the law,
Unriddle me the chapter of the week,
Show me the wing, the hand, behind the claw,
The human mouth behind the vulture beak;
Reveal, I pray you, do reveal to me
Behind the veil the vital verity;
Show me again, as you did in my youth
Behind the equivocal text the unequivocal truth!

O vintner of Troyes,
Consider the cluster of my time, its form and shape,
And say what wine will issue from this bitter grape!

I wait your answer; in the interim
I do, for you who left no son to read
The prayer before the sacred cherubim,
Intone, as one who is of your male seed,
A *Kaddish:*
　　　May it reach eternity
And grace your soul, and even bring some grace
To most unworthy, doubt-divided me.

PSALM XXXV: A PSALM OF ABRAHAM, WHICH HE MADE
BECAUSE OF FEAR IN THE NIGHT

Thou settest them about my bed,
The four good angels of the night,
Invisible wings on left and right,
An holy watch at foot and head:

Gabriel, Uriel, Raphael,
And Michael, of the angelic host
Who guard my sleep-entrusted ghost
Until day break, and break the spell.

Until day break, and shadows pass
My bones lie in a sack of flesh,
My blood lies caught in carmined mesh,
And I am wholly trodden grass.

But those the warders of life and limb
Escort my soul to distant shores,
My soul that in its dreaming soars
With seraphim and cherubim,

To lands unrecognized, to shores
Bright with great sunlight, musical
With singing of such scope and skill,
It is too much for human ears.

I see the angel's drinking-cup,
That flower that so scents the air!

233

The golden domes! The towers there!
My mind could never think them up!

Yet when the shadows flee away,
And fly the four good angels, and
I fare forth, exiled from that land,
Back to my blood, my bone, my day,

Untowered, unflowered, unscented banks,
Back to the lumpy sack of skin,
The head, the torso, and the shin,
I offer up, to Thee, my thanks.

PSALM XXXVI: A PSALM TOUCHING GENEALOGY

Not sole was I born, but entire genesis:
For to the fathers that begat me, this
Body is residence. Corpuscular,
They dwell in my veins, they eavesdrop at my ear,
They circle, as with Torahs, round my skull,
In exit and in entrance all day pull
The latches of my heart, descend, and rise—
And there look generations through my eyes.

A VOICE WAS HEARD IN RAMAH

IN RE SOLOMON WARSHAWER

On Wodin's day, sixth of December, thirty-nine,
I, Friedrich Vercingetorix, attached
to the VIIth Eavesdroppers-behind-the-Line,
did cover my beat, when suddenly the crowd I watched
surrounded, in a cobbled lane one can't pass through,
a bearded man, disguised in rags, a Jew.

In the said crowd there were a number of Poles.
Mainly, however, there were Germans there;
blood-brothers of our Reich, true Aryan souls,
breathing at last—in Warsaw—Nordic air.

These were the words the Jew was shouting:
I took them down verbatim:

"Whom have I hurt? Against whose silk have I brushed?
On which of your women looked too long?
I tell you I have done no wrong!
Send home your children, lifting hardened dung,
And let your curs be hushed!
For I am beard and breathlessness, and chased enough.
Leave me in peace, and let me go my way."

At this the good folk laughed. The Jew continued to say
he was no thief, he was a man for hire,
worked for his bread, artist or artisan,
a scribe, if you wished, a vendor or a buyer,
work of all kinds, and anything at all:
paint a mural, scour a latrine,
indite an ode, repair an old machine,
anything, to repeat,
anything at all,
so that he might eat
and have his straw couch in his abandoned stall.
Asked for his papers, he made a great to-do
of going through the holes in his rags, whence he withdrew
a Hebrew pamphlet and a signet ring,
herewith produced, Exhibits 1 and 2.

I said: No documents in a civilized tongue?
He replied:

"Produce, O Lord, my wretched fingerprint,
Bring forth, O angel in the heavenly court,
My dossier, full, detailed, bold fact and hint,
Felony, misdemeanor, tort!"

I refused to be impressed by talk of that sort.

From further cross-examination, it appeared,
immediate history: a beggar in Berlin,
chased as a vagrant from the streets of Prague,
kept as a leper in forced quarantine,
shunned as the pest, avoided like a plague,
he had escaped, mysteriously come
by devious routes, and stolen frontiers, to
the *nalewkas* of Warsaw's sheenydom.

Pressed to reveal his foul identity,
He lied:

One of the anthropophagi was he,
or, if we wished, a denizen of Mars,
the ghost of my father, Conscience—aye,
the spectre of Reason, naked, and with scars;
even became insulting, said he was
Aesop the slave among the animals . . .
Sir Incognito—Rabbi Alias . . .
The eldest elder of Zion . . . said we knew
his numerous varied oriental shapes,
even as we ought to know his present guise—
the man in the jungle, and beset by apes.

It was at this point the SS man arrived.
The Jew was interrupted; when he was revived,
He deposed as follows:

"At low estate, a beggar, and in flight,
Still do I wear my pride like purple. I
Am undismayed by frenzy or by fright,
And you are those mirrored in my pitying eye.
For you are not the first that I have met—
O I have known them all,
The dwarf dictators, the diminutive dukes,
The heads of straw, the hearts of gall,
Th' imperial plumes of eagles covering rooks!

"It is not necessary to name names,
But it may serve anon,

236

Now to evoke from darkness some dark fames,
Evoke,
Armada'd Spain, that gilded jettison;
And Russia's last descended Romanov,
Descending a dark staircase
To a dank cellar at Ekaterinoslov;
Evoke
The glory that was Babylon that now is gloom;
And Egypt, Egypt, scarcely now recalled
By that lone star that sentries Pharaoh's tomb;
And Carthage, sounded on sand, by water walled;
And Greece—O broken marble!—
And disinterred unresurrected Rome.

'These several dominions hunted me;
They all have wished, and more than wished, me dead;
And now, although I do walk raggedly,
I walk, and they are echoes to my tread!
Is it by your devices I shall be undone?

"Ah, but you are philosophers, and know
That what has been need not continue so;
The sun has risen: and the sun has set;
Risen again, again descended, yet
To-morrow no bright sun may rise to throw
Rays of inductive reason on Judaeophobic foe.

"Is there great turmoil in the sparrow's nest
When that bright bird, the Sun, descends the west?
There is no fear, there is no twittering:
At dawn they will again behold his juvenescent wing!

"Such is the very pattern of the world,
Even the sparrows understand;
And in that scheme of things I am enfurled,
Am part thereof, the whole as it was planned,
With increase and abatement rife,
Subject to sorrow, joined to joy—
Earth, its relenting and recurring life!

"Yes, but the signet ring, the signet ring!
Since you must know, barbarian, know you shall!
I who now stand before you, a hunted thing,
Pressed and pursued and harried hither and yon,
I was, I am the Emperor Solomon!
O, to and fro upon the face of the earth,
I wandered, crying: *Ani Shlomo,* but—
But no one believed my birth.

"For he now governs in my place and stead,
He who did fling me from Jerusalem
Four hundred parasangs;
Who stole the crown from off my head,
And robed him in my robes, beneath whose hem
The feet of the cock extend, the tail of the demon hangs!
Asmodeus!

"Mistake me not: I am no virtuous saint;
Only a man, and like all men, not godly,
Damned by desire—
But I at least waged war, for holy booty,
Against my human taint;
At least sought wisdom, to discern the good;
Whether of men, or birds, or beasts of the wood;
Spread song, spread justice, ever did aspire—
Howbeit, man among men, I failed—
To lay the plan, and work upon the plan
To build the temple of the more-than-man!

"But he, the unspeakable prince of malice!
Usurper of my throne, pretender to the Lord's!
Wicked, demoniac, lycanthropous,
Leader of hosts horrific, barbarous hordes,
Master of the worm, pernicious, that cleaves rocks,
The beast that talks,
Asmodeus!—

"Who has not heard the plight of his domain?
Learning is banished to the hidden cave;
Wisdom decried, a virtue of the slave;

238

And justice, both eyes seared, goes tapping with a cane.
His counsellor is the wolf. He counsels hate.
His sceptre is a claw.
And love is a high crime against the state.
The fury of the forest
Is the law.

"Upon his charnel-throne, in bloodied purple,
Hearkening to that music where the sigh
Pauses to greet the groan, the groan the anguished cry,
Asmodeus sits;
And I—"

At this point the SS men departed.
The Jew was not revived. He was carried and carted,
and to his present gaoler brought;
awaiting higher pleasure.
                              And further deponent saith not.

RABBI YOM-TOB OF MAYENCE PETITIONS HIS GOD

I am no brazen face to hale the Lord
By both His horns of glory into court,
Nor in the talons of the hawk to fix
Subpoenas to assign the heavenly horde;
I am no bailiff at a debtor's door;
I bear no writs against the angels; I
Come not to seize the moveables of the sky.
What the Lord gives, He owes; He owes no more.

Humble I stand before Thy gates,
A beggar in sackcloth, suppliant both palms,
Soliciting Thy alms.
Let them not boot me away, the keepers of Thy gates.
Let them not beat me with Thy lightning rods.
Let them not stone me with Thy thunder-weights.
Humble I stand before Thy gates.

Only in the voice of an earthworm, do I cry:
Descend from Thy tall towers in the sky;
Forsake Thy lonely hermitage; O Lord,
Grant me the Sinai of a single word.
Before Thy feet I spread my prayershawl;
The traces of Thy footsteps I wear out
With kisses; my phylacteries are kin,
Kin to Thy sandal-strings. Grant but Thy grace,
Alight upon these battlements for a space,
And in Thy talk of this and that, make clear,
Before the sun splinters to stars upon the sky,
The how and when, the wherefore and the why . . .

     Let there be light
In the two agonies that are my eyes,
And in the dungeon of my heart, a door
Unbarred. Descend, O Lord, and speak.

     Then will I say: Let cravens fear
The sword. I know it to be straw.
Let cowards quail before the spear.
To me Death is a toothless jaw.

There is no sign upon the skies,
No witness in the heavens; no
Marvel to which to raise the eyes.
Where the crow flew, there flies the crow.
(He hears not. He is busied. He
Parses the Latin of some monkish homily.)

Not so, oblivious brain, forgetting all.
Blaspheming mouth, not so.
Know what the pious know:

Who hails the cloud for love, must heed
Only the taciturn cloud in speed,—
Who climbs upon the golden stair
Of the sun goes blinded by the glare;
Who counts the stars, will ever find
More stars in the sky than in his mind;

240

And who addresses him to stone
Upon the high places, is alone.

Not in levin, not in thunder
Shall I behold the sign and wonder,
    But in the still small voice,
    Let me rejoice.
Wherefore Thy will is manifest, O Lord,
Thy will be done.

Be he who yields to baptism, abhorred;
Shunned as a leper be that one.
And unto you, virgins in Israel, be it known
No heathenish paw shall clutch you living. Aye,
Before the starved hound, eager for the bone,
Shall burst the door, lolling a fevered tongue,
Sweet bodies shall smile blithely to the sky.

Blessed this day; this day on which we shall
Make glorious His name. Blessed the sun
Accepting the *Kiddush* of the wine-filled skull.
Blessed this cellar floor, and silent stone,
And benedictions on this hallowed knife
Which pries the door to the eternal life.

BALLAD OF THE THWARTED AXE

(*Coram* the German People's Court)

The judges sat in their blood-red robes,
The victim in the dock was stood,
The clerk read a number on a writ,
And the room smelled blood.

        Headsman, headsman, whet your axe,
        Against the sparking stone,
        The blade that's eaten by the flint,
        The better eats the bone!

The perjurers recite their rote,
The body, manacled, stands mute;
It cannot be they speak of him,
If they do speak the truth.

> *Headsman, headsman, take their words,*
> *Each of a whetstone shape,*
> *And sharpen that good axe of yours,*
> *To meet a stubborn nape!*

The prosecutor weaves his phrase,
With withes of lust, and warped lore,
Accused regards his shadow, now
Lying on the floor.

> *Headsman, headsman, that skilled man,*
> *He weaves a beautiful*
> *Red basket, firm and large enough*
> *To hold a severed skull!*

The chief judge in his blood-red robe,
Opens his red-lined book,
And blows therefrom a poisoned breath,
That pales the poor man's look.

> *Headsman, headsman, catch that breath,*
> *That is as sharp as lime!*
> *O, it will eat away the limbs*
> *Of any judge's crime.*

The court is done with its assize
Of overt acts and dead intents;
Now sawdust blots the red ink of
The bleeding documents.

> *Headsman, headsman,—cheated man!*
> *Whom thorough judges mock.*
> *You shall have no use for your axe,*
> *A ghost stands in the dock!*

BALLAD OF THE DAYS OF THE MESSIAH

O the days of the Messiah are at hand, are at hand!
  The days of the Messiah are at hand!
I can hear the air-raid siren, blow away the age of iron,
  Blast away the age of iron
  That was builded on the soft quick-sand.
O the days of the Messiah are at hand!

O Leviathan is ready for the feed, for the feed!
  Leviathan is ready for the feed!
And I hold firm to the credo that both powder and torpedo
  Have so fried that good piscedo
He is ready for the eating, scale and seed!
  Leviathan is ready for the feed!

Yes, the sacred wine is ready for the good, for the good,
  The wine of yore intended for the good—
Only all that ruddy water has now turned to blood and slaughter
  Has fermented into slaughter,
Aged for so long, as it has been, in the wood—
  That wine of yore intended for the good!

O I see him falling! Will he shoot? Will he shoot?
  Will Messiah's falling herald aim and shoot?
'Tis Elijah, he announces, as he falls from sky, and bounces
  Out of all those silken flounces
Of the heaven-sent and coloured parachute:
  Messiah, he is coming, and won't shoot!

Don't you hear Messiah coming in his tank, in his tank?
  Messiah in an armour-metalled tank?
I can see the pillared fire, speeding on the metal tire
  Over muck and out of mire
And the seraphim a-shooting from its flank!
  O Messiah, he stands grimy in his tank!

243

YEHUDA HALEVI, HIS PILGRIMAGE

Liveth the tale, nor ever shall it die!
Upon his scroll the scribe has lettered it.
The learned rabbin, in his homily,
Its telling gilds with verse of holy writ.
O many a darkened Jewerie is lit
By its mere memory. It doth not fail.
Yet, in this latter day, who shall have wit,
Whose cunning of words shall in this day avail
For speech too grieving even for throat of nightingale?

Only the fingers of the wind may play
The harp of David on the willow tree;
And Solomon his song, none durst essay.
The sons of Asaph eke have ceased to be;
Dust are their temple throats; and also, he,
The chief musician is now stifled mould.
In Israel is no song save threnodie;
Shall then, for want of singer, stay untold
The tale of the pale princess and the jongleur bold?

Bard—and no Levite of degrees, no sweet
Singer in Israel, but a humble wight,
A process-server, a pleader at the leet,
Born, yea, miscarried to a pagan night,—
Sing thou the song that any other might,
Singing for supper; tell the tale as one
Who for a penny sobs his sorry plight,
And let thy words for her be orison
Of saddening evening, and dark midnight, and bright dawn.

Whilom in Toledoth, that ancient town,
Founded by Hebrews, built by the conquering Moor,
And governed now by that great Christian Don,
There dwelt the incomparable troubadour—
Bird on the lintel of the ghetto-door!
Brightest of feather of those plumaged throats,—
Melodious *ibns* of the golden lore,

244

Who sang the bubbling wine, the riddle's coats,
The ditty, merry or sad, and Love's so difficult notes!

Albeit he could joust with the wittiest,
Even with Ezra's sons, their courtesie,—
Apt at the wassail-word, the wedding jest,
The Saracen or Frankish measure, he—
Ermined in *tallith,* crown'd with phylactery,
Halevi, minnesinger of the Lord,
Liege to the manor of divinity,
Has utterly foresworn the profane word.
Homage he gives to God, and carols only at His board.

His was the ballad of the fluttering heart:
The hooded falcon on the wrist of God.
He sang its flights, its venery, its art,
Its moulting, and its final resting sod.
The jewell'd rhyming he devised to laud
The King in whose courts he carolled and was glad,
Were such as never issued from mere clod,
Or from the sage or the divinely mad,
Whether from Mantua or Lesbos or Baghdad.

Did he not also in that wondrous script
Of Al-Kazari chronicle that king,
The heathen begging of the godly-lipped
Some wisdom for his pious hearkening,—
A candle for the dark,—a signet ring
To make the impress of the soul,—that prince
Who covenanted with the mightiest King,
Abjured false testaments and alcorans,
Accepting only Torah and its puissance.

Scorn not the largess lavished on the bard
By Seigneur hearkening the bard's refrain:
The minted moon no merchant ever marr'd;
The sun, the silver currency of Spain;
The mountain flower, the flower of the plain;
And from the beaker of the soul, that wine
Which sours not; and from the bowled brain

Grape clusters torn from paradisal vine;
Honey of Samson's bees; and milk from Pharaoh's kine!

Thus, in that crowded town Castilian,
Where crypted is that psalter, writ on gold
In ink of molten ruby, th' inspired man,
Halevi, served God, luminously-souled.
Aye, and the learned glossators of old
Tell also of his leechcraft, subtil, wise,
For chills and fevers, humours hot and cold,
Simples for all who craved his remedies,—
Nazarite, Moslem, Hebrew—God's ailing entities.

Still is there aught which troubles him; it hath
No name nor appellation, yet it is.
Sometimes, it is a shadow on his path,
But thrown by whom he doth not know, y-wis!
Sometimes upon his brow, it is a kiss,—
Was it the wind or feather in the air?
He knoweth not; but there is aught amiss.
Daughter of sound? A footstep on a stair?
And in the synagogue, song heard, and no one there?

The stars are manna in the sky; the moon,
Fleshpot of Egypt. By its light he cons
Old parchment to a Babylonian tune.
He nods, he drowses. Sleep, the Cushite, fawns
Upon Halevi, and he dreams. O once
There were those wizards who could rede these things,
Make clear the dreaming to the dreaming ones—
Baker or cupbearer or young princelings—
But who shall now interpret these imaginings?

Behold in his dream, a castle on a hill,
Moated and massive, ominously-walled!
Of all its towers, one to a pinnacle
Rises, as if by constellations called
To keep all masonry abased, enthralled.
And from that tower is heard a voice, a sigh,
Bitter with Sorrow, sorrow that doth scald

Its hearer as it doth its votary,
At the barred casement of that doleful tower on high.

O beautiful beyond compare is she,
That lady in the tower of her gaol!
She is the very rose for mystery,
And like the lily is she lily-pale.
She speaketh, and it is as if a tale
Of the sharp thorn were told by the white rose,
Of fragrance that for agony doth fail,
And beauty stabbed of her dagger'd foes,
Unpetall'd, plundered, and left lying in her throes.

"I was a princess in my father's hall,
Of all his daughters, his sweet favourite!
Was there a wish, a word my lips let fall,—
The King, my father, not fulfilling it?
O did I wish—as young girls without wit
Might wish—the golden platter of the moon,
Forthwith, I swear, the chamberlain would flit
Hither and yon, send messengers,—'tis done!
So long ago that was—a dream, remembered, gone!

"Peace in the realm, my father on his throne!
The vintner, swarth, sits drinking underneath
The shadow of his grapes; the hay, new-mown,
Gladdens the peasant on the yellow heath.
And in the garden, I, the King's daughter, wreathe,
Many a flower for the King's delight,
Beauty the late summer doth bequeath,—
Peace in the realm! the generals, old, now fight
Only with bloodless chessmen throughout the noiseless night.

"Suddenly came the foe barbaric, slew,
Plundered and slaughter'd our poor scythe-arm'd youth:
They were a flame that through our hamlets flew
And left not standing palace, nor hut, nor booth.
Utterly without pity, without ruth,
Their sword proclaimed to widow and maid our shame;
The orphan, all affrighted by the uncouth

247

Stranger, remembered not his own pet name,
Remembering only, as I, the war-cry, flight, and flame.

"My father! O my father! I know not
Even to this day of his fate. I faint,
I shudder at the dark, the horrible thought.
Perhaps he fled the conqueror's constraint,
A beggar, and unrecognized, a saint,
In some far land of alien wont and word!
It may be—on his shield what blot, what taint!—
He picks the morsels flung beneath the board
By the loud drunken captains feasting with their lord!

"And me—alas!—be blotted out that day
Of ribald jest and ruffianish leer
When the barbarian spied me for his prey!
Again I see him, and again I hear
His frightening gutturals. Now, in this drear
Tower am I immured, and to be shown
Neighbouring princes entertained here,
I am their caged bird, their unwitting clown,
Their most ungracious guest, their tarnished trophied crown.

"Who shall release me from this bondage? What
Warrior, mounted and plumed, shall some great day
Gallop the highway, jump the noisome moat,
Dismount, draw sword, and leap his clanging way
Up the long staircase, bloodied with affray,
And at long last, break down this studded door?
It shall not ever be—alack-a-day!—
Ransom shall not be mine, not ever more,
And perish I shall surely on this stony floor.

"Or, if no prince shall ever bring release,
Nor any soothsayer use wizardry
Encompassing my freedom, then, God please
That soon—or I will surely cease to be—
One little precious gift be granted me!
May I soon hear my good folk speech again!
May I once more, before pale memory

248

Whitens the mind, hear talk that is like rain
Unto parched fields, like sunshine on the ripening grain!

"Hast thou some potion that will render me
A bird to flutter from these bars abhorr'd,
Halevi, bring it me; hast thou some plea
To melt the iron of this mailed horde,
Place it before the Throne; hast thou a sword,
Lift it against my gaolers; at the least,
Bring me thy ringing, winging, singing word."
The shadow lifted, and the dreaming ceased.
The moon had vanished, and the sun smiled from the east.

What fumes within the alembic of his brain
Conjured this dream? What pollen wafted from
Blossoming orchards beyond the turbulent main
Quickens the memory? What mountain drum
Beating beyond the horizon, sends its hum
Echoing softly in Halevi's ear?
In sooth, he knoweth not whence these things come;
But he hath seen a far-off princess, near,
A dark thing happening, and the Lord would make it clear!

He will no more of herbaries, nor drugs,
Nor physic that is arrogant; he will
Give, as a gift, his phials and his jugs,
And all the script of sage Aristotle.
Begone, Toledo, incense-scented gaol!
He will take staff in hand, and fare him forth
To unknown shores, across the perilous swell
Of seas uncharted, whether south or north;
And he will seek her out, that princess of great worth.

Cordova, diadem of Andaluse!
Not from thy robed scholars, splitting hairs,
Nor from thy merchants of bright silk, came news
Of her he sought, nor from the market-fairs
Loud with the gossip of strange pilgrimers.
They had not heard her fame. They knew her not.
Each lifted dinars from his stringed purse

Stamped with some royal head; alas, this wrought
Gold was not precious with the face of her he sought!

It is a ship, a full white beautiful swan,
Gliding to Africa on the Great Sea!
Alnath, alpherd, alferoz, ald'baran,—
Loveliest blossoms on the heavenly tree
Guiding the slowly-moving argosy.
The mariners sing chanties of sea-folk;
Halevi marvels at the calm blue sea
Whose little waves salaam to the oak,
Breaking the glassy waters. And then the tempest broke!

The wind plucked out the stars from heaven; and
The sea, a furious serpent, leaped at the sky,
The ship, a pebble in a tall djinn's hand,
The little men, less than homunculi.
Quoth now the Berber captain, wrathfully:
"There is in our midst an unbelieving cur,
Faring to Egypt with his heathenry!
Into the sea with him, young mariner!
In fish's belly, let him reach Iskandahar!"

Answered Halevi: "Pray unto your God!"
"Aye, that we have!" "Then let me pray to mine!"
Then was Halevi's prayer like a rod
Smiting the wild uplifted wave supine.
To liturgy heart-rending came divine
Answer unto the sea-swept wind-swept dove!
The mariners gape now at the calm brine
And now stare at the kindly sky above
Where ald'baran, alnath, alpherd, alferoz rove!

Are they not written in the annal books
The places of his perilous journeying:
The bright saharas, shimmering, with no brooks;
The deserts wild; the mountains harbouring
Assassins; and the sweet oases spring
Where tribes fanatic curl in the scimitar?
And is not, too, recorded the welcoming

250

That Cairo, Demieyet, Iskandahar,
Made for the learned minstrel coming from afar?

But nowhere did he find the face he sought.
The silent pyramids, the ancient Nile
Knowing so many secrets, knew her not.
Shereef and scarred cid and rabbin smile
At this his search, and bid him tarry awhile
In new Mizraim where no pharaoh is;
In vain: the shadow grows upon the dial;
Time flies; and in the dungeon of distress
Waits, pale, her hair hung loose, the beautiful princess.

What Asian cities did his sandals shun?
He sought them all; the cities of great bazaars;
The Gates where justice triumphs in the sun,
The village of the clanging armourers.
He sought them all; there where the gardener mars
The rose to attar, and the too-sweet air
Silences birds, and makes to swoon the stars!
He was to the fief of the crippled conjuror.
Ever he chased a shadow in a vision of nowhere.

Weary, and footsore, and in spirit low,
At length, at long last, after many days,
He is upon the dusty roads that go
Bowing to Palestine. O offer praise
Halevi, to thy Lord, for thine eyes gaze
Now upon land that is that holy stem
Whose flower, in heaven, blossoms forth ablaze
A flower, a flame, a talismanic gem—
Lift up thine eyes—the glorious Hierusalem!

O wondrous miracle that came to pass!
The blindfold of the dream is dropped away.
It is no vision, seen as through a glass,—
It is the brightness of the high noon-day.
Behold the princess in her sad array!
Certes 'tis she, and no vain stratagem!
It is she whom the vision did soothsay!

251

The princess of the fallen diadem!
Jerusalem, the princess! Fair Jerusalem!

Aye, but that dark dreaming is now bright.
The princess Zion is that princess fair
Gaoled by the cross-marked arrogant Frankish knight!
Still is she beautiful, though full of care;
Still is the jasmine fragrant from her hair
And still within her eyes is, shining, kept
Remembered sunshine. But despair, despair
Like a hot wind of the desert, overswept
Halevi, and he sang what was not song. He wept.

"Grieving for them, thy captive sons who are
The last sheep of thy flock, O Zion, take,
Accept from them their greeting from afar,
Their greeting and their longing and their ache.
Receive the homage of thy vassal, whose
Tears, like the dew of Hermon, seek thy hills,
Where he would be a jackal, all night long
        Wailing thy bitter news,
Where he would dream away thy manacles,
And be the harp melodious for thy song!

"Peniel! Bethel! Mahanayim! sod
Where walked thy saints, where rests the Immanence,
Whose gates are open to the gates of God,
Whose light is not the light of firmaments
But the illumination of the Lord!
Shrines holy! Where I would pour out my soul
As was the spirit of the sacred One
        Upon you once outpoured,
How have you fallen to an evil dole,
Where slaves now lord it from your sullied throne!

"Thy ruins, thy waste places, and thy void,
Thy dwellings rendered rubble and small rock,
The chambers of thy cherubim destroyed—
Yea, there though bleeding, barefoot, would I walk.
I will cut off my hair, and that day curse

That flung thy crowned ones among heathen foes;
I'll fast, for food and drink must surely reek
      When I behold the curs,
Tearing the lion's litter, and day shows
The eagle bleeding from the raven's beak!

"O Zion, altogether beautiful!
Thy sons rejoice them in thy time of peace,
And in thy sorrow, their cup, too, is full.
They weep thy ruins, yet they never cease
From striving towards thee from captivity,
They bend the knee upon thy gates, thy sons,
Scattered on mountains, driven over seas,
      Remembering Zion, thee,
Yearning to touch the plinth of thy shattered stones
O but to touch the boughs of thy palm-trees!

"Can Shinar and Pathros equal thee for glory?
Can Urim and Thummim be surpassed by spells?
With whom compare thy kings, thy prophets hoary,
Thy Levites and thy singers? All things else
Will pass away—idol, idolater—
Only thy crown is for eternity!
Thou art God's dwelling place, His goodly booth!
      O none is happier
Than he who with thee waits thy dawn to see
Thee once again as Thou wast in thy youth!

"God granted that I might go wandering
Where He to seer and prophet was revealed.
God gave me wings that I might fly; and fling
My broken heart upon thy broken field.
O, I will fall upon my face, and kiss
Thy very stones, so blessed in thine earth;
I will take hold of thee, thy clods, thy soil,
      Thy very dustiness,
And hold it as a thing of extreme worth—
Prized above rubies, and the richest spoil."

253

Would that with these his tears this tale might end,
Even with this sad guerdon, this poor meed!
Zion abased by the irreverend,
Yet Zion, seen; Zien beheld, in deed!
But so 'twas not ordained, not so decreed;
Lo, from afar, and shouting a wild oath
Rideth an Arab on his thundering steed.
Nameless that rider, save for war-name, Death.
Zion, O Princess, receive thy minstrel's trampled breath!

Murdered, the minnesinger of the Lord!
Where rest his bones? None knows. Surely he dwells
In the third temple of the hallowed word,
Where Zion, even now, still hears the bells
Of high-priest moving at his rituals,
Where the fair princess still hears prophecy,
And joyful music, and the oracles
Consolatory of her misery,
Saying: The daughter of the king will yet be free.

Liveth the tale, nor ever shall it die!
The princess in her tower grows not old.
For that she heard his charmed minstrelsy,
She is forever young. Her crown of gold,
Bartered and customed, auctioned, hawked and sold,
Is still for no head but her lovely head.
What if the couch be hard, the cell be cold,
The warder's keys unrusted, stale the bread?
Halevi sang her song, and she is comforted!

254

POEMS

1941-1947

PSALM 154

TO THE CHIEF MUSICIAN UPON SHOSHANNIM.
A SONG OF LOVES

Well may they thank thee, Lord, for drink and food;
For daily benison of meat,
For fish or fowl,
For spices of the subtle cook,
For fruit of the orchard, root of the meadow, berry of the wood;
For all things good,
And for the grace of water of the running brook!
And in the hallelujah of these joys
Not least is my uplifted voice.

But this day into thy great temple have I come
To praise thee for the poisons thou hast brayed,
To thank thee for pollens venomous, the fatal gum,
The banes that bless, the multifarious herbs arrayed
In all the potency of that first week
Thou didst compose the sextet of Earth spoken, made!

Behold them everywhere, the unuttered syllables of thy breath,
Heavy with life, and big with death!
The flowering codicils to thy great fiat!

The hemp of India—and paradise!
The monk's hood, cooling against fever;
And nightshade: death unpetalled before widened eyes;
And blossom of the heart, the purple foxglove!

The spotted hemlock, punishment and prize,
And those exhilarators of the brain—
Cocaine;
Blood of the grape; and marrow of the grain!
And sweet white flower of thy breath, O Lord,
Juice of the poppy, conjurer of timeless twilights,
Eternities of peace in which the fretful world
Like a tame tiger at the feet lies curled.

256

PSALM 155

TO THE CHIEF MUSICIAN, AL-TASCHITH, MICHTAM
OF ABRAHAM; WHEN ONE SENT, AND THEY
WATCHED THE HOUSE TO KILL HIM

When I in prayer beseech thy benison,
Many are they thy favours I could seek:
A long and worthy life for my only son,
A happy hearth for my wife, and for my mother
Health, and untroubled waiting in the sun,
(A golden crown in Eden for my father!)
And for my several kin, I could also speak,
Of this one's need, desire of that one,
And ask for each of thy abundant grace:—
Save that today I ask no blessings, no,
I am but one of many almoners
Who ask for him thy devastating curse!

May his flesh fall from him, and may he, living, rot
Until he is not sure he is, or he is not.
May he be flung from fever into an icy cold
And may his days be long for him, but he not old.
May strange diseases take him, doctors come
From far-off lands to twitter over him,
Matter-of-factly, without pity,
As over a strange new scum.
O may his brain be peopled by grim ghosts,
And may he wake from sleep, in sweaty fear,
Fearing four murderers at the four bed posts!
And after a fortnight of convulsions may he finally die,
And be remembered, if remembered at all,
In the name of some newly found, particularly disgusting fly,
Or in the writing on a privy wall.

PSALM 166

A PRAYER OF ABRAHAM THAT HE BE FORGIVEN FOR BLASPHEMY

Consider my speech, O Lord, not too severely;
It does not mean what it does seem to say.
With strangers I must see my tongue says merely
The hollow nought, the vacuous cliché!
For You I need not choose my language; surely
Need not measure the words with which I pray;
Surely, Lord, You would have it this way rather.
I speak to you this day
Even as once I spoke to my sire, now with You.
And I never loved one more than I did my father.

PSALM 170

TO THE CHIEF BAILIFF, A PSALM OF THE KING'S WRIT

Death, the peddler, came to my door this day.
Sold me his merchandise, old wares under a new name.
Forever and forever, piecemeal, must I pay.
Defaulting, he revendicates the same.

I shall not have peace any more.
But, every day, I shall arise,
And find him spying at my door,—
The agent with the estimating eyes:
Watching the parcels brought to me,
My mode of life, my personal mail,
And hoping most malignantly
That shortly shall those payments fail:
Whereat the bailiffs at his side

258

Unseen, like unseen creditor Death,
Shall claim their writ, hearth, home, and hide,
In lieu of merchandise, my breath.

PSALM 171

A PSALM OF ABRAHAM CONCERNING THE
ARROGANCE OF THE SON OF MAN

Consider this creature, its peculiar pride,
This braggart loud in his invented brag!
Is he not weaker than the ant, and than the dog
Duller, and than the ape but little better bred?

Yet is he arrogant: the orbit of the stars,
The wandering planets, the most marvellous sky,
Nor yet this weird earth, this terrible sea,
Induce humility in his orgulous course.

However, not all souls are violins
Evocative of music at the touch.
Indeed, there be some that no sage could teach
Nor any subtlety break through their chalky bones.

But Man, Man, Man, who perforce daily
Must in the privy take your humble seat,
A bencher of the jakes, slave to a gut,
How do you still esteem yourself, grand noble, holy?

PSALM 172

A PSALM OF ABRAHAM, PRAYING A GREEN OLD AGE

I who have expiated life in cities,
Whose lungs have inhaled dust and noisome oils,
Whose ears have heard no bird's or cricket's ditties,
Whose eyes have only surmised fruitful soils,

I who have merely guessed the bird's existence
By sparrow-droppings on the brim of a hat,
I am that one who now, with meek persistence
Pray humbly to the Lord of Eden, that

I may in such green sunny places pass
The ultimate years that when at last I leave,
My shoes be smooth with unguent of crushed grass
And green be on the elbow of my sleeve.

PSALM 173

A PSALM OF ABRAHAM OF THAT WHICH IS VISITED UPON HIM

A prowler in the mansion of my blood!
I have not seen him, but I know his signs.
Sometimes I hear him meddling with my food,
Or in the cellar, poisoning my wines.

Yet face to face with him I never come;
But by a footprint, by a book misplaced,
Or by the imprint of an inky thumb,
Or by the next day's meal, its sombre taste,

I know that he has breached my household peace.
I know that somehow he has let him in.
Shall I fling open a window, and shout *police!*
I dare not. He is of my kith and kin.

PSALM 175

A PSALM OF RESIGNATION

I shall no more complain; I shall not ask
The question that betrays the doubting soul.
Tactful my words, my face shall be a mask.
I shall say the flaws are part of the perfect whole.
Can it be otherwise?
For I am weary of the quarrel with my God,
Weary of cavilling at the works of the Lord;
For who indeed can keep his quarrel hot
And vigorous his cries,
When He who is blasphemed, He answers not,
Replies no word, not even a small sharp word?

BALLAD OF THE NUREMBERG
TOWER-CLOCK

Nuremberg tower-clock struck one:
The swastika clawed at the sun.

Ring wrong! Ring wrong! The clock struck two:
Behind a curtain trembled a Jew.

Nuremberg tower-clock struck three:
Storm-troopers shouted blasphemy,

And as the public square did roar
The clock-hands heiled, and they heiled four!

The herald, as the clock struck five,
Read out the purged from the old archive.

The Fuehrer's words, vulpine, prolix,
Annulled the song of the hour of six.

Indeed, they blared and shouted, even
As Nuremberg clock heckled: *seven.*

Somewhere, as Nuremberg clock showed eight,
With crumbs a burgher wiped his plate.

A poet, at the hour of nine,
Thought, in his cell, of the beautiful Rhine.

O, in their sleep the clock struck ten:
Men stirred in a dream of murdered men.

Gestapo music rose to heaven:
The clock, delirious, struck eleven,—

And in that last eleventh chime
Expired, as did human time.

BALLAD OF QUISLINGS

Poltroons may fear the foeman, for such are less than cattle,
But men will fear no other man who can be met in battle,
Where courage and the claymore cut apart the bitter quarrel,
Awarding one the willow, and the other one the laurel.

For the enemy who marches to the beating of his drum,
Men take their several stances: *Let him come! Let him come!*
But where shall men take counsel that they may not be beblitzed
By the renegade, the falseface, the traitor in our midst?

O not from stranger hostile, but from that cordial native
Who rattles for a pleasant noise the shackles of the caitiff,
Preserve us, and protect us, and from our congregation
Uproot him, mask and members, and fling him to damnation!

O from the subtle traitor and double-damned knave,
Inhaling breath of freeman, exhaling speech of slave,
Protect us, and Lord, save us, for we are weak before
The enemy, with roses, a-standing at our door!

For how shall men of goodwill discern his parrot-screech?
And how discern the weasel wrapt in his weasel-speech?
Is not his loud toast proffered? His hand in friendship up?
And how surmise the dagger, or poison in the cup?

God grant he be found out, and he *be* found soon thereafter
A-hanging, a fifth column, from taut rope and broad rafter,
His soul go up in sulphur, and he go out a-sizzling,
To that place where no horses are, nor any unsinged quisling!

BALLAD OF THE NURSERY RHYMES

Upon a day, and after the roar had died,
And the dust had settled, and the cities were no more,
He sat him down, alone, in a world that was wide,
As wide as is to a child his nursery floor.

And he sang all alone remembered snatches of song,
He wandered with the wandering of his mind:
Hey-diddle-diddle, and the music all gone wrong,
And the old clock turned by three mice that were blind.

His small voice cracked as he sang Cock Robin dead,
And twenty-four birds who mourned him from a pie,
And Simple Simon, begging his rationed bread,
And the poor dame whose ducks did always die.

O sad was his song when he sang Jack's tumbled crown,
And Jill who fell in channel from frying-pan,
And all the bridges that were broken down,
And fee-fi-fum, the bloods of the race of man.

And when night fell, night found him singing still:
The sheep's in the meadow, the wolf is in the corn,
And Humpty-Dumpty on a bombed window-sill,
Watching the moon, and the hornets on its horn.

POLISH VILLAGE

At length, the peasant, plodding from the woods,
Came on his village, emptied of its folk,
Save for his sisters, weeping behind their hoods,
And his father's broken body, hanging from the oak.

In his sisters' weeping, he heard no Polish phrase.
They did not name the murderers, nor sob: *why*.
They showed him geese walking their arrogant ways
And wheelmarks following the road to a broken sky.

He wept, and to his holy church he ran,
And stood before the figure of Christ, and saw
O those dear wrists re-broken! the newly-bleeding Man!
Jesus recrucified into a swastika!

VARIATION OF A THEME

Enamort have I been of bleaseful Death,
Knelled him soft names in manes a muted rhyme;
Or, vault-face, trumpeted my herald breath
Into Gold Gotha echoes of his fame:
The Lord of Ghosts; the Imperor of Bearse;
Rex Tumulus; great Sherasod the Prince;
Menhir von Wrinklemop; Barow de Hearse;
Le Comte de Funct; von Waggoner, C. G.; Sire Mintz.

Mr. O. Topsy-Turf, of Cher Noel House;
The Mausolem, Sir Koph-Ag, L.A.G.;
That mandarin chap Suo Seid; the Russ
Undone Checkofsky; Ripper R. I. P.;
Sven Swansong; Harry Carey, Samurai;
Nick Ropoulos; Regratter Abie Taff;
The Cryptic Patriark; Chief Wenanwei;
Allover Cromlech; Rotter Doestanasher, graph.

O I have skald his eili-aces rite,
And conjoured him in alles shapes and garbs,—
As heirold in black ossuary dight,
As Abbot Ware, as Coopèd haeming barbs,
As Myster Wynken brinken nods; I've seen
Hymn in his cere-monies and costumes, yea
As houriental djinn, of yestern mien,
As mielancholy Dane, and aye as Francheman gai.

His gags, his joker-knots, his escapades,
His bower, his mite, they monsternate me not.
I know his tryx, the way-pence of his trades,—
He has been sybilled blacker than he wrot.
I do not fear him, and it may well be
That I aspyre his embrass, would cry:
"Acain my brooder, comes to call for me,
And more than ever, mortal, it seems rich to die!"

SENNET FROM GHEEL

And these touched thunders, this delyredrum
Outbrasting boom from shekels of cracked steel
Arrave the whirled goon dapht, as zany in Gheel!
Mad as a hater, come, Nick knows warfrom!
Bedlam, Bicetre, and hundemonium
Are compos and sain compared to the unweal
Of these wildbats that frap in belfrydom!
Or are these horrorbingers we are guerred
And hale in Gheel, and lucid like the rest,
As good and woad as other humus merde?
If so, sweet Lord of Hosts, kind exorcist,
Fling us, un-levined, back to whence we erred,
Zuruck to our lunasylum of the blest.

COME TWO, LIKE SHADOWS

Out of the yesterday, and ages gone
Come two, like shadows on a bedroom wall,
To haggle for the psychic jettison.
It is a mighty wrestling, by my soul,
And which shall garner, at the very last
The paltry winnings, I can not foretell,
Nor which of the shadows shall give up the ghost.

Plato is one whose shadow I surmise
As one surmises the man behind a screen.
His words, however, phosphoric, to my eyes—
From whom, to whom, and what they nobly mean,—
Love that is fleshless, passion that is dry—
Betray the spirit come to keep me clean,
Clean,—tropical only in philosophy.

266

That other shadow has a bedside manner.
He holds my wrist; he bids me speak out *Ah;*
Tell him about the dream of the crimson banner
And of the carnivorous ladies that dream saw.
—O, they are two in a surrealist void
Who haunt me: Plato and his shaven jaw,
And the pudendal face of Doctor Freud.

AND IN THAT DROWNING INSTANT

And in that drowning instant as
the water heightened over me
it suddenly did come to pass
my preterite eternity
the image of myself intent
on several freedoms

   fading to
myself in yellowed basel-print
vanishing

   into ghetto Jew
a face among the faces of
the rapt disciples hearkening
the raptures of the Baalshem Tov
explaining Torah

   vanishing
amidst the water's flickering green
to show me in old Amsterdam
which topples

   into a new scene
Cordova where an Abraham
faces inquisitors

the face
is suddenly beneath an arch
whose Latin script the waves erase
and flashes now the backward march
of many

   I among them

     to
Jerusalem-gate and Temple-door!

For the third time my body rises
And finds the good, the lasting shore!

DESIDERATUM

I am no contradictor of Cabbala:
that there are nerves two hundred forty-eight—
couriers through the forest of the flesh—
is sure arithmetic, and sacred; that
organs and limbs three hundred sixty-five
give motion to this Adam's also granted;
and that these two corporeal sums add up—
gematria inspired and symbolic—
to number the six hundred and thirteen
edicts of Holy Writ, is truth most glorious!

          Yet
I would these limbs were separable, these
members divisible from their heap o'bones:
a realm compact of sovereign entities,
the body's Powers, Dominations, Thrones,
all regnant for themselves, not galley-slaves
fettered unto the simultaneous oars.
Aye, where there stood one lonely worshipper,
six hundred thirteen would run godly chores!
And this were immortality man craves!

Instance this much-desired case: the skull
though severed from unbleeding shoulders, lives.
Severed, it ambulates to some green knoll,
its eyes upon the blessed sunshine thrives,
its ears, they are two beings all of sound,
its mouth, though throatless, speaks; its sheathed brain,
a watch whose tickings were in heaven wound,
unwinding Time . . .
                                    The severed body? Let
that body, headless, go about its business,
     its grosser tasks, ejaculate, excrete,
     digest, perspire, micturate. The head
     knows no dependence, lives!

PENULTIMATE CHAPTER

The carefully-evolved and cultured tribes
     Moved blithely in their habitats and keels,
Superior in the scripture of their scribes,
     And safe in discovered fire, invented wheels.

Foretold by neither seer nor seismograph,
     The imminent earthquake of ancestral mires
Stilled not their boast, nor falsified their laugh.
     Closeted were the skeletons of their sires!

Buried; but, in the frightening-fauna'd rock,
     The dry bones quickened, in the nether plain
Stirred, and grew scales, and yearned once more to stalk
     The lesser prey. The strata burst!

                              Again
The winged reptiles in their slimy hosts,
     Their beaks saw-toothed, and their wingspread claw'd,
Swooped on the men who fled them, crying:
                    Ghosts!
     Our wild progenitors have left their sod!

269

They fled to their coasts. Out of the wallowing sea
    The ichthyosaurus! The pigmies stood unmanned
Before the horrific stare of ancestry.
    They scurried back upon the higher land—
Only to meet hooves' thunder, lightning tusks:
    Titanothere and tetrabelodon!

Terror unkerneled the dry human husks.

    The mammoths (circa 1951) . . .

ACTUARIAL REPORT

We, the undersigned
Magi of your actuarial staff
Having examined the data of the year
And drawn therefrom the hereto-appended graph
(The hanging gardens of Death, shown tier by tier)
Regretfully prognosticate a rising trend:
They will increase, our policy-holders,
Doomed to an untimely end.
We have seen the medical certificates
Guessing the cause of death; we have examined
The corpses slabbed in our filing cabinets;
We have deduced the necessary deductions.
The incidence of earthquake has been studied,
Not overlooked are pestilence and dangerous intersections.
The act of God is equated;
And the will-to-self-destruction (two premiums paid)
Is also calculated.
        Had there, however, been only these
Funereal figures on our adding-machines
It would have been easy; to wit, the status quo.
There was to be considered, unfortunately,
A state of hostilities.
It is true, of course, we have the saving war-clause.

270

Nonetheless, there are risks, perils, and bad luck
Remote from the battlefields, but laying
The dead hand on our deeds.
Such are anxiety, trouble at home, measured rations
The abnormalities of separation; in fine
General absence from felicity.
Accordingly, we have taken the measurements, and we know
The steps of death are hastened. He comes with bodyguard:
Famine, disease, and other motley personages.
His ingenuities are increased. He moves with up-to-date motion,
Certainly he gets about more than he has of recent years.
    Our contracts begin to have his personal smell. And we
    Have become the keepers of his diary.
Sirs, we had much rather come back from our spying
To say, like magi of old,
A son is born.
Regrettably, all that we can see for the present fiscal year
Is many a father dying.

AUTOBIOGRAPHICAL

Out of the ghetto streets where a Jewboy
Dreamed pavement into pleasant Bible-land,
Out of the Yiddish slums where childhood met
The friendly beard, the loutish Sabbath-goy,
Or followed, proud, the Torah-escorting band,
Out of the jargoning city I regret,
Rise memories, like sparrows rising from
The gutter-scattered oats,
Like sadness sweet of synagogal hum,
Like Hebrew violins
Sobbing delight upon their Eastern notes.

Again they ring their little bells, those doors
Deemed by the tender-year'd, magnificent:
Old Ashkenazi's cellar, sharp with spice;

The widows' double-parloured candy-stores
And nuggets sweet bought for one sweaty cent;
The warm fresh-smelling bakery, its pies,
Its cakes, its navel'd bellies of black bread;
The lintels candy-poled
Of barber-shop, bright-bottled, green, blue, red;
And fruit-stall piled, exotic,
And the big synagogue door, with letters of gold.

Again my kindergarten home is full—
Saturday night—with kin and compatriot:
My brothers playing Russian card-games; my
Mirroring sisters looking beautiful,
Humming the evening's imminent fox-trot;
My uncle Mayer, of blessed memory,
Still murmuring *maariv,* counting holy words;
And the two strangers, come
Fiery from Volhynia's murderous hordes—
The cards and humming stop.
And I too swear revenge for that pogrom.

Occasions dear: the four-legged *aleph* named
And angel pennies dropping on my book;
The rabbi patting a coming scholar-head;
My mother, blessing candles, Sabbath-flamed,
Queenly in her Warsovian perruque;
My father pickabacking me to bed
To tell tall tales about the Baal Shem Tov—
Letting me curl his beard.
Oh memory of unsurpassing love,
Love leading a brave child
Through childhood's ogred corridors, unfear'd!

The week in the country at my brother's—(May
He own fat cattle in the fields of heaven!)
Its picking of strawberries from grassy ditch,
Its odour of dogrose and of yellowing hay—
Dusty, adventurous, sunny days, all seven!—
Still follow me, still warm me, still are rich
With the cow-tinkling peace of pastureland.

272

The meadow'd memory
Is sodded with its clover, and is spanned
By that same pillow'd sky
A boy on his back one day watched enviously.

And paved again the street: the shouting boys,
Oblivious of mothers on the stoops,
Playing the robust robbers and police,
The corncob battle—all high-spirited noise
Competitive among the lot-drawn groups.
Another day, of shaken apple trees
In the rich suburbs, and a furious dog,
And guilty boys in flight;
Hazelnut games, and games in the synagogue—
The burrs, the Haman rattle,
The Torah dance on Simchas Torah night.

Immortal days of the picture calendar
Dear to me always with the virgin joy
Of the first flowering of senses five,
Discovering birds, or textures, or a star,
Or tastes sweet, sour, acid, those that cloy;
And perfumes. Never was I more alive.
All days thereafter are a dying off,
A wandering away
From home and the familiar. The years doff
Their innocence.
No other day is ever like that day.

I am no old man fatuously intent
On memories, but in memory I seek
The strength and vividness of nonage days,
Not tranquil recollection of event.
It is a fabled city that I seek;
It stands in Space's vapours and Time's haze;
Thence comes my sadness in remembered joy
Constrictive of the throat;
Thence do I hear, as heard by a Jewboy,
The Hebrew violins,
Delighting in the sobbed Oriental note.

273

THAT LEGENDARY EAGLE, DEATH

Somewhere above the innocent clouds there flies
The legendary eagle. Never yet
Have I beheld him. I have heard his cries.
And once his shadow and my shadow met.
I fear the vengeful king who sent him up!
Those claws are curled about the stones of our feud!
When will those stones fall, and that king eavesdrop
Upon the echoings of my splattered blood?
Often I hoped to make my enemy sad,
Impatient in his windy turret for
News of the eagle, and none to be had—
Lost in the skies, dead on the ocean floor.
I therefore aimed, by shadow and by call,
My arrows at what I thought his wings of jet.
The arrows rose. The eagle did not fall.
That wrathful king will have his vengeance yet.

NOT ALL THE PERFUMES OF ARABIA

Version I

Undoubtedly terror may through the widened eyes
Enter the heart, as image enters mirror;
As poison into the ears of royal Denmark
Through portals of the ears may enter Terror;—
But the real horror, the truly shuddering *nefas*
Is surely particled on the scented dust,
Is surely through the nostrils made to pass
Through the duct whispering, through the stealthy vein
Meandering, at length to thrust
Its cry of havoc into the haunted brain!

Even now, as the broadcaster at the regular hour
Announces his name, the place of his gadgets, and
His historic theme:
The evil currencies of the bloodied land—
It is not words I hear,
Nor are they sights I see,
I smell the smell of fear.

Sevastopol: and fee-fi-fum
Cordite and lilac odours fill
This powder-pollinated room;
And from each sailor-syllable
Rises upon the spindrift foam
The large green ocean-water smell.

The stukas of his speech dive down—
The dust of rubble stifles! Doom
That slinks in nether Paris-town
Evokes the stench of sewer scum;
And Hellas of the white renown
The starving mouth's effluvium!

The little panic smell of sweat
Of men who stand against a wall
Awaiting the twelve-muzzled threat—
Is that fetor judaical?
The fragrance *herrenvolk* beget?
Or is this musk dispersed from hell?

The voice of the announcer, like Mephisto's in the play
Crackles and dies.—Within the vibrating room,—
Fear, and the brimstone fume.

NOT ALL THE PERFUMES OF ARABIA

Version II

Undoubtedly terror may through the widened eyes
enter the heart, as image enters mirror;
As poison into the ears of royal Denmark
through portals of the ears may enter Terror;—
but the real horror, the truly shuddering *nefas*
surely is through the nostrils made to pass,
is inhaled, surely, and as an odour—pulver of pain!—
whirls havoc in the brain!

Even now, as the broadcaster at the regular hour
announces his name, the place of his gadgets, and
his historic theme:
They are not words I hear
nor are they sights I see,
I smell the smell of fear.

See where the mushroom
curls corruption on the air!
Shall scents and attars
avail there?

DENTIST

The planetary motion of the blood,
Also the peregrinations of routine,
And the bright pendulum of dialectic,
        All go awry,
Lose their direction and their polarhood
        Before the keen
Weltschmerz residing in a cavity!

276

Sometimes, in such a dire case, this man—
He of the aloe'd pellets against pain—
Has been to my anguish—antiseptic Hero!
   But now, to-day,
I know him different, clumsy Caliban,
   Narcoticized brain,
Gloating with pincers over my dismay!

The panic of his nightmare's still with me,
This ogre of the hypodermic claws,
Smelling of novocaine and drugged mayhem,
   Knee on my chest,
Still runs amok among the ivory,
   Distorts my jaws,
Still keeps my gurgled havoc unexpressed!

May thirty-two curses blight that torturer!
May his gums soften! May he lose his friends
Turning in silence from his exhalations!
   His tinsel wreath
Fall from his mouth, abscessed, with clotted gore
   At its forked ends!
Thirty-two curses on his thirty-two teeth!

Pity he cries? May only thirty-one
Of those foul nibs slip away from their gummy curves,
Leaving his food in lumps, uncut, unmolar'd
   For belly's sake—
And may one canine, comic and alone,
   And quick with nerves,
Remain—his *weltschmerz* and his livelong ache!

BASIC ENGLISH

(To Winston Churchill)

Of trope of testament and Caesar's wars
       Grand rhetor, voice
       Of warrior-days,
Not you, I thought, would give the lion's nod
To these eight hundred laboratory mice
Scrawny with fasting, certainly not you
       Of the armada'd phrase!

Exporters' argot, small talk of small trade,
       The agent's slang
       Bartering beads,
This is the very speech of nursery blocks,
Pidgin palaver, grunt of Caliban,
By no means the awaited syllables
       For even lesser breeds.

Reducing motion to mere come and go,
       Narrowing act
       To give and get,
Flowers no longer flower in the mind;
Fades from the eyes nuance; and eloquence
Sticks in the throat. The dumb are merely raised
       To the inarticulate.

Exhausted well of English, and defiled—
       Is it with this
       Semantic spray
You would baptize the cultured continents?
Shall Europe judge and Asia esteem
The wassail liquor of our English speech
       From this, the don's weak tea?

In jargoning ports, perhaps, in jungle-river,
       One may make use
       Of such boned gauds:
The drummer, bringing flag and bargain, may

So dragoman himself, perhaps, and thus
Close his shrewd deal,—but only after many
Gestures, head-shakes, nods.

For lettered nations this desesperanto?
For races that
Boast alphabet,
And song and synonym and subtlety?
Amused, but polite, the city-dwellers smile;
And that good-will these mumbos were to breed
We neither—give nor get.

For where among the vocables, castrate
Of Saxon strength,
O Sponsor, where
The Hellenic music or the Latin storm?
Where are the thunders of our choric voice?
And where is Shakespeare's scope and Milton's reach?
Your words triphibian, where?

Basic as bread, and English as all water—
These bread-and-water
Calories
Are not for men unpainted and in clothes!
O, rather for loincloth on some fronded isle,
Trading at beach, or at the mission chanting—
These skimmed simplicities!

Orator, organist of history,—
Much mightier tones
Have we to sound
Than these flat octaves, playing sad or glad.
Ours is a sweeping measure, resonant,
And destined, for its splendours, not its strictures,
To be renowned!

LOVE

Love, love, love,
O lyric-love, half-angel and half slut!
Uncleanest of the four-saxon-littered herd!
Foul euphemism of the apes in rut!
Laundered obscenity, the figleaf word
To hide the ambush of the treacherous gut!

It moves the sun and all the stars, this love.
Much pullulation goes on in its name.
Even reserved men wear it, with a glove.
All flatter the wench to believe herself grand dame.

The lady evangelist cries *Love:* the poet, too,
Passionate that his name be writ in water;
The playboy, likewise; and the salesman-crew
Roaming the country for the farmer's daughter.

All, all, testiculate their urgent throes:
June bridal cars sounding priapic horns,
The Ripper Jack whose luve's a red red rose,
And the monorchid, valiant among thorns.

O, oyster-swallowing gents and oat-ripe boys,
Always the jubilee turns jeremiad,
For after the long planning, brief the joys,
And after, always, every man is sad.

SPRING EXHIBIT

How pleasant are the times and their cezannes,
But pleasanter than all, the thyme of spring!
Blooms dilly-tanty fresco through God's manse,
And through its galaries, birds on the wing!
Van-terre is gone, white fogey criticans;
The paintillest buds at last are burgeoning.

280

Manet from heaven falls upon the plane
Where little fauns go fralipping the grass.
Again the babbling breukels flow, again
Riveros mighty move where marble was.
Gone is the glassic ice; the root-men reign;
The whorled is new, in fern, and furze, and grass.

Herald the vangogh of the year, its colour, flash!
O are these trees or but a dream of trees?
These flowers, of vermeils bold, chrome yellows brash,—
The world's sweet sistine day! the field's louvrese!
Youth in plenair, with all things green and fresh,
Unchagalled days in primotif release!

THE LIBRARY

On leather, beneath rafters, beside oak,
we sat and talked only of *amor intellectualis*.
The books, at their stances, on the mounting wall,
gold-lettered, crested, red,
like seventh-generation lackeys stood:
dumb, high-blood-pressured, seen and not heard. Progress
was air in that room, refinement, and soft manners:
the original robber baron bred down to
sweetness and tungsten.

His opinions were sensitive, his gestures fine,
fine, and like his cigarettes were monogrammed.
The culture of the best schools, to wit, morals and sport,
worn neatly, like his clothes.
He sighed,—from the world's lung. He had *weltschmerz*,
like a painless disease. Thinkers he quoted,
and was pure reason; poets, and was kind.
Even the blood moving his vocal cords
seemed an intrusion.

281

Yet suddenly, and for no reason at all,
his temper changed, and all his breeding sloughed,
Swiss governess and English tutor dead,
—or more than ever alive?—
it was a cinema-change. As if the books were boards,
and, at a button, had slid away, revealing
bars, and behind, cement—his secret—where wild beasts
yawned, and waved paw, circled, ran forward, reared
for the week's meat.

ADDRESS TO THE CHOIRBOYS

Another moon, and the penitential days
Will be upon us.
                   There are many signs:
My mother following her mother's ways,
Keeping two fasts the week; the ram's horn blown
Each morning, pastoral, on the city air;
The tombstone maker dusty with his stone;
And every evening, from the practising choir,
The song of the Cantor, teaching downy boys
The cantillation of the sacred prayer.

> *O Lord, thou art my Judge and Prosecutor!*
> *The Keeper of the Book which reads itself,*
> *Witness who has seen all, remembering.*

The sorrow of Rabbi Amnon made that song!
A sad and bitter day it was
That day they bore him to the House of God,
His legs cut off, that were so fleet, so strong
To serve their Maker, lopped those holy arms
That wound and wore phylacteries,—cut off:
The corners of his world, outpouring blood!

"Abjure thy faith, and there's an end to strife!"
And Rabbi Amnon—

(O but this flesh, this stalk, these leaves and petals
Do so desire life!)
The Rabbi stayed in hesitation
Between the pity of children, and his father's pride,
And hesitated.
And only, at length, defied!

> *Let us give strength to holiness this day,*
> *This day being terror-full, and full of doom,*
> *And therein raise Thy mighty Majesty.*

Therefore, these stumps, they were the Lord's dictate—
Not any that small arrogant man could utter—
Punishment for unfaith which hesitates.

Like the white petals of an eastern bloom
His limbs torn off, and he that flower, dying
The rabbi hears above him flutter
The wings of angels, angels sighing
Softly his doom.

> *O they are at the year's beginning written*
> *And on the fast day of atonement sealed:*
> *Who pass away, and who shall come to pass,*
> *Who at his time, and who before his time;*
> *Who through the death by water, who through the death*
> *By sword, by fire, by ferocious beast.*

Sing on, ye innocent choirboys, this song
The sorrow of Rabbi Amnon made
Against a day like ours, like ours a wrong!
Sing, in your innocence, O milk-sweet voices
Smooth like your cheeks your song,
Your cherry lips know nothing yet of sorrow
And only music in your throat rejoices
Nor are the tragic phrases tragic on your tongue.
O let no lips dare tell you of their meaning—
Their burden of sorrow, their weight of suffering—
But in your innocence warble, lean white throats,
And in your young unknowing jubilations, sing.

THE GOLEM

This is the golem.
He is wooden, and he is painted brown.
In walking, he carefully lifts each foot
As if to kick it out of muck
The mechanism in his throat goes cluck-cluck-cluck.
His dexter, at the hailed word, goes up and down.
Upon his upper lip, six hairs are stuck.

This is the golem.
The rabbi Nubal and his holy vessels
With pious incantation gave this clod
The strength wherewith he wrestles.
He was to serve none other but their god,
And save them from the bear of the human walk:
A hewer of wood—to keep their Sabbath hot;
A drawer of water—to fill his master's crock.

The incantation, alas, was too well wrought.
The golem ran amok!
                                        He ran amok,
And all Bohemia's forests did not suffice
For his mad hewing; before his drawing of water
The rivers trembled. Had they turned to ice—

Mortified rabbi, how will you now undo
Your doing? How revoke your invocation,
Saving you call again the abjured spell:
The horns of iron, the bladed chariot, the satanic chemical?

SONNET UNRHYMED

When, on the frustral summit of *extase*,
—the leaven of my loins to no life spent,
yet vision, as all senses, sharper,—I
peer the vague forward and flawed prism of Time,
many the bodies, my own birthmark bearing,
and many the faces, like my face, I see:
shadows of generation looking backward
and crying *Abba* in the muffled night.

They beg creation. From the far centuries
they move against the vacuum of their murder,
yes, and their eyes are full of such reproach
that although tired, I do wake, and watch
upon the entangled branches of the dark
my sons, my sons, my hanging Absaloms.

NI LA MORT NI LE SOLEIL

(On a maxim of de la Rochefoucauld)

Neither on death, nor at the blazing sun
Can mortal gaze
Without being blinded by the one
As by the other's rays:
They are two fascinations eyes reject,
Looking, yet loth
To fix themselves upon the sight elect—
Brightworlds both.

DOCTOR DRUMMOND

It is to be wondered whether he ever really
saw them, whether he knew them more than type,
whether, in fact, his occupational fun—
the doctor hearty over his opened grip—
did not confuse him into deducing
his patients' health and Irish from his own.

Certainly from his gay case-histories
that now
for two-tongued get-togethers are elocutional,
one would never have recognized his clientele.

Consider this patrician patronizing the *patois,*
consider his *habitants,* the homespun of their minds and motives,
characters out of comical Quebec,
of speech neither Briton nor Breton, a fable folk,
a second class of aborigines,
docile, domesticate, very good employees,
so meek that even their sadness
made dialect for a joke.

One can well imagine the doctor,
in club, in parlour, or in smoking car,
building out of his practice a reputation
as raconteur.
But the true pulsing of their blood
his beat ignores,
and of the temperature of their days, the chills
of their despairs, the fevers of their faith,
his mercury is silent.

THE WHITE OLD LADY

The panic jangles repeated themselves every year.
The neighbours, clutching the black cup, whispered *Police!*
The Cote des Neiges place again! Lights come on, lights go off!
    She is here!

And every evening the sergeant, wearily: Police.
And heard: She is standing at all of the windows at once.
She is pulling down white blinds, but we see her shadow.
    Monstrosities

go on in that house. The sergeant takes evidence.
Report: Someone anaemic is going whitely mad.
Ditto: That dwelling is a smuggling place for lepers,
    A cache for diamonds.

A smoke-filled den. Seek there your missing and dead—
muffled by linens, cased in the white plaster wall.
Visitors, we know, have come unseen, and there's vice
    that can't be said.

But every time the police came, stepped into the hall,
there was only a white old lady, frail, like powder,
with a pleasant smile, living alone, and no one
    else at all.

O GOD! O MONTREAL

These were but innuendo:
Louis Frechette, poet, assigning in bankruptcy,
and Butler in the Gallery of Art
(discobuli jockstrapped and brassiered nymphs),

Our century's explicit.
The scale of wages
of the municipal employees of the City of Montreal
                    Concordia Salus
ranks the librarian (assistant) just below
the first-class stableman.

Whoa, Pegasus!

MEDITATION UPON SURVIVAL

At times, sensing that the golgotha'd dead
run plasma through my veins, and that I must live
their unexpired six million circuits, giving
to each of their nightmares my body for a bed—
inspirited, dispirited—
those times that I feel their death-wish bubbling the
channels of my blood—
I grow bitter at my false felicity—
the spared one—and would almost add my wish
for the centigrade furnace and the cyanide flood.

However, one continues to live, though mortally.
O, like some frightened, tattered, hysterical man
run to a place of safety—the whole way run—
whose lips, now frenzy-foamed, now delirium-dry
cry out the tenses of the verb to die.
cry love, cry loss, being asked: *And yet unspilled
your own blood?* weeps, and makes
his stuttering innocence a kind of guilt—
O, like that man am I, bereaved and suspect,
convicted with the news my mourning breaks.

Us they have made the monster, made that thing
that lives though cut in three: the severed head
which breathes, looks on, hears, thinks, weeps, and is bled
continuously with a drop by drop longing

288

for its members' re-membering!
And, the torn torso, spilling heart and lights
and the cathartic dregs!
These, for the pit! Upon the roads, the flights—
—O how are you reduced, my people, cut down to a limb!—
upon the roads the flights of the bodiless legs.

Myself to recognize: a curio;
the atavism of some old coin's face;
one who, though watched and isolate, does go—
the last point of a diminished race—
the way of the fletched buffalo.
Gerundive of extinct. An original.
What else, therefore, to do
but leave these bones that are not ash to fill—
O not my father's vault—but the glass-case
some proud museum catalogues *Last Jew*.

A PSALM OF HORSES AND THEIR RIDERS

Chivalric more than knight on charger black;
More gallant than stiff lancer on groom steed;
Than the proud emir on the camel's back,
Kinglier; wiser than mage on mule knock-kneed;
Fleeter than he who lashed the horse that stalked
Out of the stables of King Solomon;
Nobler than Hindoo in his howdah rocked;
Stranger than centaur mounted by a faun,
Or wizard clutching hippogriffin throat,
Is this blithe waif who canters through the town,
His both feet stirruped in goat's beard, fists on horns,
Saddled upon the nape of his tamed goat!

ELEGY

Named for my father's father, cousin, whose cry
Might have been my cry lost in that dark land—
Where shall I seek you? On what wind shall I
Reach out to touch the ash that was your hand?
The Atlantic gale and the turning of the sky
Unto the cubits of my ambience
Scatter the martyr-motes. Flotsam-of-flame!
God's image made the iotas of God's name!
Oh, through a powder of ghosts I walk; through dust
Seraphical upon the dark winds borne;
Daily I pass among the sieved white hosts,
Through clouds of cousinry transgress,
Maculate with the ashes that I mourn.

Where shall I seek you? There's not anywhere
A tomb, a mound, a sod, a broken stick,
Marking the sepulchres of those sainted ones
The dogfaced hid in tumuli of air.
O cousin, cousin, you are everywhere!
And in your death, in your ubiquity,
Bespeak them all, our sundered cindered kin:
David, whose cinctured bone—
Young branch once wreathed in phylactery!—
Now hafts the peasant's bladed kitchenware;
And the dark Miriam murdered for her hair;
The relicts nameless; and the tattoo'd skin
Fevering from lampshade in a cultured home—
All, all our gaunt skull-shaven family—
The faces are my face! that lie in lime,
You bring them, jot of horror, here to me,
Them, and the slow eternity of despair
That tore them, and did tear them out of time.

Death may be beautiful, when full of years,
Ripe with good works, a man, among his sons,
Says his last word, and turns him to the wall.
But not these deaths! Oh, not these weighted tears!

290

The flesh of Thy sages, Lord, flung prodigal
To the robed fauna with their tubes and shears;
Thy chosen for a gold tooth chosen; for
The pervert's wetness, flesh beneath the rod—
Death multitudinous as their frustrate spore!—
This has been done to us, Lord, thought-lost God;
And things still hidden, and unspeakable more.

A world is emptied. Marked is that world's map
The forest colour. There where Thy people praised
In angular ecstasy Thy name, Thy Torah
Is less than a whisper of its thunderclap.
Thy synagogues, rubble. Thy academies,
Bright once with Talmud brow and musical
With song alternative in exegesis,
Are silent, dark. They are laid waste, Thy cities,
Once festive with Thy fruit-full calendar,
And where Thy curled and caftan'd congregations
Danced to the first days and the second star,
Or made the marketplaces loud and green
To welcome in the Sabbath Queen;
Or through the nights sat sweet polemical
With Rav and Shmuail (also of the slain)—
Oh, there where dwelt the thirty-six—world's pillars!—
And tenfold Egypt's generation, there
Is nothing, nothing . . . only the million echoes
Calling Thy name still trembling on the air.

Look down, O Lord, from Thy abstracted throne!
Look down! Find out this Sodom to the sky
Rearing and solid on a world atilt
The architecture by its pillars known.
This circle breathed hundreds; that round, thousands—
And from among the lesser domes descry
The style renascent of Gomorrah built.
See where the pyramids
Preserve our ache between their angled tons:
Pass over, they have been excelled. Look down
On the Greek marble that our torture spurned—
The white forgivable stone.

291

The arch and triumph of subjection, pass;
The victor, too, has passed; and all these spires
At whose foundations, dungeoned, the screw turned
Inquisitorial, now overlook—
They were delirium and sick desires.
But do not overlook, oh pass not over
The hollow monoliths. The vengeful eye
Fix on these pylons of the sinister sigh,
The well-kept chimneys daring towards the sky!
From them, now innocent, no fumes do rise.
They yawn to heaven. It is their ennui:
Too much the slabs and ovens, and too many
The man-shaped loaves of sacrifice!

As Thou didst do to Sodom, do to them!
But not, O Lord, in one destruction. Slow,
Fever by fever, limb by withering limb,
Destroy! Send through the marrow of their bones,
The pale treponeme burrowing. Let there grow
Over their eyes a film that they may see
Always a carbon sky! Feed them on ash!
Condemn them double deuteronomy!
All in one day pustule their speech with groans,
Their bodies with the scripture of a rash,
With boils and buboes their suddenly breaking flesh!
When their dams litter, monsters be their whelp,
Unviable! Themselves, may each one dread,
The touch of his fellow, and the infected help
Of the robed fauna with their tubes and shears!
Fill up their days with funerals and fears!
Let madness shake them—rooted down—like kelp.
And as their land is emptying, and instructed,
The nations cordon the huge lazaret—
The paring of Thy little fingernail
Drop down: the just circuitings of flame,
And as Gomorrah's name, be their cursed name!

Not for the judgment sole, but for a sign
Effect, O Lord, example and decree,
A sign, the final shade and witness joined
To the shadowy witnesses who once made free

292

With that elected folk Thou didst call Thine.
Before my mind, still unconsoled, there pass
The pharaohs risen from the Red Sea sedge,
Profiled; in alien blood and peonage
Hidalgos lost; shadows of Shushan; and
The Assyrian uncurling into sand;
Most untriumphant frieze! and darkly pass
The shades Seleucid; dark against blank white
The bearded ikon-bearing royalties—
All who did waste us, insubstantial now,
A motion of the mind. Oh, unto these
Let there be added, soon, as on a screen,
The shadowy houndface, barking, never heard,
But for all time a lore and lesson, seen,
And heeded; and thence, of Thy will our peace.

Vengeance is thine, O Lord, and unto us
In a world wandering, amidst raised spears
Between wild waters, and against barred doors,
There are no weapons left. Where now but force
Prevails, and over the once blest lagoons
Mushroom new Sinais, sole defensive is
The face turned east, and the uncompassed prayer.
Not prayer for the murdered myriads who
Themselves white liturgy before Thy throne
Are of my prayer; but for the scattered bone
Stirring in Europe's camps, next kin of death,
My supplication climbs the carboniferous air.
Grant them Ezekiel's prophesying breath!
Isaiah's cry of solacing allow!
O Thou who from Mizraim once didst draw
Us free, and from the Babylonian lair;
From bondages, plots, ruins imminent
Preserving, didst keep Covenant and Law,
Creator, King whose banishments are not
Forever—for Thy Law and Covenant,
Oh, for Thy promise and Thy pity, now
At last, this people to its lowest brought
Preserve! Only in Thee our faith. The word
Of eagle-quartering kings ever intends

Their own bright eyrie; rote of parakeet
The labouring noise among the fabians heard;
Thou only art responseful.

                              Hear me, who stand
Circled and winged in vortex of my kin:
Forgo the complete doom! The winnowed, spare!
Annul the scattering, and end! And end
Our habitats on water and on air!
Gather the flames up to light orient
Over the land; and that funest eclipse,
Diaspora-dark, revolve from off our ways!
Towered Jerusalem and Jacob's tent
Set up again; again renew our days
As when near Carmel's mount we harboured ships,
And went and came, and knew our home; and song
From all the vineyards raised its sweet degrees,
And Thou didst visit us, didst shield from wrong,
And all our sorrows salve with prophecies;
    Again renew them as they were of old,
    And for all time cancel that ashen orbit
    In which our days, and hopes, and kin, are rolled.

THE ROCKING CHAIR

THE ROCKING CHAIR

It seconds the crickets of the province. Heard
in the clean lamplit farmhouses of Quebec,—
wooden,—it is no less a national bird;
and rivals, in its cage, the mere stuttering clock.
To its time, the evenings are rolled away;
and in its peace the pensive mother knits
contentment to be worn by her family,
grown-up, but still cradled by the chair in which she sits.

It is also the old man's pet, pair to his pipe,
the two aids of his arithmetic and plans,
plans rocking and puffing into market-shape;
and it is the toddler's game and dangerous dance.
Moved to the verandah, on summer Sundays, it is,
among the hanging plants, the girls, the boy-friends,
sabbatical and clumsy, like the white haloes
dangling above the blue serge suits of the young men.

It has a personality of its own;
is a character (like that old drunk Lacoste,
exhaling amber, and toppling on his pins);
it is alive; individual; and no less
an identity than those about it. And
it is tradition. Centuries have been flicked
from its arcs, alternately flicked and pinned.
It rolls with the gait of St. Malo. It is act

and symbol, symbol of this static folk
which moves in segments, and returns to base,—
a sunken pendulum: *invoke, revoke;*
loosed yon, leashed hither, motion on no space.
O, like some Anjou ballad, all refrain,
which turns about its longing, and seems to move
to make a pleasure out of repeated pain,
its music moves, as if always back to a first love.

296

THE PROVINCES

First, the two older ones, the bunkhouse brawnymen,
biceps and chest, lumbering over their legend:
scooping a river up in the palm of the hand,
a dangling fish, alive; kicking open a mine;
bashing a forest bald; spitting a country to crop;
for exercise before their boar breakfast,
building a city; racing, to keep in shape,
against the white-sweatered wind; and always
bragging comparisons, and reminiscing
about their fathers' even more mythic prowess,
arguing always, like puffing champions rising
from wrestling on the green.

Then, the three flat-faced blond-haired husky ones.

And the little girl, so beautiful she was named—
to avert the evil of the evil eye—
after a prince, not princess. In crossed arms cradling her,
her brothers, tanned and long-limbed.
(Great fishermen, hauling out of Atlantic
their catch and their coal
and netting with appleblossom the shoals of their sky.)

And, last, as if of another birth,
the hunchback with the poet's face; and eyes
blue as the glass he looks upon; and fruit
his fragrant knuckles and joints; of iron marrow;—
affecting always a green habit, touched with white.

Nine of them; not counting
the adopted boy of the golden complex, nor
the proud collateral albino,—nine,
a sorcery of numbers, a game's stances.

But the heart seeks one, the heart, and also the mind
seeks single the thing that makes them one, if one.
        Yet where shall one find it? In their history—

297

the cairn of cannonball on the public square?
Their talk, their jealous double-talk? Or in
the whim and weather of a geography
curling in drifts about the forty-ninth?
Or find it in the repute of character:
romantic as mounties? Or discover it
in beliefs that say:
this is a country of Christmas trees?
                    Or hear it sing
from the house with towers, from whose towers ring
bells, and the carillon of laws?
Where shall one find it? What
to name it, that is sought?
The ladder the nine brothers hold by rungs?
The birds that shine on each other? The white water
that foams from the ivy entering their eaves?

Or find it, find it, find it commonplace
but effective, valid, real, the unity
in the family feature, the not unsimilar face?

THE CRIPPLES

(Oratoire de St. Joseph)

Bundled their bones, upon the ninety-nine stairs—
St. Joseph's ladder—the knobs of penance come;
the folded cripples counting up their prayers.

How rich, how plumped with blessing is that dome!
The gourd of Brother André! His sweet days
rounded! Fulfilled! Honeyed to honeycomb!

whither the heads, upon the ninety-nine trays,
the palsied, who double their aspen selves, the lame,
the unsymmetrical, the dead-limbed, raise

their look, their hope, and the *idée fixe* of their maim,—
knowing the surgery's in the heart. Are not
the ransomed crutches worshippers? And the fame

of the brother sanatorial to this plot?—
God mindful of the sparrows on the stairs?
Yes, to their faith this mountain of stairs, is not!

They know, they know, that suddenly their cares
and orthopedics will fall from them, and they
stand whole again.

$\qquad$ *Roll empty away, wheelchairs,*
and crutches, without armpits, hop away!

And I who in my own faith once had faith like this,
but have not now, am crippled more than they.

THE SNOWSHOERS

The jolly icicles ringing in their throats,
their mouths meerschaums of vapour,
from the saints' parishes they come, like snowmen
spangled, with spectrum colour
patching the scarf green, sash red, sky-blue the coat—
come to the crystal course. Their airy hooves
unslung from their backs are ready
to stamp their goodlucks on the solid foam.
Till then, the saints all heralded,
they snowball their banter below the angular eaves.

O gala garb, bright with assomption, flags
on limb and torso curled—
furling of white, blue zigzags, rondures red!
A candy-coloured world!
And moods as primary as their tuques and togs,—

299

of tingling cold, and the air rubbed down with snow
and winter well-being!
Like a slapdash backdrop, the street moves with colours,
the zones and rhomboids moving
toward the enhancing whiteness of the snow.

And now, clomping the packed-down snow of the street
they walk on sinews
gingerly, as if their feet were really swollen,
eager for release
from the blinders of buildings; suddenly they cut
a corner, and—the water they will walk!
Surf of the sun!
World of white wealth! Wind's tilth! Waves
of dazzling dominion
on which their coloured sails will billow and rock!

FOR THE SISTERS OF THE HOTEL DIEU

In pairs,
as if to illustrate their sisterhood,
the sisters pace the hospital garden walks.
In their robes black and white immaculate hoods
they are like birds,
the safe domestic fowl of the House of God.

O biblic birds,
who fluttered to me in my childhood illnesses
—me little, afraid, ill, not of your race,—
the cool wing for my fever, the hovering solace,
the sense of angels—
be thanked, O plumage of paradise, be praised.

GRAIN ELEVATOR

Up from the low-roofed dockyard warehouses
it rises blind and babylonian
like something out of legend. Something seen
in a children's coloured book. Leviathan
swamped on our shore? The cliffs of some other river?
The blind ark lost and petrified? A cave
built to look innocent, by pirates? Or
some eastern tomb a travelled patron here makes local?

But even when known, it's more than what it is:
for here, as in a Josephdream, bow down
the sheaves, the grains, the scruples of the sun
garnered for darkness; and Saskatchewan
is rolled like a rug of a thick and golden thread.
O prison of prairies, ship in whose galleys roll
sunshines like so many shaven heads,
waiting the bushel-burst out of the beachhead bastille!

Sometimes, it makes me think Arabian,
the grain picked up, like tic-tacs out of time:
first one; an other; singly; one by one;—
to save life. Sometimes, some other races claim
the twinship of my thought,—as the river stirs
restless in a white Caucasian sleep,
or, as in the steerage of the elevators,
the grains, Mongolian and crowded, dream.

A box: cement, hugeness, and rightangles—
merely the sight of it leaning in my eyes
mixes up continents and makes a montage
of inconsequent time and uncontiguous space.
It's because it's bread. It's because
bread is its theme, an absolute. Because
always this great box flowers over us
with all the coloured faces of mankind. . . .

UNIVERSITÉ DE MONTRÉAL

Faculté de Droit

Flaunting their canes, their jaunty berets, the students throng
slick serpentine the street and streamer the air
with ribbons of ribaldry and bunting song.
Their faces, shadowed seminary-pale,
open, flash red, announce their epaulettes,
escape from Xenophon and old Virgile.
Gaily they wind and stagger towards their own
and through the maze already see themselves
silken and serious, a gowned guild
a portrait painter will one day make traditional
beneath the Sign of the *Code Napoléon.*

This, then, their last permitted juvenal mood
kicked up by adolescence before it dons
the crown and dignity of adulthood.
Today, the grinning circle on the *Place d'Armes,*
mock trial, thumbdown'd verdict, and, singsong,
the joyous sentence of death; tomorrow, the
good of the state, the law, the dean
parting deliberate his beard
silvered and sabled with rampant right and wrong.

Thus will they note in notebooks, and will con
the numbers and their truths, and from green raw
celebrants of the Latin Quarter, duly
warp and wrinkle into *avocats.*
The solid men. Now innocence and fun.
O let them have their day, it soon will go!
Soon are begun
for haggler and schemer and electioneer—
the wizened one who is a library key,
the fat one plumped upon the *status quo*—
the fees and fetters of career.
Soon they enter
their twenty diaries, clocked and elaborate,
and soon, too soon, begin to live to leave
en bon père de famille,—a sound estate.

302

THE SUGARING

For Guy Sylvestre

Starved, scarred, lenten, amidst ash of air,
roped and rough-shirted, the maples in the unsheltered grove
after their fasts and freezings stir.
Ah, winter for each one,
each gospel tree, each saint of the calendar,
has been a penance, a purchase: the nails of ice!
wind's scourge! the rooted cross!
Nor are they done with the still stances of love,
the fiery subzeros of sacrifice.

For standing amidst the thorns of their own bones,
eased by the tombs' coolth of resurrection time,—
the pardon, the purgatorial groans
almost at bitter end,
but not at end—the carving auger runs
spiral the round stigmata through each limb!
The saints bleed down their sides!
And look! men catch this juice of their agonized prime
to boil in kettles the sap of seraphim!

O, out of this calvary Canadian comes bliss,
savour and saving images of holy things,
a sugared metamorphosis!
Ichor of dulcitude
shaping sweet relics, crystalled spotlessness!
And the pious pour into the honeyed dies
the sacred hearts, the crowns,
thanking those saints for syrops of their dying
and blessing the sweetness of their sacrifice.

303

INDIAN RESERVATION: CAUGHNAWAGA

Where are the braves, the faces like autumn fruit,
who stared at the child from the coloured frontispiece?
And the monosyllabic chief who spoke with his throat?
Where are the tribes, the feathered bestiaries?—
Rank Aesop's animals erect and red,
with fur on their names to make all live things kin—
Chief Running Deer, Black Bear, Old Buffalo Head?

Childhood, that wished me Indian, hoped that
one afterschool I'd leave the classroom chalk,
the varnish smell, the watered dust of the street,
to join the clean outdoors and the Iroquois track.
Childhood; but always,—as on a calendar,—
there stood that chief, with arms akimbo, waiting
the runaway mascot paddling to his shore.

With what strange moccasin stealth that scene is changed!
With French names, without paint, in overalls,
their bronze, like their nobility expunged,—
the men. Beneath their alimentary shawls
sit like black tents their squaws; while for the tourist's
brown pennies scattered at the old church door,
the ragged papooses jump, and bite the dust.

Their past is sold in a shop: the beaded shoes,
the sweetgrass basket, the curio Indian,
burnt wood and gaudy cloth and inch-canoes—
trophies and scalpings for a traveller's den.
Sometimes, it's true, they dance, but for a bribe;
after a deal don the bedraggled feather
and welcome a white mayor to the tribe.

This is a grassy ghetto, and no home.
And these are fauna in a museum kept.
The better hunters have prevailed. The game,

304

losing its blood, now makes these grounds its crypt.
The animals pale, the shine of the fur is lost,
bleached are their living bones. About them watch
as through a mist, the pious prosperous ghosts.

KRIEGHOFF: CALLIGRAMMES

Let the blank whiteness of this page be snow
and majuscule the make of Cornelius:
    then tented A's inverted V's
may circumflex and shade the paysage page
    with French-Canadian trees;
or equal the arrows of the frozen flow
    by the last minus of degrees
stopped in their flight; or show
the wigwams and the gables—
of Krieghoff the pat petted verities.

And any signs will do:
the ladder H that prongs above the chimney;
prone J's on which the gay sleighs run;
the Q and her papoose;
crucifix Y; or bosomed farmwife B—
wanting an easel and the painter's flourish
with alphabet make free,
make squares, make curlecues
of his simplicity.

But colours? Ah, the two colours!

These must be spun, these must be bled
out of the iris of the intent sight:
red rufous roseate crimson russet red
    blank candid white.

BREAD

Creation's crust and crumb, breaking of bread,
Seedstaff and wheatwand of all miracles,
By your white fiat, at the feast-times said,
World moves, and is revived the shrouded pulse!

Rising, as daily rises the quickening east,
O kneading of knowledge, leaven of happiness,
History yearns upon your yearning yeast!
No house is home without your wifeliness.

No city stands up from its rock-bound knees
Without your rustic aid. None are elect
Save you be common. All philosophies
Betray them with your yokel dialect.

O black-bread hemisphere, oblong of rye,
Crescent and circle of the seeded bun,
All art is builded on your geometry,
All science explosive from your captured sun.

Bakers most priestly, in your robes of flour,
White Levites at your altar'd ovens, bind,
Bind me forever in your ritual, your
Worship and prayer, me, and all mankind!

POLITICAL MEETING

(For Camillien Houde)

On the school platform, draping the folding seats,
they wait the chairman's praise and glass of water.
Upon the wall the agonized Y initials their faith.

306

Here all are laic; the skirted brothers have gone.
Still, their equivocal absence is felt, like a breeze
that gives curtains the sounds of surplices.

The hall is yellow with light, and jocular;
suddenly some one lets loose upon the air
the ritual bird which the crowd in snares of singing

catches and plucks, throat, wings, and little limbs.
Fall the feathers of sound, like *alouette's.*
The chairman, now, is charming, full of asides and wit,

building his orators, and chipping off
the heckling gargoyles popping in the hall.
(Outside, in the dark, the street is body-tall,

flowered with faces intent on the scarecrow thing
that shouts to thousands the echoing
of their own wishes.) The Orator has risen!

Worshipped and loved, their favourite visitor,
a country uncle with sunflower seeds in his pockets,
full of wonderful moods, tricks, imitative talk,

he is their idol: like themselves, not handsome,
not snobbish, not of the *Grande Allée! Un homme!*
Intimate, informal, he makes bear's compliments

to the ladies; is gallant; and grins;
goes for the balloon, his opposition, with pins;
jokes also on himself, speaks of himself

in the third person, slings slang, and winks with folklore;
and knows now that he has them, kith and kin.
Calmly, therefore, he begins to speak of war,

praises the virtue of being *Canadien,*
of being at peace, of faith, of family,
and suddenly his other voice: *Where are your sons?*

He is tearful, choking tears; but not he
would blame the clever English; in their place
he'd do the same; maybe.

Where *are* your sons?
                    The whole street wears one face,
shadowed and grim; and in the darkness rises
the body-odour of race.

THE SPINNING WHEEL

You can find it only in attics or in ads,
heirloom a grandmother explains, woodcut
to show them native, quaint, and to be had
at the fee feudal; but
as object it does not exist, is aftermath
of *autre temps* when at this circle sat
domesticity,
and girls wearing the black and high-necked blouse
at its spokes played house.

Now it is antique, like the *fleur de lys,*
a wooden fable out of the olden time,—
as if the epileptic loom and mad factory
that makes a pantomime
out of this wheel do so for picturesqueness
only, and do achieve a fine excess,
not for the dividend
surely. No. Just to preserve romance,
the rites, the wage-rates of old France.

Symbol, it still exists; the seigneur still,
though now drab and incorporate, holds domain
pre-eminent; still, to his power-foaming mill
the farmer brings his grain
his golden daughters made banality;

and still, still do they pay the seigneury
the hourly *corvée,*
the stolen quotient of the unnatural yields
of their woven acres and their linen fields.

FRIGIDAIRE

Even in July it is our winter corner,
hill 70 of our kitchen, rising white
and cool to the eye, cool to the alpenfinger.
The shadows and wind of snowfall fall from its sides.

And when the door swings away, like a cloud blown,
the village is Laurentian, tiered and bright,
with thresholds of red, white roofs, and scattered greens;
and it has a sky, and clouds, and a northern light.

Is peopled. On its vallied streets there stands
a bevy of milk, coifed like the sisters of snow;
and beaded bosoms of butter; and red farmhands;
all poised, as if to hear from the distant meadow,

there on the heights, with its little flowers of white,
the cubes that seem to sound like pasture bells.
Fixed to that far-off tingle they don't quite
hear, they stand, frozen with eavesdropping, like icicles.

And there on the heights, the storm's electric, thriving
with muffled thunder, and lightning slow and white!
It is a private sky, a weather exclusive,
a slow, sensational, and secret sight.

AIR-MAP

How private and comfortable it once was,
our white mansard beneath the continent's gables!
But now, evicted, and still there—
a wind blew off the roof?—
we see our fears and our featherbeds plumped white
on the world's crossroads.

DRESS MANUFACTURER: FISHERMAN

In his wandered wharf on the brake side of the lake;
in boots bucolic;
thatched and eaved with brim and circle of straw,
he'll sit for hours, himself his boat's prow
dangling the thread of his preoccupation.

Far from the lint and swatches, among lilies
chinned upon glass,
among the bulrushes his childhood only read,—
over cool corridors
pearled with bubbles, speckled with trout,
beneath the little songs, the little wings,
his city ardours all go out
into the stipple and smooth of natural things.

And he becomes, at the end of his filament,
a correspondent of water and of fish,
one who casts line and riches—
the glittering foolish spoon the rainbow fly—
to hide within the wish
that for so many years beat from the heat
of his enterprise and city sky
the simmering emphasis of his summer loss.

Here he would sink the curbstones!
And on the granite of his effort
grow a moss!
Back to the hotel, tanned, percer-proud
with the ransom of his youth—
a hero with private trout—
he's familiar in the kitchen, a fisherman
all evening in the lobby kidded and praised;
is modest, but encourages talk; and knows
with every compliment and trout
his childhood summers from the water raised.

PAWNSHOP

May none be called to visit this grim house,
all cup-boards, and each cup-board skeleton'd
with ghost of gambler, spook of shiftless souse,
with rattling relict of the over-dunned!
Disaster haunts it. Scandals, once-renowned,
speak from its chattels. In its darkness glow
the phosphor-poor who stalk its rooms at night.
One should have razed it to the salted ground
antitheses ago,
and put its spectres long ago to flight!

Near waterfront, a stone's throw from the slums,
it lifts, above its wreckage, three gold buoys;
yet to its reefage tattoo'd flotsam comes
unsnaring bag and baedeker of toys.
Also those stranded on their own dear shores,—
the evicted tenant, the genteel with false name,
the girl in trouble, the no-good sons and heirs,
waver, and pause before its brass-bound doors,
look right and left, in shame,
enter, and price, and ticket their despairs.

Oh, for a coloured cardboard, wave out of sight
the dear, the engraved, the boasted inventory:
(a) family plate—hocked for the widow's mite;
(b) birthday gifts; the cups marked *champion* (c);
(d) tools; (e) special, vase picked up in Crete;
en bloc: watch; ring, endowing bride;
camera; medal; crushed accordion;—
rich votives of penultimate defeat,
weighed, measured, counted, eyed
by the estimating clerk, himself in pawn.

Whose lombard schemes, whose plotting kapital
thrusts from this lintel its three burnished bombs
set for a time, which ticks for almost all
whether from fertile suburbs or parched slums?
The architect is rusted from his plaque.
Was his name Adam? Was his trade a smith
who thought a mansion to erect of wealth
that houses now the bankrupt bricabrac,
his pleasure-dome made myth
his let-do hospitality made stealth?

This is our era's state-fair parthenon,
the pyramid of a pharaonic time,
our little cathedral, our platonic cave,
our childhood's house that Jack built. Synonym
of all building, our house, it owns us; even
when free from it, our dialectic grave.
Shall one not curse it, therefore, as the cause,
type, and exemplar of our social guilt?
Our own gomorrah house,
the sodom that merely to look at makes one salt?

THE GREEN OLD AGE

Pity who wear the castoffs of the years
dressing in clown's clothes the unclownish ones,
with baldness on head, and hairiness in ears,
and cellophane upon the chalky bones,
  and in concealed sacking, stones!

Sweet flakes in the blood, the mouth exhaling acid;
the bowels becalmed, and the loud bile in rage;
the artery hardened, and the member flaccid;
nor ever at normal the pulsating gauge—
  metathesis of age

which strives again toward its babyhood
where neither the shanks nor sphincters will behave,
nor syntax stand, and where, as if it would
be joined again, the spinal cord does crave
  the navel of the grave.

Be blessed the doctors who with toxic ease,—
coned odour, marrowed needle, candid pill,—
the waxing of these mooned monstrosities
forestall; and give into the hand and will
  the proleptic miracle.

THE BREAK-UP

They suck and whisper it in mercury,
the thermometers. It is shouted red
from all the Aprils hanging on the walls.
In the dockyard stalls
the stevedores, their hooks rusty, wonder; the
wintering sailors in the taverns bet.

313

A week, and it will crack! Here's money that
a fortnight sees the floes, the smokestacks red!
Outside *The Anchor's* glass, St. Lawrence lies
rigid and white and wise,
nor ripple and dip, but fathom-frozen flat.
There are no hammers will break that granite lid.

But it will come! Some dead of night with boom
to wake the wagering city, it will break,
will crack, will melt its muscle-bound tides
and raise from their iced tomb
the pyramided fish, the unlockered ships,
and last year's blue and bloated suicides.

COMMERCIAL BANK

Flowering jungle, where all fauna meet
crossing the marbled pool to thickets whence
the prompted parrots, alien-voiced, entreat
the kernel'd horde, the efflorescent pence,—

wondrous your caves, whose big doors must be rolled
for entrance, and whose flora none can seek
against the armed unicorn, furred blue and gold,
against the vines fatal, or the berries that touched, shriek.

How quiet is your shade with broad green leaves!
Yet is it jungle-quiet which deceives:
toothless, with drawn nails, the beasts paw your ground—
O, the fierce deaths expiring with no sound!

QUEBEC LIQUOR COMMISSION STORE

Nonetheless Ali Baba had no richer cave,
nor lamps more sensitive Aladdin's thumb
than this cave, and these lamps which, at the touch,
evoke the growing slave,
and change the rag-poor world to purple-rich.
"O Vizier, wrapped in all knowledge and experience,
bring me, bring me in a flower of air,
the scent of the world's motion, the pollen, the fire,
the fumes, of magnificence!"
"Your servant, my Lord, has done according to your desire!

"And brought you also the pleasures of the skin about the round,
the sycophancy of glass, the palm's cool courtier,
and the feel of straw, all rough and rustical,
by some king's daughter donned;
and for your royal eyes, your Ishmael
with rub and abracadabra and obeisance brings
these forms and shapes, that harem opulence
that my Lord dotes on; and, of the same scope
their voices, like happenings
on cushions behind curtains, like whispers at the thrilled ear's lobe."

"Well done! thou gurgling knave, and above all, well done,
in the conjuring of those mischievous genii
who nip at the paps of palate, hop on the tongue,
in the throat make merry and fun!
Lithe, they go tumbling in the paunch's nets! And rung
by rung, disporting, they climb into the brain's bazaar!
Wonderful are their tricks and somersaults,
such ingenuities as do make a king forget
the troubles that there are
even for kings, the rag-poor past, the purple that may set."

MONTREAL

O city metropole, isle riverain!
Your ancient pavages and sainted routs
Traverse my spirit's conjured avenues!
Splendour erablic of your promenades
Foliates there, and there your maisonry
Of pendant balcon and escalier'd march,
Unique midst English habitat,
Is vivid Normandy!

You populate the pupils of my eyes:
Thus, does the Indian, plumed, furtivate
Still through your painted autumns, Ville-Marie!
Though palisades have passed, though calumet
With tabac of your peace enfumes the air,
Still do I spy the phantom, aquiline,
Genuflect, moccasin'd, behind
His statue in the square!

Thus, costumed images before me pass,
Haunting your archives architectural:
Coureur de bois, in posts where pelts were portaged;
Seigneur within his candled manoir; Scot
Ambulant through his bank, pillar'd and vast.
Within your chapels, voyaged mariners
Still pray, and personage departed,
All present from your past!

Grand port of navigations, multiple
The lexicons uncargo'd at your quays,
Sonnant though strange to me; but chiefest, I,
Auditor of your music, cherish the
Joined double-melodied vocabulaire
Where English vocable and roll Ecossic,
Mollified by the parle of French
Bilinguefact your air!

Such your suaver voice, hushed Hochelaga!
But for me also sound your potencies,
Fortissimos of sirens fluvial,
Bruit of manufactory, and thunder
From foundry issuant, all puissant tone
Implenishing your hebdomad; and then
Sanct silence, and your argent belfries
Clamant in orison!

You are a part of me, O all your quartiers—
And of dire pauvrete and of richesse—
To finished time my homage loyal claim;
You are locale of infancy, milieu
Vital of institutes that formed my fate;
And you above the city, scintillant,
Mount Royal, are my spirit's mother,
Almative, poitrinate!

Never do I sojourn in alien place
But I do languish for your scenes and sounds,
City of reverie, nostalgic isle,
Pendant most brilliant on Laurentian cord!
The coigns of your boulevards—my signiory—
Your suburbs are my exile's verdure fresh,
Your parks, your fountain'd parks—
Pasture of memory!

City, O city, you are vision'd as
A parchemin roll of saecular exploit
Inked with the script of eterne souvenir!
You are in sound, chanson and instrument!
Mental, you rest forever edified
With tower and dome; and in these beating valves,
Here in these beating valves, you will
For all my mortal time reside!

WINTER NIGHT: MOUNT ROYAL

Slowly, and flake by flake . . . At the drifted frond
of the terraces and ski-runs over me
there falls a snow of sound:
tinkle of frost   minims of mercury
        campanile cold

Horseman and horse among the chandeliers
parting the crystal twigs? Some belfry burst
frozen, and fractured into chips of sound?
The air itself
made little globes,
their rounds ringing in Fahrenheit descant?

White innocence the mountainside is mist,
its bells as secret as the bells of its flowers.

Now nearer, and jollier, and fourtimed, canters
the bend of the road this jingle of this silver!
Big-eyed, equestrian, trotting
the nickle blossoms,
the bells and hellos of his yoke and harness!

Heraldic, guled, the sleigh in a flurry of sound—
hooves upon snow the falsettos of water
and bells cavalier—
passes before me, is festive, and passes beyond
the curve of the road, the heels of its runners
scrolling it into the mist.

They are now fainter, have no direction, lost.
One would say the hidden stars were bells
dangling between the shafts of the Zodiac.
One would say
the snowflakes falling clinked together their sparkles
to make these soft, these satin-muffled
tintinnabulations.

LOOKOUT: MOUNT ROYAL

Remembering boyhood, it is always here
the boy in blouse and kneepants on the road
trailing his stick over the hopscotched sun;
or here, upon the suddenly moving hill;
or at the turned tap its cold white mandarin mustaches;
or at the lookout, finally,
breathing easy, standing still

to click the eye on motion forever stopped:
the photographer's tripod and his sudden faces
buoyed up by water on his magnet caught
still smiling as if under water still;
the exclamatory tourists descending the *calèches*;
the maids in starch; the ladies in white gloves;
other kids of other slums and races;
and on the bridle-paths
the horsemen on their horses like the tops of f's:

or from the parapet make out
beneath the green marine
the discovered road, the hospital's romantic
gables and roofs, and all the civic Euclid
running through sunken parallels and lolling
in diamond and square, then proud-pedantical
with spire and dome
making its way to the sought point, his home.

home recognized: there: to be returned to—

lets the full birdseye circle to the river,
its singsong bridges, its mapmaker curves, its
island with the two shades of green, meadow and wood;
and circles round that water-tower'd coast;
then, to the remote rhapsodic mountains; then,
—and to be lost—
to clouds like white slow friendly animals
which all the afternoon across his eyes
will move their paced spaced footfalls.

319

THE MOUNTAIN

Who knows it only by the famous cross which bleeds
into the fifty miles of night its light
knows a night-scene;
and who upon a postcard knows its shape—
the buffalo straggled of the laurentian herd,—
holds in his hand a postcard.

In layers of mountains the history of mankind,
and in Mount Royal
which daily in a streetcar I surround
my youth, my childhood—
the pissabed dandelion, the coolie acorn,
green prickly husk of chestnut beneath mat of grass—
O all the amber afternoons
are still to be found.

There is a meadow, near the pebbly brook,
where buttercups, like once on the under of my chin
upon my heart still throw their rounds of yellow.

And Cartier's monument, based with nude figures
still stands where playing hookey
Lefty and I tested our gravel aim
(with occupation flinging away our guilt)
against the bronze tits of Justice.

And all my Aprils there are marked and spotted
upon the adder's tongue, darting in light,
upon the easy threes of trilliums, dark green, green, and white,
threaded with earth, and rooted
beside the bloodroots near the leaning fence—
corms and corollas of childhood,
a teacher's presents.
And chokecherry summer clowning black on my teeth!

The birchtree stripped by the golden zigzag still
stands at the mouth of the dry cave where I
one suppertime in August watched the sky

320

grow dark, the wood quiet, and then suddenly spill
from barrels of thunder and broken staves of lightning—
terror and holiday!

One of these days I shall go up to the second terrace
to see if it still is there—
the uncomfortable sentimental bench
where,—as we listened to the brass of the band concerts
made soft and to our mood by dark and distance—
I told the girl I loved
I loved her.

LONE BATHER

Upon the ecstatic diving board the diver,
poised for parabolas, lets go
lets go his manshape to become a bird.
Is bird, and topsy-turvy
the pool floats overhead, and the white tiles snow
their crazy hexagons. Is dolphin. Then
is plant with lilies bursting from his heels.

Himself, suddenly mysterious and marine,
bobs up a merman leaning on his hills.

Plashes and plays alone the deserted pool;
as those, is free, who think themselves unseen.
He rolls in his heap of fruit,
he slides his belly over
the melonrinds of water, curved and smooth and green.
Feels good: and trains, like little acrobats
his echoes dropping from the galleries;
circles himself over a rung of water;
swims fancy and gay; taking a notion, hides
under the satins of his great big bed,—
and then comes up to float until he thinks
the ceiling at his brow, and nowhere any sides.

His thighs are a shoal of fishes: scattered: he
turns with many gloves of greeting
towards the sunnier water and the tiles.

Upon the tiles he dangles from his toes
lazily the eight reins of his ponies.
An afternoon, far from the world
a street sound throws like a stone, with paper, through the glass.
Up, he is chipped enamel, grained with hair.
The gloss of his footsteps follows him to the showers,
the showers, and the male room, and the towel
which rubs the bird, the plant, the dolphin back again
personable plain.

PASTORAL OF THE CITY STREETS

i

Between distorted forests, clapped into geometry,
in meadows of macadam,
heat-fluff-a-host-of-dandelions dances on the air.
Everywhere glares the sun's glare,
the asphalt shows hooves.

　　　　　　　In meadows of macadam
grazes the dray horse, nozzles his bag of pasture,
is peaceful. Now and then flicks through farmer straw
his ears, like pulpit-flowers; quivers
his hide; swishes his tempest tail
a black and sudden nightmare for the fly.
The sun shines, sun shines down
new harness on his withers, saddle, and rump.

On curbrock and on stairstump the clustered kids
resting let slide some afternoon: then restless
hop to the game of the sprung haunches; skid

to the safe place; jump up: stir a wind in the heats:
laugh, puffed and sweat-streaked.

O for the crystal stream!

Comes a friend's father
with his pet of a hose,
and plays the sidewalk black
cavelike and cool.

O crisscross beneath the spray, those pelting petals and peas
those white soft whisks
brushing off heat!
O underneath these acrobatic fountains
among the crystal,
like raindrops a sunshower of youngsters dance:
small-nippled self-hugged boys
and girls with water sheer, going *Ah* and *Ah*.

ii

And at twilight,
the sun like a strayed neighbourhood creature
having been chased
back to its cover
the children count a last game, or talk, or rest,
beneath the bole of the tree of the single fruit of glass
now ripening,
a last game, talk, or rest,
until mothers like evening birds call from the stoops.

M. BERTRAND

Oh, but in France they arrange these things much better!
M. Bertrand who always, before kissing the female wrist
rolls the *r* in *charmante*
admits he owes everything to those golden Sorbonne years.
Returned now to our forest, he is sad and nostalgic;
indeed, pained; he winces when his brother says *icitte*.
O, he can never forget fair Paris, its culture and cuisine,
particularly as he stalks deaf and hungry
among the barbarians who never were seasick.
     Still, he has one consolation—the visitor from
         abroad,
the old classmate, the *conferencier,* perhaps, even
a bearded *maître* of the Academy.
Then is he revived, like a dotard by the *Folies Bergères,*
revived, stimulated, made loquacious with *argot,*
and can't do enough for his guest, but would lavish on him
jowl-kiss, hand-kiss, and other kisses Parisian.

THE NOTARY

Next to the *curé,* he is hierarch,
the true poet functional of this place,
laureate of its lands.
O, as longing's redacted, hope given witnesses,
its scarlet seal ambition, through him work
the larger myths and motives, and the heart
counts its beats on the margin, and our county lies
cadastral on his hands!

Formal in black, gold watch, and lyric collar,
he's ceremonial a priest a bard;
money and love are his themes.
He speaks, for all, the imprescriptible word;

324

and with his name, sacred upon the roll,
makes rich a date, and permanent a wish,
giving desire its deed, and the blessing of the hands
to the English-measured dreams.

And with a flourish moves the immoveable,
gratifies the unborn of the unborn!
The certainties are his!
Yes, so to our custom dedicate and sworn,
he it is makes all getting honourable,—
truly our poet, coining the bride her song,
and making even out of the last will
our cherished elegies!

MONSIEUR GASTON

You remember the big Gaston, for whom everyone predicted
a bad end?—
Gaston, the neighbour's gossip and his mother's cross?
You remember him *vaurien,* always out of a job,
with just enough clinking coinage
for pool, bright neckties, and blondes,—
the scented Gaston in the poolroom lolling
in meadows of green baize?
In clover now. Through politics. *Monsieur* Gaston.

They say the Minister of a certain department does not move
without him; and they say, to make it innocent,—
chauffeur.
But everyone understands. Why, wherever our Gaston smiles
a nightclub rises and the neons flash.
To his slightest whisper
the bottled rye, like a fawning pet-dog, gurgles.
The burlesque queen will not undress
unless Monsieur Gaston says yes.
And the Madame will shake her head behind the curtain-rods
unless he nods.

325

A changed man, Gaston; almost a civil servant,
keeps records, appointments, women; speaks tough English;
is very much respected.
You should hear with what greetings his distinguished approach is
    greeted;
you should see the gifts he gets,
with compliments for his season.

LIBRAIRIE DELORME

Among the penny arcades and the dime shows,
attic above the dark racked secondhand stores
its number; neighbour to cubicles in heat,
hashjoints, vodvils, poolrooms—the scruffed doors
the derelict swings, the cop on the corner knows—
Far from the pomp epopic of its themes,
far from the pemmican West, out of the storm
confederate, upon a city street:
Canadiana: Librairie Delorme:
door grated: wooden stairs: the incunabulate dreams

stacked: shadows catalogued. The runted past
grows only the thickness of dust and greys frustrate
the Intendants' enterprises, and Laval's—
in brochures bandied. Though Jesuits relate,
and explorers claim, and statesmen think they last
none come to listen, save the bibliophile;
or Hollywood for manners; or the bright
young candidate who'd show *de facto* false;
an abbé, perhaps, beatified with sight
of green Laurentia kneeling to church-bell.

Monsieur Delorme . . . Stooped and with doctoral beard
he is all anecdote and courtesy,
one who loves bindings and the old regime
that in his mind is gobelin'd *fleur de lys*

326

and in the chapel of his speech revered.
Nonetheless seems at peace with the conqueror's state,
is casual, diffident, a-political;
and from his manner you would never dream
he was a man was putting up for sale
his family heirlooms and his family plate.

SIRE ALEXANDRE GRANDMAISON

When Sire Alexandre Grandmaison, Seigneur of Biche,
read the final draft of the bill, placed by his secretary,
(who watched such things,) upon his heirloom desk,
he was desolate.
That day was a lost day, and Sire Alexandre
outraged, forgot those lesser domains and fiefs:
    Quebec Paper Products, Ltd.
    Champlain Industries, Inc.
    Laurentian Cold Storage, Ltd.
    La Societé de Fiducie, and subsidiaries
of all of which he had been duly elected president.

To think of it!
The ancient rights attaching now commuted!
King Louis' honour, which not even the English would touch
paid off at six per cent:
pious ceremony reduced
to legal tender at a banker's wicket!

Mais, que voulez-vous? It was a parliament
of grocers, notaries, farmers' sons who would
crate custom, barter the *fleur de lys* for leeks.
It was a too commercial age.

HORMISDAS ARCAND

Hormisdas Arcand, about to found a new party
manufactures him historic manifesto.
Alas, he can not get
beyond the principal
first blast.
It keeps repeating itself, like a youpin meal.
Et, pour vrai dire, what more political
is there to say after you have said:
A bas les maudits Juifs!

LES FILLES MAJEURES

Evenings, they walk arm in arm, in pairs,—
as if to emphasize their incompleteness,—
and friendly together make an ambiguous form,
like a folded loneliness,
or like mirrors that reflect only each other.

And in the daytime, they are aunts; they pet,
they censor their sisters' children, take them for walks,
help them with privacies, and buy them presents.
It is baby talk
and precocity that is their topic, their event.

Their life is like a diary, to be filled.
Therefore they'll sit at concerts where music invents
them love-affairs; or lectures—for the mind's eye;
or, almost male, will tend
their gardens; or social service. Thus, the days hold.

Sometimes, having found another grey hair
they will put on the uniform of conventional dress
with the single item florid, the single feather

328

for the elusive one. Alas
always they return, and sighs the sisterly mirror.

Thereafter they shield themselves, brood on, avoid,
hate the entire vocabulary of love.
The shine of left-handed rings makes them feel odd,
and certain small words grieve
them, insult their spinsterhood.

For them, for them the world lacks symmetry!
And they themselves seem to themselves
like vases, broken in half, the halves perversely
stood upon shelves
unfinished, and rich with flowers never to be.

FILLING STATION

With snakes of rubber and glass thorax,
like dragons rampant,
statistical, red with ambush,
they ambuscade the highway.

Only in the hinterland, and for neighbours,
the extant blacksmith drives
archaic nails into the three-legged horse.

But on Route 7
the monsters coil and spit from iron mouths
potent saliva.

(Beyond the hills, of course;
the oxen, lyric with horns, still draw
the cart and the limping wheels.)

ANNUAL BANQUET: CHAMBRE DE COMMERCE

And as the orators, rewarded roars, scored, soared, bored—
The man of capital:
You certainly have a wonderful country. Why don't you
Exploit it?

To which his neighbour and host
Seeking in pocket and pouch
Bosom and hip and thigh
At last produced it, bold and double-column.

> *Quebec: The place for industry*
> *Cheap power. Cheap labour.*
> *No taxes (first three years).*
> *No isms (forever).*

Verso, the guest beheld; and smiled:
Photograph of Mr. & Mrs. Damase Laberge
on the occasion of their 25th wedding anniversary,
surrounded by their children and grandchildren
to the number of thirty-two; from left to right. . .

O love which moves the stars and factories. . . .

PORTRAIT OF THE POET AS LANDSCAPE

i

Not an editorial-writer, bereaved with bartlett,
mourns him, the shelved Lycidas.
No actress squeezes a glycerine tear for him.
The radio broadcast lets his passing pass.
And with the police, no record. Nobody, it appears,

330

either under his real name or his alias,
missed him enough to report.

It is possible that he is dead, and not discovered.
It is possible that he can be found some place
in a narrow closet, like the corpse in a detective story,
standing, his eyes staring, and ready to fall on his face.
It is also possible that he is alive
and amnesiac, or mad, or in retired disgrace,
or beyond recognition lost in love.

We are sure only that from our real society
he has disappeared; he simply does not count,
except in the pullulation of vital statistics—
somebody's vote, perhaps, an anonymous taunt
of the Gallup poll, a dot in a government table—
but not felt, and certainly far from eminent—
in a shouting mob, somebody's sigh.

O, he who unrolled our culture from his scroll—
the prince's quote, the rostrum-rounding roar—
who under one name made articulate
heaven, and under another the seven-circled air,
is, if he is at all, a number, an x,
a Mr. Smith in a hotel register,—
incognito, lost, lacunal.

ii

The truth is he's not dead, but only ignored—
like the mirroring lenses forgotten on a brow
that shine with the guilt of their unnoticed world.
The truth is he lives among neighbours, who, though they will allow
him a passable fellow, think him eccentric, not solid,
a type that one can forgive, and for that matter, forgo.

Himself he has his moods, just like a poet.
Sometimes, depressed to nadir, he will think all lost,
will see himself as throwback, relict, freak,
his mother's miscarriage, his great-grandfather's ghost,

331

and he will curse his quintuplet senses, and their tutors
in whom he put, as he should not have put, his trust.

Then he will remember his travels over that body—
the torso verb, the beautiful face of the noun,
and all those shaped and warm auxiliaries!
A first love it was, the recognition of his own.
Dear limbs adverbial, complexion of adjective,
dimple and dip of conjugation!

And then remember how this made a change in him
affecting for always the glow and growth of his being;
how suddenly was aware of the air, like shaken tinfoil,
of the patents of nature, the shock of belated seeing,
the loneliness peering from the eyes of crowds;
the integers of thought; the cube-roots of feeling.

Thus, zoomed to zenith, sometimes he hopes again,
and sees himsedf as a character, with a rehearsed role:
the Count of Monte Cristo, come for his revenges;
the unsuspecting heir, with papers; the risen soul;
or the chloroformed prince awakening from his flowers;
or—deflated again—the convict on parole.

iii

He is alone; yet not completely alone.
Pins on a map of a colour similar to his,
each city has one, sometimes more than one;
here, caretakers of art, in colleges;
in offices, there, with arm-bands, and green-shaded;
and there, pounding their catalogued beats in libraries,—

everywhere menial, a shadow's shadow.
And always for their egos—their outmoded art.
Thus, having lost the bevel in the ear,
they know neither up nor down, mistake the part
for the whole, curl themselves in a comma,
talk technics, make a colon their eyes. They distort—

332

such is the pain of their frustration—truth
to something convolute and cerebral.
How they do fear the slap of the flat of the platitude!
Now Pavlov's victims, their mouths water at bell,
the platter empty.
                    See they set twenty-one jewels
into their watches; the time they do not tell!

Some, patagonian in their own esteem,
and longing for the multiplying word,
join party and wear pins, now have a message,
an ear, and the convention-hall's regard.
Upon the knees of ventriloquists, they own,
of their dandled brightness, only the paint and board.

And some go mystical, and some go mad.
One stares at a mirror all day long, as if
to recognize himself; another courts
angels,—for here he does not fear rebuff;
and a third, alone, and sick with sex, and rapt,
doodles him symbols convex and concave.

O schizoid solitudes! O purities
curdling upon themselves! Who live for themselves,
or for each other, but for nobody else;
desire affection, private and public loves;
are friendly, and then quarrel and surmise
the secret perversions of each other's lives.

iv

He suspects that something has happened, a law
been passed, a nightmare ordered. Set apart,
he finds himself, with special haircut and dress,
as on a reservation. Introvert.
He does not understand this; sad conjecture
muscles and palls thrombotic on his heart.

He thinks an impostor, having studied his personal biography,
his gestures, his moods, now has come forward to pose

333

in the shivering vacuums his absence leaves.
Wigged with his laurel, that other, and faked with his face,
he pats the heads of his children, pecks his wife,
and is at home, and slippered, in his house.

So he guesses at the impertinent silhouette
that talks to his phone-piece and slits open his mail.
Is it the local tycoon who for a hobby
plays poet, he so epical in steel?
The orator, making a pause? Or is that man
he who blows his flash of brass in the jittering hall?

Or is he cuckolded by the troubadour
rich and successful out of celluloid?
Or by the don who unrhymes atoms? Or
the chemist death built up? Pride, lost impostor'd pride,
it is another, another, whoever he is,
who rides where he should ride.

v

Fame, the adrenalin: to be talked about;
to be a verb; to be introduced as *The:*
to smile with endorsement from slick paper; make
caprices anecdotal; to nod to the world; to see
one's name like a song upon the marquees played;
to be forgotten with embarrassment; to be—
to be.

It has its attractions, but is not the thing;
nor is it the ape mimesis who speaks from the tree
ancestral; nor the merkin joy. . .
Rather it is stark infelicity
which stirs him from his sleep, undressed, asleep
to walk upon roofs and window-sills and defy
the gape of gravity.

vi

Therefore he seeds illusions. Look, he is
the nth Adam taking a green inventory

334

in world but scarcely uttered, naming, praising,
the flowering fiats in the meadow, the
syllabled fur, stars aspirate, the pollen
whose sweet collusion sounds eternally.
For to praise

the world—he, solitary man—is breath
to him. Until it has been praised, that part
has not been. Item by exciting item—
air to his lungs, and pressured blood to his heart—
they are pulsated, and breathed, until they map,
not the world's, but his own body's chart!

And now in imagination he has climbed
another planet, the better to look
with single camera view upon this earth—
its total scope, and each afflated tick,
its talk, its trick, its tracklessness—and this,
this, he would like to write down in a book!

To find a new function for the *déclassé* craft
archaic like the fletcher's; to make a new thing;
to say the word that will become sixth sense;
perhaps by necessity and indirection bring
new forms to life, anonymously, new creeds—
O, somehow pay back the daily larcenies of the lung!

These are not mean ambitions. It is already something
merely to entertain them. Meanwhile, he
makes of his status as zero a rich garland,
a halo of his anonymity,
and lives alone, and in his secret shines
like phosphorus. At the bottom of the sea.

POEMS

1948-1952

CANTABILE: A REVIEW OF THE CANTOS OF EZRA POUND

De litteris, et de armis, praestantibusque ingeniis

And when they brought him back
the fibbiest fabricator of them all
      il miglior fabbro
they didn't know what to do with him
      at the customs he had nothing to declare
saving and except a number of synonyms, to wit:
zhid, sheeny, jewboy, youpin, kike, yitt, shweef.
             and the ballad
    But bye and rade the Black Douglas
    And wow but he was rough!
    For he pulled up the bonny brier
    And flang't in St. Mary's Lough.

didn't know what to do with him . . . hang him?
old, *exhaussé*, a poet, there was a question of ethics, moreover
      one kuddent make a martyr of him, cood one?
          St. Ezra Benedict

So the seven psychiatrists feigned insanity
committed him.

U S U R A: that his offence
that he sought to extract an exorbitant interest
          from a limited talent.
speculated in the cultural exchanges
passed off

      χρύσω   χρυτοτέρα
the Dante coinage, Provencal, Chinese yen
not as his own, but his for increment.
It must be admitted, however, that as a pawnbroker
he was distinguished.
He invented a new way to ring a coin on the table
was expert in the bite for counterfeit,
trafficked only in the best mdse. and to his friends gave discounts
for the rest was fierce, bearded like the pard, like his Jew.

Pound   Libra   £

USURA

The cantos? 'The art of conversation' said Tate (Allen) meaning
small talk shouted.
80 of them 80
anecdote, persiflage, ideogram, traduction
                    traductore—tradittore
all to the same if any effect—the syphilisation of our gonorera
                    and Pound its thunder clap,
a good role but the wrong actor.

Don't you think said the lady from Idaho on tour at Rapallo
that he will be remembered?   Yes
As the author of a Gradus ad parnassum
 " a compiler of several don'ts
 " a perpetrator of ditto
 " a dropper-down of learning's crumbs
and as the stoic of the empty portals.

Otherwise, as Jimmy, quoting himself and poor Mr. Breen
            E. P.: E P
            'EP.   *Est Perditus.*

PARADE OF ST. JEAN BAPTISTE

Bannered, and ranked, and at its stances fixed
the enfilade with vestment colours the air.
Roll now the batons of the tambours round
ruminant with commencement, and now sound
annunciative, ultramontane, the
fanfares of jubilee!
It moves festive and puissant the chivalry
advances chief, law crouped and curvetting—
finish and force, undulant muscle and braid—
O centaurs en gambade!

339

They move as through a garden, moving between
gay altitudes of flowers, populous
of all the wards and counties burgeoning hero
ribbons and countenances, joys and colours—
nuances of meridian, the blue
the rose, the vert, the blond, all lambencies
to this rich spectacle turned heliotropic,
graceful and levitant: Quebec, its people:
flotation of faces: badinage of petals:
profound from suburbs surfaced on
the Real to spy Imagination.

Applause! Ovation of hourras! There pass
before the flowering faces, imaged, the
animal fables, myths of the crayon'd class,
the nursery's voyage and discovery:
redeemed and painted is the Indian;
lake sirens chant again; and sorcery
again makes princess out of Cendrillon,
(by Massicotte, research; and courtesy
of Simpson's and of Eaton T. and Son)
last! last! the coachmen of *chasse-gallerie.*
Oh, all,—parents; their infant epaulettes—
All here are dauphins of a vanished empery.

The grand progenitor! Herbert! Salute
as acted en tableau revivified
the pioneer fiat, the patrimonial geste
deracinating forest into prairie!
Surge, visions of farms the river parcelled out!
Conjured, the parish parallelograms,
the chapel's verdant foyer! (Does not this scene,
habitants of the fumed and pulverous city
immured in granite canyons and constrict,
does it not veil the eyes with memories
sylvan, campestral? Does it not palpitate pain
current nostalgic away from the factory
to the mountain liberties and large champaign?)

340

Now, into their vision, from the parishes
with gonfalons emergent juvenal
the schools and seminaries, potent with race:
name after name, catena of grand fame,
tradition—orgulous. Martyr and saint
chrysostomate their standards. Aspiration
surrounds them, and the future dowers with power—
regenerate, augmentative: the nation.
The berceuses are its anthems; thus survives
philoprogenitive Quebec; thus grants survival
unto the spired culture elsewhere tom'd
Yes, here with students and their cassock'd doctors,
the angels of Aquinas dance their dances,
and march the pious mascots of St. Francis.

Quebec, Quebec, which for the long blanched age—
infidelium partes—multiplied
pagan its beasts and painted savages—
(while Rome was rounded with St. Peter's dome
and Europe vertical with tower and cross
supported constellations)—is still rich
of realms spiritual the Jesuits founded,
and Sabbaths of the monks of Yamachiche.
Crosses of clergy, luxe armorial,
still vivify with their insignia
the evangelical air, and benedictions
douce-digital from priest and eminence
still quadrilate the inhospitable tense.

And sudden! camaraderie and jokes.
Ablute and pompous, staid, the rotund mayor
(remember in Maisonneuve his gestured discourse—
Cyrano, né p'tit gars de Ste. Marie?)
with chain of office now, and magistral,
promenades, flanked by seniors of the city.
These are not allegorical; the people
familiar still, as if with candidates,
cry out allusions, scandals; parodize
the clichés and the rhetoric suave.
But unconcerned and bland, the market elect

march recognitions through the colonnade—
ineffably correct.

Patronial, of recent heraldry:
the piston sinistral, the scutcheon coin,
blazon and bar of blank,—the seigneurie
of capital, new masters of domain.
See, this is he, the pulp magnifico,
and this the nabob of the northern mine;
this man is pelts, and this man men allow
factotum. To the servants of their wage,
le peup' the docile, the incognito
paupers, they do offer the day's homage,
but know their seasons appertain to them,
they being loyal, inexpensive, leige.

O who can measure the potency of symbols?
The hieratic gesture murdering grief?
The gloss on suffering? The jewelled toy
that sports away quotidian the anguish?
For the gray seasons and the frustrate heart,
therefore, these rituals, which are therapy,
a ceremonial appeasement. O
single and sole upon the calendar
the baptist's day with rite and rapture tints
dolour that for its annuair of day
will dance, refract, this one day's images.

Departed is the enfilade; the people
in groups chromatic through the boulevards
disperse; spectators benched and poled, descend;
the traffic gauntlets gesture; klaxons sound;
all motion is pastelled; gala and gay
the picnic—loud tramway.
It is a prelude for the pleiades
that pyrotechnic will this night illume
pères de famille idyllic and content,
and in the dense boskage the ancient intimate experiment.

342

OF THE MAKING OF GRAGERS

The following are the proper instruments wherewith Haman and
all of that ilk may best be confounded:

   clappers   utterants & mutterants
   racketrakers   funaphores   hullabellows
   flippics   titus-taps   sonorosnorers
   fracasators   clangabangs & clackacousticons
   drums and bimbamboomicores   vociferators
   nazinoisicans   palmapats   gourds
   ratatats   cymbals & stridors
   knuckleknacks & castanets   brekekex
   ton'o'thunders   datadiscords
   panpandemonia   torquemadatumps   borborigmi
   brontobronks   chmelnizzicatoes   pharophonics
   hellodeons   whistles & fee-fi-fo-fifers
         etceterows

BENEDICTIONS

For that he gave to a stone understanding to understand direction.
For that he made no slave for me.
For that he clothes the naked with the nudities of beasts.
For that he erects the contracted.
For that he smites me each dawn with a planet.

WHO HAST FASHIONED

  Blessed art thou, O Lord,
   Who in Thy wisdom hast fashioned man as Thou hast
fashioned him; hollowed and antrious, grottoed and gutted,
channelled; for mercy's sake gifted with orifice, exit, and vent!

Did one of these only suffer obstruction, survives not the hour that man!

Thy will according, there drops the baneful excess: the scruff falls; from the pores surreptitious the sweat; and the nails of the fingers are cut; the demons are houseless.

Be blessed for the judgment of the eight great gates who dost diminish us to make us whole; for the piecemeal deaths that save; for wax and cerumen, which preserve all music, and for flux of the sinus, which gives the brain coolness, its space, and for spittle prized above the condiments of Asia; even for tears.

OF REMEMBRANCE

Go catch the echoes of the ticks of time;
Spy the interstices between its sands;

Uncover the shadow of the dial; fish
Out of the waters of the water-clock
The shape and image of first memory.

Recall:
The apple fallen from the apple tree:
O child remembering maternity!

The candle flickering in a mysterious room:
O foetus stirring in the luminous womb!

One said he did remember, he did know
What time the fruit did first begin to grow:
O memory of limbs in embryo!

Another did recall the primal seed—
Conceiver of conception of the breed!

A third, the sage who did the seed invent—
O distant memory of mere intent!

Recall the fruit's taste ere the fruit was fruit—
Hail memory of essence absolute!

Recall the odour of fruit when no fruit was,
O Spirit untainted by corporeal flaws!

Recall the fruit's shape ere the fruit was seen,
O soul immortal that has always been!

Said one, and he the keenest of them all:
No thing is what I vividly recall—
O happy man who could remember thus,
The Mystery beyond the mysterious.

STANCE OF THE AMIDAH

O Lord, open Thou my lips; and my mouth shall declare Thy praise:

God of Abraham, God of Isaac, God of Jacob, who hast bound
to the patriarchs their posterity and hast made Thyself manifest
in the longings of men and hast condescended to bestow upon
history a shadow of the shadows of Thy radiance;
Who with the single word hast made the world, hanging before
us the heavens like an unrolled scroll, and the earth old manuscript,
and the murmurous sea, each, all-allusive to Thy glory, so that
from them we might conjecture and surmise and almost know Thee;

> *Whom only angels know*
> *Who in Thy burning courts*
> *Cry:* Holy! Holy! Holy!
> *While mortal voice below*
> *With seraphim consorts*
> *To murmur:* Holy! Holy!
> *Yet holiness not know.*

Favour us, O Lord, with understanding, who hast given to
the bee its knowledge and to the ant its foresight, to the sleeping

345

bear Joseph's prudence, and even to the dead lodestone its instinct for the star, favour us with understanding of what in the inscrutable design is for our doomsday-good;

Oh, give us such understanding as makes superfluous second thought; and at Thy least, give us to understand to repent.

At the beginning of our days Thou dost give—oh, at the end, forgive!

Deem our affliction worthy of Thy care, and now with a last redeeming, Redeemer of Israel, redeem!

Over our fevers pass the wind of Thy hand; against our chills, Thy warmth. O great Physician, heal us! and shall we ailing be healed.

From want deliver us. Yield the earth fruitful. Let rain a delicate stalk, let dew in the bright seed, sprout ever abundance. Shelter us behind the four walls of Thy seasons, roof us with justice, O Lord, who settest the sun to labour for our evening dish!

Thyself do utter the Shma! Sound the great horn of our freedom, raise up the ensign of freedom, and gather from the four corners of the earth, as we do gather the four fringes to kiss them, Thy people, Thy folk, rejected Thine elect.

Restore our judges as in former times restore our Judge. Blessed art Thou, O Lord, King, who loves righteousness and judgment.

Favour them, O Lord, Thy saints Thy paupers, who do forgo all other Thy benedictions for the benediction of Thy name.

Oh, build Jerusalem!

Anoint Thy people David!

Our prayers accept, but judge us not through our prayers: grant them with mercy.

Make us of Thy love a sanctuary, an altar where the heart may cease from fear, and evil a burnt offering is consumed away, and good, like the fine dust of spices, an adulation of incense, rises up.

Oh, accept, accept, accept our thanks for the day's three miracles, of dusk, of dawn, of noon, and of the years which with Thy presence are made felicitous.

Grant us—our last petition—peace, Thine especial blessing, which is of Thy grace and of the shining and the turning of Thy Face.

346

BEAVER

He lifts his middle-aged cabby-face from roots,
hears the far ferment of the fall. *The time!*
Soon drunk with juice of timber, he smiles logs:
the joy of habitat.

Twigs, branches, bitten bole—they teeth him and tusk him;
mud webs his feet, he shines as if with sweat;
now in deep water builds his forest, fruited
with fish, by currents breezed, by quivering quiet.

Come frost, and ice his mud!
                              Come flakeful fall
his herbage hibernate!
                              Come flurrying months
and whitely roof him over his crystal plinths:
he waits the spring—a merman animal.

EPITAPH

The coffin-board has now been planed;
The spade has bit the bitter earth;
The worm has spanned my meagre girth;
My hollow home has been attained.

And you, O traveller, may laugh
Seeing what is the end of me;
You may revile my threnody
And you may scorn my epitaph.

But I beneath this fertile sod
Will surely find a peaceful lapse,
Yea, I may lay my head, perhaps,
Upon the very knees of God.

APPENDIX

FOREWORD TO *HATH NOT A JEW . . .*,
BY LUDWIG LEWISOHN

It is several years ago now that there began to appear in one or two not very conspicuous periodicals, poems signed ABRAHAM M. KLEIN that both refreshed and excited me. I had then no notion who Klein was, and it was to be some years before I was to learn that a young Montreal attorney was destined to be the first contributor of authentic Jewish poetry to the English language. This statement can be at once abbreviated and enlarged: the first Jew to contribute authentic poetry to the literatures of English speech. For until his appearance all or nearly all Jews writing verse in English (and there were few enough even of those) had sought to make themselves more or less indistinguishable from the non-Jewish poets. Hence none of these men and women had gone to that core and visceral centre whence poetry springs, and had therefore had no substance of their own which, given the talent, they could have transformed into a personal and therefore, if only the personality was salient and rich enough, an ultimately universal form.

The matter sounds intricate and is really simple enough. We are not born on the day of our birth; we are not abstract and unfathered creatures. As we are born into the use of a given language or of several given languages, so are we born into a group, a tradition, a religion, a set of memories and attitudes concerning love and death, man and God. We need not blindly accept our heritage; we may legitimately rebel against it. But he who blankly "represses" it, denies it, flees from it, cannot evidently be a poet. For deep and strong poetry is the concrete, as Goethe was never tired of declaring, that *becomes* the universal. That perishable thing which is only symbol is an immensely concrete, individualized thing—a thing that has taken generations to grow, to become itself, never a thing contrived and constructed or imitated. Only the poet who has a substance of his very own will be able to create a style of his very own. And so an apparent paradox becomes a necessary truth: Abraham Klein, the most Jewish poet who has ever used the English tongue, is the only Jew who has ever contributed a new note of style,

350

of expression, of creative enlargement to the poetry of that tongue. He is a far better English poet than the Jewish poets who tried to be non-Jewish English poets. In high things and low, honesty is not only the best policy; it is the only policy that makes for life.

The thing was illustrated to me with almost amusing emphasis upon my next contact with Klein's work. In a volume of *The American Caravan* published some years ago, a poetic work of Abraham Klein was placed next to a group of poems by another young American Jew who is rather spectacularly in flight from his Jewishness and therefore from his authentic self and authentic humanity. And this far from untalented young man wrote of inchoate images in borrowed manners. He had recourse to the latest eccentricities to veil the poverty of concrete meanings in his heart. Abraham Klein, on the other hand, did not have to be frightened of the great tradition of English poetry. For he had that substance and that power of passionate meaning within him, which could take that tradition and forge within it in the magnificent *Design for Mediaeval Tapestry* an instrument of expression which none had ever used except himself:

> *The wrath of people is like foam and lather*
> *Risen against us. Wherefore, Lord, and why?*
> *The winds assemble; the cold and hot winds gather*
> *To scatter us. They do not heed our cry.*
> *The sun rises and leaps the red horizon,*
> *And like a bloodhound swoops across the sky.*

Klein had the luck, of course, to be born into a family and into an environment in which the lore and tradition of our people were things so alive that the quiver of this aliveness, so tense that it can humorously turn upon itself, has accompanied all his years. Therefore he has been able to turn the Berditshever's cries to the Eternal concerning the fate of Israel, and the dark tragedies of the Crusades, and Chelm, the fabled town of fools, and the Pesach Haggadah, and the legend of Prague, and the dances of Chassidim, and the humours and ruling passions of a *Minyan,* and the vision and life of Baruch Spinoza into some of the most authentic and exciting English poetry of our day. He knows the Talmudic sages great and small as he knows the men and women on Saint Lawrence Street in Montreal, and into his English poetic style, even to the

351

wild wit and sparkle of his rhymes, he has transfused their ardours, their dreams, their exquisite goodness, their storming of the very courts of God.

Few modern poets have been able to utter more than a lyric cry. Or else they have sought a depersonalization in the mass which is and must be the death of poetry. Klein occupies the classic middle station within which all important literature has hitherto been produced. As the Greek poets, according to Keats, left "great verse unto a little clan" which was *their* clan, so Klein writes as an intense individual out of one of those clans of which the texture of humanity is composed.

INDEX OF FIRST LINES

354

TITLE INDEX